Inaugural
Wounds

Inaugural Wounds

The Shaping of Desire in Five
Nineteenth-Century English Narratives

Robert E. Lougy

OHIO UNIVERSITY PRESS — ATHENS

Ohio University Press, Athens, Ohio 45701

Ohio University Press books are printed on acid-free paper ⊗™

12 11 10 09 08 07 06 05 04   5 4 3 2 1

Earlier versions of chapter 1 appeared in *Dickens Studies Annual* 21 (1992) as
"Repressive and Expressive Forms: The Bodies of Comedy and Desire in *Martin Chuzzlewit*," and in *Criticism* 36, no. 4 (Fall 1994) as "Dickens and the Ideology of Violence: America in Charles Dickens's *Martin Chuzzlewit*." An earlier version of chapter 2 appeared in *Modern Language Quarterly* 50, no. 3 (1991) as "Narrative Form and Meaning in Thackeray's *Notes of a Journey from Cornhill to Grand Cairo*." I am grateful for the permission to reprint this material.

Library of Congress Cataloging-in-Publication Data

Lougy, Robert E.
    Inaugural wounds : the shaping of desire in five ninetenth-century
    English narratives / Robert E. Lougy.
            p. cm.
    Includes bibliographical references and index.
    ISBN 0-8214-1563-8 (alk. paper)
    1. English fiction—19th century—History and criticism.
    2. Psychoanalysis and literature—England. 3. Desire in literature.
    I. Title.
    PR868.P74L68 2004
    823'.809353—dc22

                                                                2004002988

For Cameran, Lesley, Rob, and Erin

It is in the nature of desire to be radically torn. The very image of man brings in here a mediation which is always imaginary, always problematic, and which is therefore never completely fulfilled. It is maintained by a succession of momentary experiences, and this experience either alienates man from himself, or else ends in destruction, a negation of the object.

Jacques Lacan, *Seminar II*, 166

Contents

Acknowledgments   ix

Introduction   Insupportable Absence and the Writing of Desire   1

1   *Martin Chuzzlewit*   23

2   Exile and Desire in Thackeray's *Notes of a Journey from Cornhill to Grand Cairo*   57

3   Death, Desire, and the Site of the Prostitute in Elizabeth Gaskell's *Ruth*   79

4   Entangled Desire: Wanting and Narrative Structure in Wilkie Collins's *The Woman in White*   113

5   Yearning and Melancholia: Obscure Objects of Desire in *Jude the Obscure*   137

Notes   165

Works Cited   185

Index   199

Acknowledgments

This book is, among other things, concerned with the impossibility of fulfilled desire, and my desire to acknowledge all who have had a hand in the final realization of this project must also fall short. Colleagues too numerous to name, both here at Penn State and elsewhere, have given me their time, their patience, and their advice. I would also like to thank the English Department and Penn State's College of Liberal Arts for their support of my project and for providing travel funds that allowed me to develop my ideas before different forums.

If this project has a beginning, and as Wordsworth tells us, beginnings are terribly difficult to locate, it would be the Lacanian conference "History and Hysteria," held at the University of Missouri in 1991. I would like to thank Ellie Ragland for organizing this conference and for inviting me to participate in it. I found there the opportunity to take part in some wonderful discussions of Freud and Lacan and to breathe in the air of a charged atmosphere that made me realize that such conversations do matter. I would also like to thank the members of my graduate seminars on Freud and Lacan for helping me to refine and flesh out my arguments and readings of psychoanalytic texts. Similarly, I wish to express my gratitude to my undergraduate honors seminars for giving me such exciting and challenging opportunities to explore the complex and mysterious windings of desire in literary texts.

I would like to thank the anonymous readers of my manuscript for Ohio University Press, both for their encouragement and for their suggestions as to how the manuscript could be improved. Their comments were wise, judicious, and helpful. My editor, Sharon Rose, has been there from the beginning, and her help has been invaluable. And finally, my gratitude to Gwen, without whose love and support none of this would have been possible.

Introduction

Insupportable Absence and the Writing of Desire

> Most of our longings go unfulfilled. This is the word's wistful implications—a desire for something lost or fled or otherwise out of reach.
>
> DON DELILLO, *Underworld*

Language and Narrative Desire

Toward the end of *Underworld*, the novel's central figure, Nick Shay, reflects on the meaning of the word "longing," on why it is, as he puts it, that "most of our longings go unfulfilled." He argues that "this is the word's wistful implications—a desire for something lost or fled or otherwise out of reach" (803). This book should be regarded as an inquiry into the wistful implications of longing that DeLillo speaks of, an examination of the various ways in which the "desire for something lost or fled or otherwise out of reach" is mapped out in five nineteenth-century narratives: Charles Dickens's *Martin Chuzzlewit* (1843–44), William Thackeray's *Notes of a Journey from Cornhill to Grand Cairo* (1846), Elizabeth Gaskell's *Ruth* (1853), Wilkie Collins's *The Woman in White* (1860), and, finally, Thomas Hardy's *Jude the*

Obscure (1895). I have characterized these narratives as mapping out the various shapes of desire, but "desire" is a term frequently invoked to refer to a wide range of specific ends or objects—political or economic power, for example, or sexual fulfillment, personal freedom, and so on.[1] When I speak of desire, however, I am referring specifically to desire as Jacques Lacan has theorized it, and, in fact, when Nick Shay describes the "wistful implications" of longing and how it always involves "a desire for something lost or fled or otherwise out of reach," his understanding of desire closely resembles Lacan's. But while DeLillo's character ponders this question for only a moment, Lacan examines it throughout his writings, and I return to Lacan and desire later in the introduction. At this point, I want to look at the narratives themselves and the ways in which I approach them.

While each of these narratives considers the question of desire, each does so in its own way, and thus I have tried to heed Lacan's admonition that we "start from the text, start by treating it, as Freud does and he recommends, as Holy Writ" (*Seminar II*, 153), for I am persuaded that whatever we say as readers must begin with the text.[2] "Critique," J. Hillis Miller reminds us, "is a testing of the grounding of language in this or that particular text, not in the abstract or in abstraction from any particular case," and, as he also notes, any "attempt to take the language of literature for granted and shift from the study of word with word to the study of the relations of words with things or subjectivities, will only lead back in the end to the study of language" ("Search," 31). When, however, the texts in question are Victorian narratives, this "study of word with word" can seem like an overwhelming task. As Robert Polhemus has noted, "One of the greatest problems in literary studies is that the prose of a long novel can be as dense and highly charged as the language of poetry," but because "we cannot give the language of huge novels the intense scrutiny we give to a few lines of verse, our study of fiction . . . has been comparatively spotty and superficial" (*Comic*, 21). While it is difficult to approach novels with the same "intense scrutiny" that we are able to give, for example, to poetry, we must nevertheless make the effort (as Polhemus certainly does), for when we read the books that nineteenth-century novelists wrote instead of those that we think they should have written or those that we have been told they wrote, the books often astound us not only by the resonance and range of their language, but also by their ability to take us to strange and haunting places.

The earliest text examined in this study, Charles Dickens's *Martin Chuzzlewit* (1843–44), was published more than a decade before Darwin's *Origin of the Species*, while the latest, Thomas Hardy's *Jude the Obscure* (1895), was published shortly before the turn of the century. Dickens was only seven years old when John Keats, himself but twenty-four years old and already dying of tuberculosis, was writing his great odes in 1819, while Thomas Hardy, born in 1840, lived long enough into the twentieth century to read a popular exposition of Einstein's *Theory of Relativity* late in his life.[3] But however differently these five writers might have inhabited the nineteenth century, they were all children of their age, and thus I am mindful of William Baker's admonition that we must keep such genealogies in mind and not impose "Lacan, Barthes, Derrida, Foucault, Kristeva et al. in an ahistorical fashion," and that we should avoid, as he puts it, the "imposition of ideas from other cultures, traditions, and generations" ("Afterword," 232). And although I have drawn extensively on the theoretical inquiries of Freud and Lacan, and have turned at one point or another to virtually all of the writers identified by Baker, I would nevertheless agree with what he has to say, adding only that what we need to guard against is not the application of ideas from other cultures or traditions, but rather careless or casual applications.

When Freud turns toward artists as different as Sophocles, Shakespeare, and Leonardo da Vinci, or when Lacan similarly explores the dynamics of desire in Shakespeare's *Hamlet* and Edgar Allen Poe's "The Purloined Letter," they do so because they are persuaded, as am I, that desire insinuates itself in complex but discernible ways into the varied narrative histories of all human subjects. Victorian texts continue to surprise us, and we need to be wary of drawing too many sharp distinctions between their age and our own. At one point in *David Copperfield*, for example, Dickens describes the schoolmaster, Mr. Creakle, noting his "*delight* at cutting at the boys, which was like the *satisfaction of a craving appetite*" (91, emphasis mine). He also tells us that Creakle "couldn't resist a chubby boy, especially; that *there was a fascination in such a subject, which made him restless in his mind,* until he had scored and marked him for the day" (91, emphasis mine). Freud's essay "A Child Is Beaten" and his other inquiries into sadism and fetishism, as well as James Kincaid's work on the Victorian eroticization of the child, might help open up or gloss this passage, but it is Dickens's richly precise and disturbing

language that lays bare Creakle's sadistic and compulsive pedophilic appetites.[4] This moment remains Dickens's, and his alone, and it would be difficult, if not impossible, to "impose" twentieth-century psychoanalytic theory
on a text in which the sexual dynamics interrogated by that theory resonate
so powerfully.

The writers examined in this study are situated in historical moments that
defined and to some extent shaped the directions of their art, for while each
artist tells the story of desire in his or her own way, the choices the writers
make, the metaphors they draw on, and the narratives they weave depended
in no small part on their own personal histories and the various cultural
sites in which their writing was located. Studies that have examined the relationship between writers and these locations, such as Gillian Beer's *Darwin's
Plots: Evolutionary Narrative in Darwin, George Eliot, and Nineteenth-
Century Fiction* and Catherine Gallagher's *The Industrial Reformation of
English Fiction: Social Discourse and Narrative Form, 1832–1867*, have
shown that such examinations can yield fruitful readings of the nineteenth-
century British novel. My readings of the five narratives in the chapters that
follow are, I hope, grounded on a similar awareness of the importance of
such historical moments and sites. Thus, it does matter, for example, that
Elizabeth Gaskell writes *Ruth* at a moment in British history when the
question of prostitution seemed to dominate both political and social discourse, or that Thomas Hardy's *Jude the Obscure* both gives voice to and is
haunted by that lassitude or malaise that permeates the later decades of the
nineteenth century. But as Jacques Derrida and others have reminded us,
we need to be careful in drawing on such sites, for they are themselves texts,
no less than the texts they are sometimes used to ground or stabilize. In speaking of Rousseau's *Confessions*, for example, Derrida argues that we cannot
move outside the text to get to the "real" Rousseau, for "there is nothing outside of the text [there is no outside text; *il n'y a pas de hors-texte*]" (*Of Grammatology*, 158). This is so not because we are uninterested in the life of
Rousseau or Mama or Thérèse, but because "there has never been anything
but writing; there have never been anything but supplements, substitutive
significations which could only come forth in a chain of differential references" (158–59).[5]

Such cautionary notes aside, however, I am arguing that if we try to
regard our sense of the historical reality or cultural context in which artists

write as the final ground of meaning for their texts, we come to realize the inadequacies of such an approach, for figural language and the inscription of desire in it contest or destabilize the historical, disturbing texts in such ways as to modify the ways in which we can understand their relationship to such sites. As we will see in chapter 2, for example, Thackeray shared with his age a number of the attitudes toward race and empire that we find expressed in William Kinglake's *Eothen,* and he actually speaks admiringly of Kinglake's book in his *Journey from Cornhill to Grand Cairo.* Nevertheless, the power and strange beauty of his narrative are only remotely connected to such attitudes, but arise instead from a desire that has its origin in wounds that Thackeray's language explores and articulates, even as the narrative voice remains only obscurely aware of them. The existence of the unconscious, what Freud referred to as a "new place," "*ein anderer Schauplatz,*" or another scene, means that we inhabit a split or divided subjectivity, and that we therefore often write from sites of which we remain unconscious.[6] As Freud often admits, artists were familiar with this "new place" long before he discovered it, as when, for example, Charlotte Brontë writes in her 1850 preface to *Wuthering Heights* of how "the writer who possesses the creative gift owns something of which he is not always the master—something that strangely wills and works for itself" (40). Such strange workings, as we will see, are much in evidence in Thackeray's narrative.

Now, however, I would like to turn to Daniel Defoe's *Robinson Crusoe* (1719), looking at the ways in which the presence of an unnamed but nevertheless articulated desire in its language punctures or unravels the tight weave of its narrative frame. *Robinson Crusoe* is a considerably earlier text than the others I consider, but it is exemplary not only in the ways in which its language alerts us to the presence of Freud's "new place," but also in how it contests our attempts to read the text strictly along materialist or historicist lines. It is not that we should attempt to separate his text from the eighteenth-century sites of capitalism and commerce in which it is situated, but rather that we should recognize that we cannot understand it solely through such sites. The section of the novel I look at occurs after Crusoe has been on the island for almost twenty-five years and hears one night offshore the sounds of gunfire associated with a ship in distress. He awakens the next morning to discover that there has indeed been a shipwreck but no survivors, the ship having foundered on the same concealed rocks that had once enabled him to salvage much from his own ship before it finally sank. As he comes to realize his own good fortune, Crusoe praises God's providential design: "It is very rare that the providence of God casts us into any condition of life so low, or any misery so great, but that we may see something or other to be thankful for; and may see others in worse circumstances than ourselves" (192).

As he continues to look out on this fatal watery scene, however, he becomes intensely but peculiarly aware of his isolation: "I cannot," he writes, "explain by any possible energy of words what *a strange longing or hankering of desires* I felt in my soul upon this sight" (192, emphasis mine). "In all the time of my solitary life," he adds, "I never felt so earnest, so strong a desire after the society of my fellow-creatures, or so deep a regret at the want of it" (192). At this point, Crusoe begins to reflect on the mysterious origins of such "a strange longing or hankering of desires": "There are some secret moving springs in the affections, which when they are set a-going by some object in view, or be it some object, though not in view, yet render'd present to the mind by the power of imagination, that motion carries out the soul by its impetuosity to such violent eager embracings of the object that the absence of it is insupportable" (193). Desire, he suggests, is set into motion by "some secret moving springs in the affections," which, once "set a-going," carry the soul in impetuous and peculiar directions toward such "violent eager embracings of the object" that its absence, as he puts it, "is insupportable." In some respects, this account of the origin and directions of desire corresponds fairly closely to what is happening to Crusoe himself, the object in question in his case being, of course, the ship and the human companionship that it promised to hold. But Crusoe's remarks, although occasioned by this particular moment, also raise some important questions involving the nature of desire itself, for what is especially striking or curious about this scene is not the nature of his feelings, but rather the ways in which it calls our attention to their obscure or ambiguous origins. Clearly the prospect of "the society of my fellow-creatures," first raised and then dashed by the violence of a capricious sea, would be enough to unsettle anyone who had been alone for as long as Crusoe had been. And yet, by emphasizing the "strange longing or hankering of desires," the scene resists this explanation, or, more precisely, it resists our inclination to accept just this explanation. The ways in which Crusoe's language emphasizes his bewilderment make us attentive and curious as to why he should be con-fused and baffled. Why call our attention, in other words, to the strangeness of his longings when what he wants—namely, the company of other human beings—would seem to be so self-evident and understandable?

Nevertheless, his body, as well as his language, registers the obscure conflicts with which this scene is invested, for as Crusoe imagines the pos-sibility of even one survivor, he writes of how "the desires were so moved by it that when I spoke the words my hands would clinch together and my fin-gers press the palms of my hands, that if I had had any soft thing in my hand, it would have crushed it involuntarily" (193). Again, he is able to tell us what he does, but he cannot tell us why: "Let the naturalists explain these things, and the reason and manner of them," he writes. "All I can say to them is to describe the fact, which was even surprising to me when I found it" (193). Genuinely astonished not only by what he is feeling, but by his very gestures, their presence as well as their origin, Crusoe confesses that he cannot explain them or account for them—"I knew not from what it should proceed"—and because, as he admits, his own language fails him, he turns to other discourses, such as that of naturalists, in hopes of finding out what is going on. At one point he attempts to account for his anguish by suggesting that it arises from his "ardent wishes" for "the conversation of one of my fellow-Christians" (193), but his remarks here are finally unper-suasive, suggesting that Crusoe, although seeking some explanation, is no more convinced by the reasons he advances than he believes that "natural-ists" could actually explain what is happening to him. Narrative, Peter Brooks has suggested, is "condemned to saying other than what it would mean" (56), and Crusoe's narrative registers the pressure of this condemnation.

Freud discovered the unconscious in language by listening carefully to the spoken word, paying attention not only to what was said but also to *how* it was said, especially to the places in which a text stumbles, in which we detect semantic lurches or erratic movements.[7] This scene from *Robinson Crusoe*, I would suggest, is characterized precisely by such stumbles and discontinuities, giving us the sense that there is something unusual about it, something not quite right.[8] For Freud, Jacqueline Rose has argued, lan-guage "was always redolent of what is both hardest to articulate and most pressingly in need of speech" (*States of Fantasy*, 149), and we find such a language in this passage, for its narrative impulses direct our attention to something that is felt but not understood, to something in the passage that fractures or agitates whatever logical or reasonable explanations might be applied to it, either by Crusoe or ourselves. It is not, as Crusoe realizes, that such explanations would be wrong, but rather that they would be incomplete or lacking, and what they would lack is precisely the ability to get at the fundamental but unconscious presence of lack or loss itself, as desire makes itself felt by means of the pressure exerted on a language through which it momentarily escapes. Drawing on the myth of Orpheus and Eurydice, Lacan has argued that the unconscious is "a discovery [that] becomes a rediscovery and, furthermore, is always ready to steal away again, thus establishing the dimension of loss" (*Concepts*, 25). A "dimension of loss" saturates this scene from *Robinson Crusoe*, but what it is that has been lost remains problematic and elusive, for while we are most certainly talking about the loss of human companionship, something more is involved as well, a surplus of meaning that refuses to be silenced or denied.

And it is, I would argue, psychoanalysis rather than historicism that enables us to identify what this lack or loss might be. For what is disclosed here is precisely the ways in which desire lacerates the appearances and things of this world, testifying to a want or gap in the human subject that the world and its structures and sites can never fill in or satisfy. For although Robinson Crusoe at first considers himself providentially blessed as he looks on the foundering ship, thinking of how he avoided the death that befell this ship's mariners, he almost immediately also comes to feel or know another loss or death, namely, the loss of that part of himself from which he is forever removed—what Lacan refers to as the "objet a," that from which we must be separated if we are to be constituted as a subject in language. Crusoe's reactions during this scene, characterized as they are by a powerful feeling of being incapacitated, disabled, and disoriented, correspond in many ways to Freud's description of the act of mourning, when the world as we have known it is suddenly shattered and we are unable to negotiate the new one thrust on us. Mourning is how we attempt to cope with the hole in the real caused by loss or death, or, as Lacan puts it, "The work of mourning is first of all performed to satisfy the disorder that is produced by the inadequacy of the signifying elements to cope with the hole that has been created in existence" ("Desire," 38). But, at the same time, as he points out, mourning "impeaches" the "systems of signifiers in their totality" (38), for it discloses the fact that the symbolic cannot heal or close such a hole. We draw on the symbolic in order to patch up the holes in our lives, to repair or heal the tears or wounds of human subjectivity itself, but there is always something that escapes its nets, a surplus, as it were, that refuses to be contained. Readers of *Robinson Crusoe* have observed that it is a text in which the symbolic order, spelled out by the novel's numerous inventories of goods and descriptions of various mercantile systems of exchange, is tightly structured and drawn together, and historicist approaches toward Defoe's text have correctly identified the text's close relationship to the colonial and capitalist projects of eighteenth-century England.[9] And yet, moments such as this one disclose the precariousness and final insufficiency of this symbolic order, and, in this respect, the moment becomes especially traumatic, similar to the dreams, hallucinations, and visions of cannibals and cannibalism that tear holes in the otherwise tightly knit fabric of Crusoe's narrative. Like the plaintively uncanny cry of Polly, his parrot, "Robin, Robin, Robin Crusoe, poor Robin Crusoe, where are you, Robin Crusoe? Where are you? Where have you been?" (152), this moment asks questions of Crusoe that he would just as soon not listen to, but questions that nevertheless insist on being heard.

This richly layered scene deserves more attention than I can give it here, but what I want to emphasize is how the language of Defoe's text discloses pressures, conflicts happening somewhere in such a way that, although Crusoe can feel their effects, he is confused or baffled by their presence. Unconscious desire makes itself known, Lacan suggests, in the moments "where the subject surprises himself in some unexpected way" (*Concepts*, 28), and this scene is riddled with surprise and bewilderment, disclosing the presence of another site or origin, that other place being the unconscious as the site of desire. Crusoe's stumbles, the discontinuities in the seams of his narrative, call our attention to important things happening on levels that are felt but not understood by the narrator. Similar moments, as we will see, are found in a number of the texts I will be looking at—a peculiar confrontation late in Dickens's novel, for example, between Tom Pinch and young Martin Chuzzlewit, in which much that is unsaid is nevertheless able to make itself known, or an episode in *A Journey from Cornhill to Grand Cairo* in which Thackeray lingers in fascination over the disturbing image of a hidden trapdoor as he imagines the bodies of lovely young women who have disappeared through it. There is also a particularly striking scene in *Jude the Obscure* in which the sight of Arabella's breasts and Jude's sudden lack of appetite for liquor become caught up together in the dynamics of conflicted desire. I am interested in that desire that has its origins in what Defoe refers to as "some secret moving springs in the affections," a desire that is often mysterious and violent, painful, impulsive, and, as we will see in *Martin Chuzzlewit* and *Ruth*, self-destructive as well. "The goals we pursue are always veiled," Milan Kundera tells us; "The thing that gives our every move its meaning is always totally unknown to us" (*The Unbearable Lightness of Being*, 122). Like the desire identified by *Robinson Crusoe*, disclosed through an anxious narrative voice that confesses to its own perplexity and confusion, the desire I will be looking at most often remains veiled, making itself known only indirectly.

As we might expect, a number of nineteenth-century British writers other than those I will be looking at have also explored the shapes of this desire. Let me give a few brief examples. In "The Child in the House"—an essay I will in fact return to in chapter 2—Walter Pater writes of how its central figure, Florian Deleal, recalls his boyhood, describing how "a touch of regret or desire mingled all night in the remembered presence of red flowers, and their perfume in the darkness about him; and *the longing for some undivined, entire possession of them* was the beginning of a revelation to him, growing ever clearer" (1,474, emphasis mine). Or in the case of *Wuthering Heights*, when the revenant Cathy beats on the window beside Lockwood's bed, pleading to be let in and saying, "I'm come home. I'd lost my way on the moor" (67), we hear the desire to crash through separation or division that is behind the unnamable sense of loss that haunts both Cathy and Heathcliff to their graves. And, finally, in speaking of the conclusion to *The Mill on the Floss*, Garrett Stewart has noted that "George Eliot has drawn for us the reversionary desires that are death" (*Death Sentences*, 118); and when Maggie Tulliver tells her brother Tom of her fear that "everything is going away from us—the end of our lives will have nothing in it like the beginning" (*The Mill on the Floss*, 325), she testifies to such reversionary desires, hungering for something that can be approached only asymptotically through the apocalyptic violence of death that enfolds brother and sister in its arms toward the end of the novel.[10]

However, one of the most sustained meditations on these particular aspects of desire is found in Amitav Ghosh's postmodern novel *The Shadow*

Lines (1988). At one point early in the novel, the narrator tells of a conversation that took place between his cousin and himself on the nature of "real desire": "He said to me once that one could never know anything except through desire, real desire, which was not the same thing as greed or lust; a pure, painful and primitive desire, a longing for everything that was not in oneself, a torment of the flesh, that carried one beyond the limits of one's mind to other times and other places, and even, if one was lucky, to a place where there was no border between oneself and one's image in the mirror" (29). The cousin, Tridib, makes it clear that what he has in mind is not "greed or lust," but "real desire," that which is "pure, painful, and primitive." Invoking the image of a damaged or pained body, Ghosh argues that desire has its origin in a wound or split, a fissure between oneself and the other, that which "was not in oneself." Desire for Ghosh is a "torment of the flesh" that compels us to seek beyond ourselves, in other places or other times, for that which is more than ourselves, or that which possesses whatever it is that we do not have. As when Crusoe describes the crushing pressure of his fingers on his palms or when his teeth struck "together and set against one another so strong that for some time I could not part them again" (169), the torment that Ghosh speaks of can be painful, even wrenching. Ghosh's narrator tells of how he listened to his cousin, "bewildered, wondering whether I would ever know anything at all, for I was not sure whether I would ever experience desire of that kind" (30). The five narratives I will be examining all testify to the fact that such desire does exist, but, at the same time, each also denies the existence of "a place where there was no border between oneself and one's image in the mirror." Instead, they argue that desire is grounded in a fundamental human lack, a tear in the fabric of being itself that can be known only indirectly or obliquely—as in, for example, our desire for a place without divisions or borders.

Lacan and the Structure of Desire

Like the longings DeLillo speaks of in the epigraph to this chapter, Ghosh's account of the trajectory of desire is strikingly similar to desire as Lacan understands it, and thus this would be a good point to turn to the question of Lacanian desire. I would like, first of all, to indicate what I understand such desire to be, and, secondly, to identify more fully some of the directions that this study will be pursuing. While Lacan often turns to the question of desire, he perhaps does so nowhere more effectively than in "The Direction of the Treatment and the Principles of Its Power." In this 1958 essay, Lacan sets out to "articulate that which structures desire" (*Ecrits*, 263), and he does so in important ways. Desire, he writes, "is that which is manifested in the interval that demand hollows out within itself, in as much as the subject, in articulating the signifying chain, brings to light the want to be, together with the appeal to receive the complement of the Other, if the Other, the locus of speech, is also the locus of this want, or lack" (*Ecrits*, 263). At times Lacan's style can be intimidating—he acknowledges at one point, in fact, that he prefers "to leave the reader no other way out than the way in, which I prefer to be difficult" (*Ecrits*, 146). But in this case, the initial or apparent difficulty of the passage stems from the fact that Lacan says a good deal in a relatively small number of words. Desire, he tells us, is manifested or found "in the interval that demand hollows out within itself," and makes itself known or felt through the articulation of the signifying chain, namely, through the ways in which language discloses or "brings to light" the "want to be," or that "want of being" that Lacan refers to as *"manque à être."* He also notes that this articulation of the signifying chain addresses or appeals to the "Other," insofar as this other, "the locus of speech," is also "the locus of this want, or lack." As Lacan often reminds us, "desire" is distinct from both "need" and "demand," for while need registers biological require-ments on the part of the infant and demand the infant's insistence that the parent or caretaker provide love and recognition as well as food and shel-ter, desire addresses the fact that such an insistence is always made from a position of lack or want, what Lacan often refers to as a gap (*béance*) or split.[11] Thus desire occupies the site or the interval that "demand hollows out within itself," situated in the spaces structured by the fact that when we demand, we are always seeking or asking for something more than we can get, and also more than we even realize we are demanding. In his "The Mirror Stage as Formative of the Function of the I as Revealed in Psycho-analytic Experience" (1949), Lacan explores some of the reasons for this particular trajectory of desire. In that early essay, he argues that the ego, or "I," is structured around a series of illusory or mirror images of identity, what he refers to as "a succession of phantasies" (*Ecrits*, 4). However, such images—for example, that image of wholeness and equilibrium that the infant sees when she looks in the mirror in a moment of what Lacan identifies as "spatial identification" (*Ecrits*, 4) — do not succeed in concealing or doing away with the child's awareness of the fact that there is a profound difference between her own bodily self, filled with all of "the turbulent movements that the subject feels" (*Ecrits*, 2), and the illusory image of intactness and balance.

This sense of the fragmented body that is born at this time stays with us throughout our life, as it makes itself felt in our dreams, for example, or is captured on the canvasses of Hieronymus Bosch and Picasso. Similarly, the dialectics of Self and Other that are structured by this mirror stage do not end when we grow out of infancy. On the contrary, Lacan argues that the moment when the mirror stage itself comes to an end "decisively tips the whole of human knowledge into mediatization through the desire of the other" (*Ecrits*, 5). In other words, we continue throughout our lives to seek in the Other that which we do not have, not knowing that this Other, similarly grounded in lack or want, does not and cannot possess that which we seek. Or, as Joan Copjec puts it, "Desire is produced not as a striving for something, but only as a striving for something else or something more. It stems from the feeling of our having been duped by language, cheated of something, not from our having been presented with a determinate object or goal for which we can aim" (*Read My Desire*, 55). This longing for something that might close or narrow this split or gap, giving us back what we have been cheated of, is precisely what Lacan means by desire.[12] Desire is neither need nor demand, but that which is beyond both, carved out in the hollows created by the fact that buried within our demands are certain requests or desires that cannot be answered.

As Copjec's remarks suggest, desire makes itself felt and known in and through language, for language is born out of lack or want, and testifies by its presence to the fact that desire cannot be satisfied. Insofar as we are constructed by language, we are separated from any possibility of wholeness or intactness, or, as Lacan puts it in an often-cited passage, "The moment in which desire becomes human is also that in which the child is born into language" (*Ecrits*, 103). Desire thus makes itself felt through the signifying chain of language, always reaching unconsciously for that which it cannot have or be; it cannot be satisfied, for it is located at the point at which demand asks for something more than the need it expresses. In this respect, desire is metonymic, always the desire for something else, and, as Lacan points out, it is especially when the need articulated by demand is met that we become most acutely deprived of the desire that lies behind this demand.[13] Freud first glimpsed this relationship between language and desire as he watched his one-and-a-half-year-old grandson playing a game in which he tossed a spool into his bed and then pulled it back out with a string, saying "fort" (gone) or "da" (there) as he did so, in a gesture of play that allowed him to cope with his mother's absence from the room. But, as Lacan notes, Freud saw in his grandson's behavior much more than simply a child's play: "Through the word—already a presence made of an absence—absence itself gives itself a name in that moment of origin whose perpetual recreation Freud's genius detected in the play of the child. And from this pair of sounds modulated on presence and absence . . . there is born a world of meaning of a particular language in which the world of things will be arranged" (*Ecrits*, 65).[14] In his final lecture in Caracas, Venezuela, in 1980, Lacan underscored the continuous and fundamental presence of Freud in his own work when he told his audience, "It's up to you to be Lacanians, if you want. As for me, I am a Freudian."[15] And while I am not sure that I am a Freudian, Freud certainly occupies a prominent place in this study.

Like John Irwin in *Doubling and Incest/Repetition and Revenge*, I consider Freud's writings as "problematical as any speculative philosophic writings" (2), and I too am interested in those areas of inquiry—for example, repetition compulsion, the death instinct, the nature of the uncanny, and the dynamics of mourning and melancholia—in which Freud, as Irwin puts is, "is at his most metaphysical, at his most philosophical" (2). But while Irwin's study of Faulkner presents structures such as the Oedipus complex and the repetition compulsion in what he identifies as "their classically Freudian form, devoid of later revision" (4), I am also interested in Lacan's return to Freud. As Juliet Mitchell notes, Lacan "dedicated himself to the task of refinding and reformulating the work of Sigmund Freud" (*Feminine Sexuality*, 1), convinced that the originality and radical nature of Freud's thought had been lost or trivialized by an age that was unwilling to read what Freud actually wrote. In the seminars that he gave over the years, first at Hôpital Saint-Anne and then later at the École normale supérieure, Lacan attempted to recover Freud's texts and to teach them to others, exploring the ways in which they constitute a fundamental redefinition of our place in the scheme of things.[16]

Among those who regularly attended the seminars that Lacan gave at Saint-Anne from 1953 onward was Michel Foucault, and, in fact, as David Macey notes, Foucault was "one of the first to bring to the rue d'Ulm news of the 'return to Freud,' or in other words of Lacan's reformulation of psychoanalytic principles in the light of modern linguistics, anthropology, and philosophy and of his dismissing of the 'ego-psychology' which, he claimed, was reducing psychoanalysis to banal psycho-social engineering" (*The Lives of Michel Foucault*, 56). And although Macey also points out that Foucault had "a long and fraught relationship with psychoanalysis" (68), there is no doubt that Foucault, like Lacan, was fascinated by the abyss in which thought makes itself heard by agitating and disturbing the surface of language. I have had the opportunity on several occasions to draw on Foucault's writings. His stunning analysis of the creation and control of docile bodies in his *Discipline and Punish*, for example, figures into my reading of *The Woman in White*, and my chapter on Elizabeth Gaskell's *Ruth* is informed by his inquiry into the various dynamics of the "multiple, fragmentary, and mobile sexualities" (*The History of Sexuality*, 46) that we find in the Victorian age. In fact, any reading of nineteenth-century fiction concerned with the question of desire must recognize Foucault's presence, if only to acknowledge the ways in which, until rather recently, his theories of power and sexuality have tended to be at the center of critical conversations concerning Victorian literature, with his followers arguing along historicist lines that we need to regard desire as an effect of cultural production.

Recent studies, however, such as Joan Copjec's *Read My Desire* and Christopher Lane's *The Burdens of Intimacy: Psychoanalysis and Victorian Masculinity*, have asked us to reopen the conversation between historicism and psychoanalysis. In her introduction to *Read My Desire*, for example, Copjec maintains that her arguments are less with Foucault in general than with the directions in his thought that move him away from a position he articulates elsewhere—namely, the notion of "a surplus existence that cannot be caught up in the positivity of the social" (4).[17] Historicism, she suggests, persists in "the reduction of society to its indwelling network of relations and power" (6), and attempts "to ground being in appearance and wants to have nothing to do with desire," (14), whereas psychoanalysis maintains not only that desire is real, but also that it can articulated. Arguing against the notion of a metalanguage that can somehow exist outside of the structure it signifies, she asks us to recognize that society is split "between its appearance—the positive relations we observe in it—and its being, that is to say, its generative principle, which cannot appear among these relations" (9). And in contemplating what she identifies as a notion of transcendence, "a principle or a subject that 'transcends' the regime that he [Foucault] analyzes" (7), Copjec turns to Lacan's discourses and concept of the real as well as to Freud's analyses of such concepts as the primal father and the death wish. Without such a notion of transcendence, she maintains, social space cannot help but be reduced to the "relations that fill it" (7), and it is psychoanalysis, and especially the work of Lacan, that enables us to understand the constraints of such an approach.

Although Copjec addresses what she considers to be the essential or fundamental differences between psychoanalysis and historicism, other readers have asked us to acknowledge the fact that the projects of Freud and Foucault are not necessarily at odds with one another. Thus, although she concedes the differences between historicism and psychoanalysis, Ann Laura Stoler argues in *Race and the Education of Desire* that "there are surprising ways in which their [Freud's and Foucault's] projects can and do converge" (168–69).[18] Christopher Lane develops this argument further in *The Burdens of Intimacy*, noting that while readers often speak of Foucault's remark in *Madness and Civilization* (1961) to the effect that psychoanalysis "has not been able, will not be able, to hear the voices of unreason" (*Madness*, 278), they tend to ignore his later comments in *The Order of Things* (1966) that would seem to say *"the exact opposite"* (*Burdens*, 21, emphasis Lane's). In this later work, Foucault speaks of the relationship of psychoanalysis to the human sciences, arguing that psychoanalysis, by "setting itself the task of making the discourse of the unconscious speak through consciousness" (*Order of Things*, 374), advances "in the direction of that fundamental region in which the relations of representation and finitude come into play" (374). In this respect, Foucault stresses, there is a fundamental difference between psychoanalysis and other areas of inquiry, for while the other human sciences "advance towards the unconscious only with their back to it," psychoanalysis "points directly towards it, with a deliberate purpose," toward "what is there and yet is hidden, toward what exists with the mute solidity of a thing, of a text closed in upon itself, or of a blank space in a visible text, and uses that quality to defend itself" (374).[19] Many followers of Foucault,

Lane remarks, underestimate the proximity "between Foucault and Freud" (4), and he adds that, given the existence of such rich passages as this one, "it is odd that many Anglo-American readers of Foucault have consistently ignored this dimension of his work" (22). Foucault may not have been, in Lane's words, "a closet Freudian" (21), but he was certainly not the enemy of Freud that he is often made out to be.

The reading of Victorian fiction is a project certainly large enough and complex enough to accommodate a multiplicity of voices, for if, as I am arguing, we cannot understand a text by attempting to ground it wholly in its historical or cultural sites, neither can we read such texts satisfactorily without an awareness of these sites. As John Bowen has noted, it is precisely the resistance of literary texts "to be interpreted by a consistent set of principles and methods" that constitutes "the (paradoxical) condition of their (impossible) condition" (*Other Dickens*, 2), and we should celebrate this paradoxical, impossible, and resistant nature of textuality. The act of reading asks us to remain open to the possibility of doubt, uncertainty, even disorientation, and I do not for a moment believe that the approach taken in this study (or any other single approach for that matter) establishes the ways in which all texts can or should be read or explored.

The Textual Unconscious and Five Narratives of Desire

"Dehiscence" is a term botanists use to describe the process in which a seed or pod, when it splits open, develops a gaping hole or wound. Lacan draws on this term in characterizing the human condition, when he speaks of the human subject as a figure of "dehiscence within the world" (*Seminar II*, 166). But if language testifies to our wounded relationship with the world, it also grounds our being in it, and because both Freud and Lacan emphasize the fact that unconscious desire makes itself known through language, their inquiries have particular meaning for students of literature.[20] As Ned Lukacher has suggested, although "the future of psychoanalysis as a therapy is likely to remain in question for some time to come, its theoretical and textual relation to literary and philosophic history should not be regarded as either inconsequential or obvious." Lukacher argues, in fact, that in the case of psychoanalysis, "its interpretive rather than therapeutic ends may finally predominate" (*Primal Scenes*, 23).[21] These interpretive ends, however, are often ambiguous, indeterminate. Foucault, for example, has spoken of the "structurally open, structurally gaping character of interpretation" ("Nietzsche, Freud, Marx," 3), and in *The Interpretation of Dreams*, Freud writes of how there is "at least one spot in every dream at which it is unplumbable—a navel, as it were, that is its point of contact with the unknown" (143, 564). As readers of literary texts, we often come into contact with such navels, sites of the mysterious and unknowable, but the presence of these black holes in literary texts should be every bit as exhilarating as their existence within the universe.

As Steven Hawking and others have pointed out, cosmic black holes, because of their density, draw everything into themselves, allowing nothing, including light itself, to escape, and thus they can be studied only indirectly, by observing, for example, the often peculiar and violent activity taking place around them.[22] And in his *A Theory of Literary Production*, Pierre Macherey has argued that literary texts have their own black holes, their own sites of conflict and tension, suggesting that we must seek their meaning as well through indirect gestures and signs, through the silences and ruptures disclosed by the text. In order to "reach utterance," he observes, "all speech envelops itself in the unspoken," and thus for a book to say some things, "there are other things that must not be said" (85). And just as Lacan argues that Freud's discovery of the unconscious implies the vision of a split or decentered human subjectivity, Macherey similarly locates in the literary text evidence of a schism or division, what he refers to as its textual unconscious: "We must show," he writes, "a sort of splitting from within the work: this division is its unconscious" (92). It is "not a question of redoubling the work with an unconscious, but a question of revealing in the very gestures of expression that which it is not" (94). When we read a literary text, he argues, we need to pay attention not to "that false simplicity that derives from the apparent unity of its meaning, but [to] the presence of a relation, or an opposition," a conflict in the text that "reveals the inscription of an *otherness* in the work" (80, 85). It is this opposition or otherness that bestows structure on the work, and even though the text cannot speak of such division, it identifies it through its silences: "In its every particle, the work *manifests*, uncovers, what it cannot say. This silence gives it life" (84). Macherey is not talking about finding "the hidden meaning" of a text; on the contrary, he stresses the fact that the literary text "has no interior, no exterior; or rather, its interior is like its exterior, shattered and on display. Thus it is open to the gaze, peeled, disemboweled" (96). In order for a work to say one thing, however, it must also say something else, and what we need to look for is the contrast between the two, the hollow that "separates and unites them" (100). It is in this sense and this sense only that Macherey refers to the unconscious of the work (as opposed to that of the author), and this is the meaning that I too have in mind when I speak of the textual unconscious.

"In the culture of psychoanalysis," Ned Lukacher suggests, "Dickens has always been the figure of both its prehistory and its future" (336), and thus it is only appropriate that my first chapter turns its attention to Dickens and specifically to *Martin Chuzzlewit*. This early novel (1843–44) had its origin in turbulence and conflict, as Dickens attempted to come to terms with the profound disappointments he had experienced during his 1842 visit to America. But while conflict and psychic violence are, in part at least, behind the complex impulses that drive this novel, they are also responsible in some mysterious way for the fact that it is a wonderful comic novel, one rightfully included by Robert Polhemus in the great tradition of the British comic novel. Not only was Sairey Gamp William Faulkner's favorite literary character (*Lion in the Garden*, 251), but she remains one of the most memorable characters in English literature. Freud's *Jokes and Their Relation to the Unconscious* is still the best discussion of humor that we have, and in it he reminds us that jokes are almost always subversive, unashamedly politically incorrect, and often violent and sexual. In this respect, *Martin Chuzzlewit* might be read as a joke writ large, with Mrs. Gamp as both its punch line and its lead stand-up comic. But the novel looks at the sexual and the violent in other ways as well. The central scene I consider, occurring fairly late in the novel, is initiated by a fight between Tom Pinch and Jonas Chuzzlewit, but Charity Pecksniff also figures prominently in it. This particular scene embodies one of the textual ruptures or hollows that Macherey speaks of, a site of forbidden wishes or desires, including those of patricide and incest, that cannot be given voice but must instead be articulated indirectly through ambiguous and sometimes violent gestures, as well as through the awkward or aberrant behavior that surrounds them.

In the second section of this chapter, I look at the American episodes of *Martin Chuzzlewit*, arguing that Dickens finds in America's myths and legends about itself evidence of a repressed narrative that testifies to the ways in which the desire that Ghosh speaks of, namely, the desire to find a

place without borders, works itself out in America's history. In the case of
Dickens's America, such a desire leads to violence and aggression, for the
body politic of America, the novel argues, is a fragmented body torn away
from its origins or beginnings and desperate in its pain to reclaim that
which has been lost. In the American sections of *Martin Chuzzlewit*, desire
gives birth to a death wish that wears the face of a demonic child, separated
from its childhood and willing to do whatever is necessary to return to it
once again. The language, myths, and legends of the Americans in *Martin
Chuzzlewit* are symptomatic gestures that disclose an unconscious desire
that manifests itself, like hysteric symptoms, in patterns of repetition and
return characterized by violence and self-deception.

I next turn my attention to Thackeray's *Journey from Cornhill to Grand
Cairo* (1846), an account of a voyage that Thackeray, at the invitation of a
friend, took in 1844 through the Middle East and what was then referred
to as the Orient. Thackeray's *Journey*, I argue, is a site of unacknowledged
conflicts, telling a story rather different from the one Thackeray's narrator
claims to tell. It is the only narrative examined in this study that is not a
novel, and thus its inclusion calls for some comment. Like Dickens's *Martin Chuzzlewit* and Elizabeth Gaskell's *Ruth, Journey from Cornill to Grand
Cairo* is a fascinating and powerful text by a major author that has received
comparatively little attention. But even more importantly, Thackeray's narrative raises important questions regarding subjectivity, especially in regard
to the identity of the writing subject. As indicated earlier, the existence of
the unconscious implies the notion of a decentered subjectivity, the possibility that we write and speak from somewhere other than where we think
we write and speak from, and as much as any text examined in this study,
Thackeray's narrative invites us to explore the implications of such a possibility. It is precisely this dislocation of subjectivity that lies behind much of
this text's haunting and troubling tone, for in the text we find a narrative of
exile, as Thackeray's narrator wanders through a world that invites his gaze,
but does not allow him to inhabit it.

Elizabeth Gaskell's *Ruth* (1853), the subject of my third chapter, is a
text that various readers have characterized as distressed and uneven, a novel
filled with conflict and errant cross-purposes, and I too am interested in
these aspects of Gaskell's novel. I am especially intrigued by what *Ruth* does
not say, but what is nevertheless acted out by the elaboration of certain utter-

ances in it. Gaskell's novels frequently explore the domain of the erotic. *Ruth* too participates—brilliantly, in fact—in such an exploration, but, at the same time, it is a death-haunted novel, just as Ruth herself is an intensely passionate woman around whom an aura of death and dissolution lingers throughout the novel. Desire in *Ruth* is often death haunted or death ridden, seeking from the beginning darkened spaces and corners that anticipate the plague-infected topography of the novel's closing pages. The prostitute is not only the other of the Victorian age itself, as Sarah Webster Goodwin has suggested ("Romanticism and the Ghost of Prostitution," 159–60), but also the other of Gaskell's text, a floating signifier embodying this strange and troubled merging of the erotic and death, and her presence in the text testifies to Elizabeth Gaskell's own rich and complex imagination.

In Wilkie Collins's *The Woman in White* (1860), the focus of the next chapter, we find a narrative that would seem to call our attention to the ways in which we should read it, as we hear Walter Hartright telling of "something hidden below the surface," and Marian Halcombe speaking of "the hidden contents" of texts. But there are no hidden depths or concealed meanings in this narrative, for, like Freud's unconscious, the textual unconscious of Collins's novel is disclosed through language, making itself known, for example, through the ways in which what is said is said—namely, in the very nature of Walter's narrative itself (how he tells the story he tells) as well as in the lacunae and wounds, in part Oedipal in nature, that punctuate his narrative, creating disequilibria and textual tears or gaps in its lines of filiation and chronology. And in my final chapter, I turn to *Jude the Obscure* (1895), both the last novel Hardy wrote and, I would argue, the last novel of the Victorian age. Both Hardy and his readers have suggested a number of reasons why he wrote no more novels after *Jude the Obscure*, but it is possible that he had nowhere else to go, nothing else to say, or at least nothing else that he wanted to say as a novelist. In writing about the art of Wagner and Turner, Hardy suggested that he especially admired their later work because neither man was content to rest complacently in what he had done so well, but instead continued to push the limits of his art: "When a man not contented with the grounds of his success goes on and on, and tries to achieve the impossible," Hardy said, "then he gets profoundly interesting to me."[23] Like Wagner and Turner, Hardy was too good an artist to simply do again what he had done earlier, refusing to rest content "with the grounds of his success." Instead of going backward or standing still, he moved into poetry, letting *Jude the Obscure* stand as his last novel. And although Hardy was not happy with *Jude the Obscure*—"Alas, what a miserable accomplishment it is," he confessed, "when I compare it with what I meant to make it"—his last novel is considerably more of an accomplishment than Hardy's remark acknowledges.[24]

Marjorie Garson points out in *Hardy's Fables of Integrity* that "Jude Fawley wants" (152), but Sue Bridehead also "wants," and in her case as well as Jude's, "want" implies both lack and desire. But the object of desire in *Jude the Obscure* remains hidden, obscured, and Hardy invokes ancient voices of classical literature, not only in order to develop his own voice more fully, but also to explore the nature of this desire, identified in *Jude* as "yearning." Coming at the end of Hardy's career as a novelist as well as at the end of the century, *Jude the Obscure* is appropriately enough a fiction about ends, exploring the nature of closure itself. In looking at the question of closure and its relationship to what Hardy identifies as the condition of modernism, I have drawn on Freud's *Beyond the Pleasure Principle*, one of our century's most haunting and disturbing inquiries into these questions, for it can tell us much, I think, about the nature of the concealed desires in *Jude* and the ways in which they make their presence felt. My final chapter on *Jude the Obscure* allows my study to come full circle. In *Martin Chuzzlewit*, Sairey Gamp and the world of the folk and carnivalesque that she represents stand in sharp contrast to the death-haunted and violent impulses that govern much of the novel, and in Hardy's last novel, its final words are spoken by Arabella Donn, a woman who is, like Mrs. Gamp, utterly at home in her own body, an anomaly in a world otherwise inhabited by lonely wanderers taking part in a futile search for that place without borders, experiencing a sense of absence that is, like Robinson Crusoe's, insupportable.

1

Martin Chuzzlewit

The Bodies of Desire in *Martin Chuzzlewit*

> He who has eyes to see and ears to hear may convince himself
> that no mortal can keep a secret. If his lips are silent, he chatters
> with his fingertips; betrayal oozes out of him at every pore.
>
> SIGMUND FREUD, "Fragment of an Analysis of a Case of Hysteria"[1]

Dickens is intrigued by the depressions and protuberances inscribed on the surface of the human body, by noses, pimples, Adam's apples, beards and bare cheeks, bare legs and wooden legs, by snowy breasts and waving hands, mouths with teeth and mouths without them, by various bodily odors and emanations, and by the ways in which bumps, abrasions, or errant thoughts can cause the surfaces and appendages of our body to change shape or color, become moist or dry, larger or smaller, hotter or colder. Throughout the novel, Dickens is fascinated by the bodily concavities and convexities that shatter, disrupt, or violate the images of wholeness and intactness we attempt to present to the world. He is drawn not to the individual body per se, but rather to its capacity for sudden growths, eruptions, and transformations. The bodies we find in *Martin Chuzzlewit* are not seamless texts, but

are instead characterized by various shapes and often bizarre combinations
of parts and pieces, invested with their own configurations and power to
intrigue and attract.

In speaking of Rabelais's fascination with the grotesque body, Mikhail
Bakhtin notes that "all these convexities and orifices have a common characteristic; it is within them that confines between bodies and between the
body and the world are overcome: there is an interchange and interorien-
tation" (*Rabelais and His World*, 317).[2] Dickens, like Rabelais, is fascinated
by such bodies and writes about them with comparable enthusiasm, albeit
without Rabelais's scatology. Such, for example, is the case in a scene in
which young Martin becomes, as Jerome Meckier has described him, "a
violated man" (*Innocent Abroad*, 7), his body carefully investigated by several Americans:

> Two gentlemen . . . agreed to divide the labour. One of them took him
> below the waistcoat; one above. Each stood directly in front of his subject
> with his head a little on one side, intent on his department. If Martin put
> one boot before the other, the lower gentleman was down upon him; he
> rubbed a pimple on his nose, and the upper gentleman booked it. He
> opened his mouth to speak, and the same gentleman was on one knee
> before him, looking at his teeth, with the nice scrutiny of a dentist. . . .
> They had him in all points of view: in front, in profile, three-quarter face,
> and behind. . . . New lights shone in upon him, in respect of his nose.
> Contradictory rumours were abroad on the subject of his hair. (316)

The novel, Bakhtin suggests, enables us to "encounter new forms for making public all unofficial and forbidden spheres of human life" (*The Dialogic Imagination*, 165–66). This examination of young Martin makes
public a previously concealed landscape of the body, and like Gulliver's
view of the Brobdingnagian breast, it perhaps shows us more than we would
prefer to see. Priggish and rather stuffy throughout much of the novel, Martin becomes the grotesque body of orifices and protuberances (the gaping
mouth and pimpled nose), examined from all angles, from the rear as well
as from the front and sides. If young Martin's body, like his contradictory
hair, is open to various interpretations, Dickens's attitude toward the bodies
that populate his fictional landscapes is similarly ambiguous. "Spitting to

Dickens," S. J. Newman has observed, "is as shitting to Swift" (*Dickens at Play*, 109), and Dickens is disturbed or unsettled by the body and its functions. But his imagination is fueled rather than constrained by such misgivings, and he is drawn, whether in fascination, horror, or both, to images of the body and its various openings that destabilize boundaries, collapsing the categories of inside and outside, self and other, body and earth.

If we interpret such images in Dickens's novels as simply serving the cause of satire, we not only diminish his fiction, but cheat ourselves as well. In reading *Martin Chuzzlewit*, for example, we should imitate the methodology of the curious Americans, for its fictional landscape is filled with bodies, often dismembered or fragmented, its world resembling at times the fecundity and corporeality of a Fellini film, at other times the *corps morcelé* of Salvador Dali's canvasses. In the epigraph for this section, taken from his case history of Dora, Freud states that human beings cannot keep secrets, for even if we keep our mouth shut, other parts of our body will talk: we chatter with our fingertips and the truth betrays us by oozing through our pores.[3] Dickens's bodies are virtual chatterboxes, and in reading the body in *Martin Chuzzlewit*, we need to pay close attention to the surface of the text, to its fissures, blushes, and changes, as well as to the extraordinary gestures and movements through which repressed desire finds articulation. "We never know what's hidden in each other's breasts," Mrs. Gamp observes, "and if we had glass winders there, we'd need to keep the shutters up, I do assure you" (400). But as this novel demonstrates, the hidden does find ways of making itself known, even while the shutters are up. Before I turn my attention to three of Dickens's bodies, however, I indicate briefly the ways in which the two sections of this chapter share a common focus, other than the fact that they examine the same novel.

For although the first section examines a scene late in the English section of *Martin Chuzzlewit*, and the second focuses almost exclusively on the American sections, the question of fantasy figures prominently in both sections; and in order to look at the ways in which it does so, I would like to jump ahead somewhat, turning to the passage from Jacqueline Rose's *States of Fantasy* that serves as one of the epigraphs for this chapter. In it, she writes that "fantasy shapes the contours of our political worlds," and that "it circulates and empowers itself in other more public, collective domains" (79). Throughout her aptly named book, Rose argues that we need to think of fantasy as something other than wholly private and secretive, suggesting that "there is no way of understanding political identities and destinies without letting fantasy into the frame" (4). Although she asks us to expand and deepen our understanding of fantasy, she does not suggest that we should abandon its more common usage. For fantasy does indeed identify our licentious and asocial imaginings and daydreams, that hunger or curiosity that calls forth with both fascination and horror the realms of human experience that are private, secretive, buried deep in dark closets where the gaze of public scrutiny never penetrates—or so it is hoped.[4] In the first section of this chapter, I consider almost exclusively this latter meaning of fantasy, as I examine the ways the body becomes a theater in which are staged various private fantasies and desires that insist on making themselves felt and known as sites of *jouissance*. In the opening chapter of *Martin Chuzzlewit*, however, Dickens reminds us that our most disturbing and private fantasies have also found their way into the collective history of the human race, inscribed in its legends and its various cultures, and it is toward this more shared or public meaning of fantasy that I turn my attention in the second part of this chapter. I look at Dickens's exploration of what Rose identifies as "the unconscious dreams of nations" (3), arguing that his novel suggests that we cannot understand either the identity of America or the trajectory of its history without taking into account the fantasies that shaped it.

Let me turn now to *Martin Chuzzlewit* and to a rather peculiar scene in chapter 24; given the length of this novel, a brief synopsis of the scene might be helpful. It begins with a fight between Jonas Chuzzlewit and Tom Pinch that results in Jonas being struck on the head with his own walking stick. Along with Tom Pinch, Jonas soon returns to the Pecksniff residence, where his wounds are tended to by Pecksniff and his daughter, Mercy, while Pecksniff's other daughter, Charity, recently jilted by Jonas, sits quietly by with a strange smile on her face. The second section takes place later that same evening when Charity, having already guessed the origin of Jonas's injury, comes to Tom Pinch's room, and, with unusually intimate gestures, expresses her gratitude to him and tells him that she wants to be his friend. During the third section, Tom contemplates the significance of Charity's visit as well as the implications of his earlier fight with Jonas. As Tom reflects on his position in the ambiguous and shifting entanglements of the Pecksniff and Chuzzlewit families, his thoughts or dreams—the whole passage is ambiguously suspended between sleep and wakefulness—turn to Mary Graham and conclude with what Michael Steig has described as "one of the most remarkable passages in Dickens" ("*Martin Chuzzlewit*: Pinch and Pecksniff," 184):

> It must be acknowledged that, asleep or awake, Tom's position in reference to this young lady was full of uneasiness. The more he saw of her, the more he admired her beauty, her intelligence, the amiable qualities that even won on the divided house of Pecksniff. . . . When she spoke, Tom held his breath, so eagerly he listened; when she sang, he sat like one entranced. She touched his organ; and from that bright epoch even it, the old companion of his happiest hours, incapable as he had thought of elevation, began a new and deified existence. (340)

Steig argues, "Dickens would no doubt have expunged this last sentence had he been consciously aware of its extended sexual pun" (184). Perhaps Dickens would have, perhaps not, but in any case, it was not deleted, and, as Steig notes in "The Intentional Phallus," it is difficult to conceive of such a passage as the result of a mere accident (53–55). Steig also raises the question of authorial intentionality, but such questions, while interesting, remain extremely problematic, since, at best, we can only hazard a guess about what Dickens intended or did not intend, and whether such intent, if it does exist, is inscribed in the design and/or execution of the particular text under examination.[5] More importantly, however, if Freud, Lacan, and countless artists have taught us anything, it is that we are not in full control of the meaning of the words we use or the language we create. Moreover, the passage involving Tom Pinch does not exist in isolation, but rather, like the fight between Jonas and Tom and Charity's visit to Tom's room, it provides exemplary evidence that the body is a theater in which our desires are acted out, a text on which are transcribed narrative histories repressed by language. As such, these three sections exemplify Peter Brooks's concept of "textual binding," in which textual energies are organized into a "serviceable form," such as repetition, recurrence, or symmetry, which "allows us to bind one textual moment to another in terms of similarity or substitution rather than mere contiguity" (*Reading for the Plot*, 101).

In each of the three moments that constitute this scene, desire is betrayed by means of libidinal sites marked by the presence of blood, and thus it is appropriate that the scene itself begins with a violent fight between Tom Pinch and Jonas Chuzzlewit: "He [Jonas] flourished his stick over Tom's head; but in a moment, it was spinning harmlessly in the air, and Jonas himself lay sprawling in the ditch. In the momentary struggle for the stick, Tom had brought it into violent contact with his opponent's forehead; and the blood welled out profusely from a deep cut on the temple" (338). A shaken Tom Pinch later confesses to Charity, "I didn't mean to hurt him so much" (339), but even more significant than Tom's ambiguously phrased admission (How much is "so much"?) is the disclosure of a capacity for violence on Tom's part that is both registered and erased by a text that informs us that his "apparently" violent designs are "really" directed toward healing: "Tom Pinch, in his guilty agitation, shook a bottle of Dutch Drops until they were nothing but English Froth, and in his other hand sustained a formidable carving-knife, really intended to reduce the swelling, but apparently designed for the ruthless infliction of another wound as soon as that was dressed" (338–39).

What is most peculiar about this scene, however, is not the fight itself, since Jonas's belligerence virtually forces Tom's hand, but rather Jonas's response to his own wound. Throughout the novel, he is moved quickly to anger, easily offended, and, as Montague Tigg later discovers, dangerous to cross, and yet his subdued response to his injury is so out of character that even Tom is bewildered, interpreting it as evidence of a new magnanimity on Jonas's part. With a passivity insufficiently accounted for by his mild concussion, Jonas stares at his bloodstained handkerchief ("several times he took his handkerchief from the cut to look vacantly at the blood upon it" [338]), as if he were attempting to interpret the stain itself. If we are to understand the enigmatic nature of Jonas's wound, we need to regard it as the site of psychic as well as physical trauma, and thus as a symptomatic mark or metonymic cultural scar.

For from the beginning, *Martin Chuzzlewit* announces that it is interested in examining the nature of the wound we experience by virtue of our insertion into human culture and history. The original title of the novel, for example, identified the centrality of kinship and genealogy to the novel, offering its readers a key that would enable them to enter "the House of

Chuzzlewit," while its original motto—"*Your* homes the scene. *Yourselves* the Actors, here"—made it clear that the novel was concerned with the conflicts and desires found in all "houses," not just the Chuzzlewits'.[6] In this respect, the Chuzzlewit family embodies not only the tensions, conflicts, and desires inscribed in the family romance, but also what Dickens in the opening chapter refers to as the "innumerable repetitions of the same phase of character" that are passed on from one generation to the next. Woven into the novel as an Oedipal Ur-plot that amplifies or brings into sharper focus other tensions (for example, those between Tom Pinch and Pecksniff and between young and old Martin), Jonas's story is unusual not because it tells of parricidal desires, but rather because in his case repressed desires have momentarily escaped interdiction.[7] It is through Jonas's wound as mark or fissure that his blood, at once familiar and unfamiliar, and thus uncanny, pours forth, inscribing an enigmatic text on a handkerchief. The handkerchief will show up later even more bloodstained, reappearing with Montague Tigg's clothes, "stained with clay, and spotted with blood" (675), when Nadgett retrieves them from the river into which Jonas threw them.

The repressed returns in other ways as well. The strength of the symbolic father, Lacan's "Name of the Father," derives from the fact that it is the voice of interdiction, that which intervenes between child and mother, as it says no to our desire, and thus thrusts us into culture, or, as Lacan expresses it, "The Father, the Name of the Father, sustains the structure of desire with the structure of the law" (*Concepts*, 34). The power of "the Father" derives from the fact that the sons internalize his prohibitions after his death, yielding to his patriarchal interdictions through what Freud characterizes as "deferred obedience" (*SE*, 13:143). Freud argues, in works such as *Totem and Taboo* and *Civilization and Its Discontents*, that the death of this father at the hands of his sons set up the superego, and thus the construction of a community based on remorse and guilt. As Joan Copjec notes, this notion of the primal father has often been seen as "one of Freud's most crackpot ideas" (*Read My Desire*, 12): "But to call it crackpot is to miss the point that if this father of the primal horde is indeed preposterous, then he is objectively so. That is to say, he is unbelievable in the regime in which his existence *must* be unthinkable if relations of equality are to take hold" (12, emphasis Copjec's). Arguing, as does Lacan, that structures are real, albeit never capable of being wholly contained within language itself, Copjec suggests that it is precisely the structure proposed by this "crackpot" theory that enables us to account for "a society of equals, which is thus shown to be irreducible to the labile relations of equality that never obtain absolutely" (12).[8] "Since civilization obeys," writes Freud, "an internal erotic impulse which causes human beings to unite in closely-knit groups, it can only achieve this aim through an ever-increasing reinforcement of the sense of guilt" (*Civilization and Its Discontents*, 80). But, as he also reminds us, the same aggression, what he will refer to as "trends of death" (80), that originally led to the murder of the father still exists, destabilizing and frustrating any hope of the realization of an unthreatened or stable community or society.

Dickens too knew of these "trends of death," and argues in the opening chapter of *Martin Chuzzlewit* that human history is written with the violent patterns of "innumerable repetition" in which guilt and aggression struggle against each other for control. In the case of Anthony and Jonas Chuzzlewit, the father's voice is heard once again, demanding a punishment born of guilt, for as Anthony's judgment returns from beyond the grave, spoken through the choric voices of Chuffey and Lewsome, it speaks of the violation of prohibited desires, and thus sets into motion the punishment that follows. Jonas's passive response to his wound and his "reading" of his blood acknowledge the strength of the dead father's presence, and, as fissure or mark, the wound also prefigures his later attempts to atone for his crime through self-inflicted punishment. Before atonement can take place, however, Jonas's body is once again marked or scarred, this time with the taboo, and exposed to public scrutiny and repulsion. The horror that Jonas's presence invokes suggests that the community is responding to him not as the murderer of Montague Tigg, but rather as the parricide, albeit an unsuccessful one: "They turned away," Dickens writes, "from him as if he were some obscene and filthy animal, repugnant to the sight. . . . As he crouched on the floor, they drew away from him as if a pestilence were in his breath. They fell off, one by one, from that part of the room, keeping him alone on the ground" (671, 675).

The taboo, Freud argues, arises in response to our most powerful fantasies and unconscious desires, and the strength of the repulsion it evokes measures the strength of these desires (*SE*, 13:35). Regarded as contagious, as a "pestilence," Jones incites what Freud alludes to as the community's "fear of an infectious example" (*SE*, 13:71–72), and he brings out such a response only because the community is, in fact, already "infected" with Jonas's disease, finding in him the embodiment of its own unconscious desires. Having actually done (or tried to do) that of which the community has only fantasized, Jonas is more correct than he realizes when he observes at one point in the novel, "I dare say I'm no worse than other men. We're all alike, or nearly so" (545). Ritualistically summoned to public exposure and punishment by the patriarchal voice of old Martin, who still presides over the house of Chuzzlewit—"'Let no one leave the house,' said Martin. 'This man is my brother's son. Ill-met, ill-trained, ill-begotten'" (666)— Jonas is condemned to death. However, in a brilliant intuitive stroke on Dickens's part, Jonas is unable to hang himself, but instead must drink poison, thus killing himself by the same instrument of destruction he attempted to use against his father. Like the hero of Kafka's "The Judgment," Jonas is condemned to death by an internalized patriarchal voice and carries out the sentence on himself.

As Mercy Pecksniff and her father tend to Jonas's wounds, Charity does not help, but sits "upright in one corner, with a smile upon her face" (338). As in Jonas's case, the textual body gives voice to a desire that language itself attempts to repress, literally speaking in this case through its pores. Similar to the scene in *Great Expectations* in which Estella, "a bright flush upon her face, as though something had happened to delight her" (121), first allows Pip to kiss her, having secretly witnessed a fight between him and Herbert Pocket, this moment involving Charity and Tom Pinch is situated in the erotic dynamics of violence.[9] "Underlying eroticism," writes Georges Bataille, "is the feeling of something bursting, of the violence accompanying an explosion" (*Erotism*, 93), and Charity's flushed or blood-suffused face reveals the *jouissance* she experiences through her vicarious participation in the scene between Jonas and Tom Pinch. In *Martin Chuzzlewit*, the opening of what should be closed alerts us to the escape of repressed desire, and like Jonas's wound, the scene involving Charity and Tom Pinch begins with such an opening. For as Charity quietly sneaks to Tom's room and knocks on his door, Tom "heard a gentle tap at his door, and opening it, saw her, to his great astonishment, standing before him with her finger on her lip" (339). The gesture of the "finger on her lip" calls attention to the precarious containment of secrets that threaten to escape through the fissures or seams of the body, and Charity's body, her gesture of conspiratorial silence notwithstanding, testifies to the presence of such secrets, as she elaborates on her remark to Tom "I am your friend from tonight. I am always your friend from this time" (339): "She turned her flushed face upon Tom to confirm her words by its kindling expression; and seizing his right hand, pressed it to her breast, and kissed it. And there was nothing personal in this to render it at all embarrassing, for even Tom, whose power of observation was by no means remarkable, knew that she would have fondled any hand, no matter how bedaubed or dyed, that had broken the head of Jonas Chuzzlewit" (339).

It is hard to take Dickens's feeble narrative disclaimer ("there was nothing personal in this to render it at all embarrassing") seriously, except insofar as it calls our attention to the transgressive nature of erotic gestures directed toward someone who virtually occupies the position of her brother in the Pecksniff household. The blush, Monique David-Ménard notes in *Hysteria from Freud to Lacan,* "points up the insistence of a long experience of pleasure that has always been situated at the point of articulation between body and language" (60). Like the Victorian novelist's "virginal blush," which belies its adjectival demure, the flushed face testifies to sublimation or the displacement upward of what is below.[10] For although the "kindling expression" of Charity's flushed face "confirms her words," her words themselves, with their allusions to a wished-for friendship, attempt to evade or avoid the desire that empowers them. The erotics of the scene, however, are identified not only by the configurations of Charity's body or by a blush that will not remain repressed, but also by a series of acts that complete or provide closure for the desire articulated by her blood: as she "fondles" Tom's hand, which has been marked ("bedaubed or dyed") by association with the blood or violence of Jonas's wound, first pressing it to her breast and then kissing it (gestures that both recall and preempt the "snowy breasts" that throw kisses at Tom because they see "no harm" in him), she enacts a pantomime of sexual activity and *jouissance,* caught up in the dynamics of violence and desire that permeate this scene.

If the narrator willfully attempts to misread Charity's gestures, Tom does not. And if we in turn are to understand Tom Pinch, we cannot dismiss him, as Barbara Hardy does, as a "grossly sentimental figure" ("The Change of Heart in Dickens's Novels," 112). Mould, the undertaker, alerts us to the significance of surnames in *Martin Chuzzlewit*, and Tom Pinch's surname suggests not only his distorted and prematurely wizened nature, but also the pain associated with his body. Anticipating *David Copperfield*'s Mr. Dick, Tom is an early Dickensian version of the man-child as sage and artist who hides behind his simplicity or even simple-mindedness values and perceptions against which the rest of the characters are judged. He is, however, problematic in ways that Mr. Dick is not, for while Mr. Dick remains essentially asexual, we find in Tom an ambiguous but nevertheless discernible growth of sexual awareness and erotic desire.

Tom's body is the arena in which this growth is registered, and, both as Dickens describes it and as Hablot K. Browne draws it, it is an ambiguous text, which, like his clothes, has been "twisted and tortured into all kinds of odd shapes." The unconscious expresses itself through the body, and someone familiar with its articulations or "symptomatic acts," Freud suggests in *The Psychopathology of Everyday Life*, might "feel like King Solomon who, according to oriental legend, understood the language of animals" (*SE*, 6:199). However, such articulations can be puzzling, and Tom's body is an enigmatic text. He is described as

> an ungainly, awkward-looking man, extremely short-sighted, and prematurely bald. . . . He was far from handsome certainly; and was dressed in a snuff-coloured suit, of an uncouth make at the best, which, being shrunken with long wear, was twisted and tortured into all kinds of odd shapes; but notwithstanding his attire, and his clumsy figure, which had a great stoop in his shoulders, and a ludicrous habit he had of thrusting his head forward, by no means redeemed, one would not have been disposed . . . to consider him a bad fellow by any means. He was perhaps thirty, but he might have been any age between sixteen and sixty: being one of those strange creatures who never decline into an ancient appearance, but look their oldest when they are very young, and get over it at once. (17)

Tom's body bewilders and intrigues us, concealing its true age even as we attempt to decipher its history. Other erotic bodies similarly misread it. "Sparkling eyes and snowy breasts came hurriedly to many an upper casement as he clattered by, and gave him back his greeting; not stinted either, but sevenfold, good measure. They were all merry. They all laughed. And

Fig. 1. "Meekness of Mr. Pecksniff and his charming daughters," by Hablot K. Browne. From *Martin Chuzzlewit* by Charles Dickens, edited by Margaret Cardwell (New York: Oxford University Press, 1982), 17. The illustration appeared in the first edition of *Martin Chuzzlewit* (London: Chapman and Hall, 1844).

some of the wickedest among them even kissed their hands as Tom looked back. For who minded poor Mr. Pinch! There was no harm in *him*" (59, emphasis Dickens's). Even "the wickedest" of the "sparkling eyes and snowy breasts" regard Tom as a eunuch, as a man who has "no harm" in him; John Westlock similarly regards him as lacking that which a man should possess when he tells Tom, "You haven't half enough of the devil in you" (20).[11] Although Tom's body invites misinterpretation by others, it reveals the truth, for Tom's knowledge, registered in the text as both somatic and psychic pain, is experienced as moments of "uneasiness" or discomfort. Thus, although the narrator denies any "personal" significance to Charity's gestures, Tom Pinch knows better, as he goes to bed, "full of uncomfortable thoughts":

> That there should be any such tremendous division in the family as he knew must have taken place to convert Charity Pecksniff into his friend, for any reason, but, above all, for that which was clearly the real one; that Jonas, who had assailed him with such exceeding coarseness, should have been sufficiently magnanimous to keep the secret of their quarrel; and that any train of circumstances should have led to the commission of an assault and battery by Thomas Pinch upon any man calling himself the friend of Seth Pecksniff, were matters of such deep and painful cogitation, that he could not close his eyes. His own violence, in particular, so preyed upon the generous mind of Tom, that coupling it with the many former occasions on which he had given Mr. Pecksniff pain and anxiety (occasions of which the gentleman often reminded him), he really began to regard himself as destined by a mysterious fate to be the evil genius and bad angel of his patron. But he fell asleep at last, and dreamed—new source of waking uneasiness—that he had betrayed his trust, and run away with Mary Graham. (339–40)

Like Jonas's wound and Charity's flushed face, Tom's discomfort brings to light previously repressed desire. As he reflects on familial patterns of secrets, betrayals, and violence unnoticed by him earlier, Tom becomes aware not only of a "tremendous division" in the Chuzzlewit family, but also of his own ambiguous position in these structures. As he realizes, his "assault and battery" of Jonas, the "friend of Seth Pecksniff," was a reenactment of earlier assaults on Pecksniff, and thus he correctly associates or "couples" his violence toward Jonas with the occasions on which he had given Pecksniff "pain and anxiety." Tom regards himself as "destined by a mysterious fate to be the evil genius and bad angel of his patron," as someone taking part in hidden scenarios, acting out a script not of his own making.

"The text itself," Roland Barthes writes, "can reveal itself in the form of a body, split into fetish objects, into erotic sites" (*The Pleasure of the Text*, 56); and the wound that flows from Jonas's temple, the blood suffusing Charity's face, and the tumescence of this scene's final paragraph all tell of the word made flesh. As in the two earlier sections (with their corresponding gestures of the violent "touch" that wounds Jonas and Charity's touching of Tom's hand to her breast and lips), the libidinal area here is identified by the touch ("She touched his organ; and from that bright epoch even it, the old companion of his happiest hours, incapable as he had thought of elevation, began a new and deified existence"). The touch calls our attention to the particular site of Tom's *jouissance*. If the sliding of signified under signifier seems especially evident in this scene, the musical metaphor barely containing the elevated organ it only half-heartedly attempts to conceal, it is because of symptoms that demand to be heard, because of desires, such as those that empower Tom's dreams, that will not remain silent.

The presence of the Oedipus in the family romance, Edward Said suggests, disturbs patterns of kinship and genealogy, creating what he refers to as "a tangling up of the family sequence" (*Beginnings*, 170), and such entanglements pervade *Martin Chuzzlewit*. Some time ago, George Orwell spoke of the "incestuous atmosphere" we sometimes find in Dickens's novels ("Charles Dickens," 448), and Tom's uneasiness or discomfort has its origin not only in his feelings of violence or aggression toward Pecksniff, but also in the fact that Mary's presence in his fantasies or dreams screens even more forbidden desires. At one point, this screen momentarily collapses altogether, and Tom and Ruth Pinch stumble on that which should be hidden. Initiated, like the previous such scene, by the opened door and the violent gesture, this puzzling scene begins with young Martin bursting into Tom's apartment and accusing him of an unnamed treachery or betrayal. Tom repeatedly asks young Martin to be more explicit—"I don't know what is in your mind," he tells Martin at one point, "or who has abused it, or by what extraordinary means" (652), and he later repeats this protest, reminding Martin near the end of their conversation, "you have not told me what your accusation is" (654). But neither Tom nor the reader ever finds out what Tom is specifically accused of or why Martin will not be more direct. At one point, Martin turns to Ruth, telling Tom, "I appeal to your good sister to hear me," but he is immediately interrupted by Tom, who says, "Pray, do not appeal to her. She will never believe you" (653), and, Dickens adds, "He drew her arm through his, as he said it" (653), in a gesture of both affection and control. Ruth in turn makes it quite clear that she does not want to listen to any unkind words about her brother, and Martin quickly backs away from a strategy bound to fail, claiming that he "never meant to appeal to you against your brother" (653).

But this moment, like Martin's earlier verbal pirouettes, creates large gaps of silence that bestow on this scene a peculiarly enigmatic quality, as if something is missing, as if something has been left unsaid that was straining to be heard or to be given a voice. Young Martin eventually leaves the room, but the tensions created by his refusal to be more specific about the nature of his accusation linger. Tom and Ruth, moving to fill in the holes of silence created by Martin's departure, begin to speak of secrets, but in doing so they create silences of their own, as they too refuse to name the subject of their discourse. Her arms already clasping Tom's neck as she kneels beside his chair, Ruth responds to a sudden burst of tears on his part by moving even closer to him ("More closely yet, she nestled down about him, and wept as if her heart would break" [654]), telling him, "I know your secret heart. I have found it out; you couldn't hide the truth from me. Why didn't you tell me?" (654). He answers, "I am glad . . . that this has passed between us . . . because it relieves my mind of a great weight" (655), and he then continues: "'My dear girl,' said Tom: 'with whatever feelings I regard her,' they seemed to avoid the name by mutual consent; 'I have long ago—I am sure I may say from the first—looked on it as a dream. As something that might possibly have happened under very different circumstances, but which can never be'" (655). As with Martin's outburst, what is most striking about this passage is its evasiveness, not what is said, but what is unsaid. Tentatively coming close to the subject, but never approaching it directly, Tom and Ruth participate in such a circuitous dialogue that the narrator actually intervenes, noting that they "seemed to avoid the name by mutual consent."

Like Jonas's body, the name of the sister as the object of desire remains unspoken, although it makes itself felt through the similarly elided name of Mary. David Holbrook argues that Dickens was able to avoid "the fear of sex" by presenting "a man-woman relationship from which the libidinal elements are excluded, as with Tom Pinch's relationship with his sister, or by father-daughter relationships" (10). But if the libidinal elements are excluded, it is precisely their exclusion, I would argue, that compels us to acknowledge their power and their reality. In other words, what gives such relationships in Dickens the power to stay with us—Tom and Ruth Pinch, for example, or Jarndyce and Esther Summerson in *Bleak House*—is precisely the presence in them of strong and even compelling libidinal elements. When Esther, for example, tells us on two different occasions (670, 894) that she kissed Jarndyce as a woman would kiss a man, traces or residues of these occasions linger, regardless of how much the later plot of the novel attempts to deflect our attention from them, shaping in part at least the ways in which we understand the ending of the novel and hear its language. When Peggy Lee sang "my heart belongs to Daddy," she had in mind, I would suggest, something rather different from what we see going on in *Bleak House*. Similarly, whatever else might be excluded from this scene between brother and sister in *Martin Chuzzlewit*, it is most certainly not the presence of desire. Testifying to the chasm between desire and need as well as to the indestructibility of unconscious desires, Tom and Ruth both cry out in their symptoms, afraid to come any closer, but even more terrified, as the language of their bodies makes clear, of moving farther apart. Tom dreams of a world in which desire might find fulfillment, but his vision of closure, rooted in fictional scenarios no longer available to him, is haunted by death as well as by desire—"someone who is precious to you might die," he tells Ruth, "and you may dream that you are in Heaven with the departed spirit, and you may find it a sorrow to wake to the life on earth" (656).[12] If, as Peter Brooks observes, incest is "the exemplary version of a temptation of short-circuit from which protagonist and text must be led away, into detour, into the cure that prolongs narrative" (109), Tom realizes that such a short circuit, however tempting, cannot be. But, at the same time, the novel's final illustration demonstrates how powerful this desire can be.

Dominating the center of this illustration, "Warm Reception of Mr. Pecksniff by his Venerable Friend," is old Martin Chuzzlewit, Freud's "obscene, ferocious figure" of the primordial father (Lacan, *Ecrits*, 176), his face distorted by rage and his walking stick raised high, ready to strike. He revenges himself on Pecksniff, who cowers by the desk while other members of the clan look on with various expressions of relief, bemusement, and curiosity. A patriarchal bust presides over this scene from atop the bookcase, and a copy of *Paradise Lost*, a text similarly concerned with patriarchy, loss, and transgressive desire, lies on the floor, one more victim of the violence of this scene.[13] Standing in front of the bookcase are Tom and Ruth Pinch, their arms and hands still entangled and their bodies touching, as if they have been interrupted in the midst of an embrace, pantomiming interdicted desire, even in the presence of patriarchal rage. Hablot K. Browne's brilliant final illustration is visual testimony to the text's refusal to separate brother and sister, for they remain bound together in a ménage à trois legitimized by Ruth's marriage to John Westlock, itself a screen for deeper motives that we find articulated in Ruth's insistence to her future husband that she will not tolerate separation from her brother. Tom and Ruth seem destined to reenact, in a Sadean comedy of erotic terror and joy, narrative scripts wherein *jouissance* is always anticipated, the fulfillment of desire forever deferred.

The Violence of Desire in *Martin Chuzzlewit*

> Fantasy shapes the contours of our political worlds. It breaks
> through the boundary separating inner and outer space. To think
> of fantasy as private *only* is a form of possession; holding on to our
> fantasy, we blind ourselves to the way it circulates and empowers
> itself in other more public, collective domains.
>
> JACQUELINE ROSE, *States of Fantasy*

Jacques Lacan has described with some eloquence how our lives are surrounded or "enveloped" even before we are born, by symbolic structures:

> Symbols in fact envelop the life of man in a network so total that they join
> together, before he comes into the world, those who are going to engender him "by flesh and blood"; so total that they bring to his birth, along
> with the gift of the stars, if not with the gift of the fairies, the shape of his

Fig. 2. "Warm Reception of Mr. Pecksniff by his venerable friend," by Hablot K. Browne.
From *Martin Chuzzlewit* by Charles Dickens, edited by Margaret Cardwell (New York:
Oxford University Press, 1982), 798. The illustration appeared in the first edition of *Martin
Chuzzlewit* (London: Chapman and Hall, 1844).

destiny; so total that they give the words that will make him faithful or renegade, the laws of the acts that will follow him right to the place where he is not yet and even beyond his death. (*Ecrits*, 68)

Dickens too was fascinated with the various configurations that destinies can assume and with the network of signifiers that govern not only our birth into the social order, but also our exit from it. Intrigued by the ways in which we are the unconscious heirs of codes and laws that constitute human culture, Dickens realizes that the shape of our destiny, if not bestowed by the stars or fairies, is the gift of equally ambiguous or mysterious forces. As noted earlier, the original title and title-page motto for *Martin Chuzzlewit* were deleted before it was published in its three-volume format in 1844, and the motto was, in fact, never used, having been dropped even earlier by Dickens on the advice of John Forster. But their presence in the genealogy of the text, like the buried archeological artifacts that Freud compares to the unconscious, testifies to the fact that the novel from its very beginning focused on questions of genealogy, kinship, and family structure.[14]

John Bowen has described the first chapter of *Martin Chuzzlewit* as "one of the most remarkable of any novel" (*Other Dickens*, 185), and in it Dickens traces the relationship between the Chuzzlewits and what Dickens refers to as "the antiquity of the race," following the lineage of the Chuzzlewit family back to Adam and Eve.[15] The unconscious, Freud reminds us, is eternal and timeless, and both the English and American sections of *Martin Chuzzlewit* chart the return of ancient and powerful desires as they are plotted along what Ellie Ragland-Sullivan has referred to as the "path of repetition in the here and now" (111). However, in the American episodes of the novel, these desires assume their own particular paths and narrative patterns. The stormy and complex history of Dickens's relationship with America resembles that of a painful love affair, for it is a tale of love and hate, dreams nurtured and then betrayed. The editors of the third volume of the Pilgrim Edition of Dickens's letters, by far the single most important source for anyone interested in the full history of that relationship, suggest, for example, that Dickens's response to America moved from "delighted gratification at his welcome to disenchantment and even repulsion" (vii). As they also point out, "English travellers naturally read each others' books" (viii), and Dickens, prior to his first American visit, read the writings of those who had preceded him to America, including Harriet Martineau's three-volume work, *Society in America* (1837), her *Retrospect of Western Travel* (1838), and Frederick Marryat's *A Diary in America* (1839). After he returned from America, he also spoke warmly of Mrs. Trollope's *Domestic Manners of the Americans* (1832).

But Dickens's representation of America in *Martin Chuzzlewit* is distinctly his own, differing not only from the works of other authors that come before it, but also from his earlier *American Notes*. Questions of kinship and genealogy are at the heart of both the English and American sections of *Martin Chuzzlewit*, but the latter focus more on the question of human nature itself—in other words, on the relationship between *human* and *nature*, and specifically the ways in which we as human subjects cannot remain in nature, but rather must enter into the various symbolic structures that constitute culture.[16] Introduced into the novel as early as the first chapter, with its references to the eighteenth-century theories of J. F. Blumenbach and Lord Monboddo—both concerned with the origin and nature of human nature, as they trace our beginnings back to the swine and the orangutan, respectively—this particular line of inquiry also suggests the degree to which Dickens's concerns touch on some of the central philosophical questions of his age. Jean-Jacques Rousseau's and Karl Marx's formulations, for example, concerning the relationship between the human and the natural are particularly helpful in amplifying the issues explored by *Martin Chuzzlewit*.

Readers such as Myron Magnet and Jerome Meckier have spoken of Dickens's disillusionment with America—not only his disenchantment with the American experiment itself, but also his loss of faith in Rousseau's vision of nature and the possibilities of human fulfillment or happiness in it. However, one could argue that Dickens does not abandon Rousseau's vision, but rather approaches some of its more troubling or ambiguous aspects. Rousseau found the relationship between the natural and the human to be problematic, arguing, for example, that sublimation and repression are the price we must pay to enter human culture, and that they take their toll in fire, war, and other acts of violence and aggression. In chapter 9 of his *On the Origin of Language*, Rousseau ponders the question of what could have prompted human beings to exchange a life of nature for a life of language and culture. "The earth nourishes men," he writes, "but when their initial needs have dispersed them, other needs arise, and it is only then that they speak, and that they have any incentive to speak" (39).[17] But what, he asks, would make them give up a life of nature, especially when the "life of language and culture" inevitably leads to misery and crime? "I cannot imagine how they would ever be induced to give up their primitive liberty, abandoning the isolated pastoral life so fitted to their natural indolence, to impose upon themselves unnecessarily the labors and the inevitable misery of a social mode of life" (38–39). Rousseau may not know how or why this move took place, but he does know, as Judith N. Shklar has observed, that "no worse disaster had or has ever befallen us than our departure from nature to culture." "What greater cosmic injustice," she asks, "can be imagined than an accident that dooms us to insuperable inequality and oppression?" (53). Finally Rousseau does not have an answer to the questions he poses, but can observe only that "he who willed man to be social, by the touch of a finger shifted the globe's axis into line with the axis of the universe" (39). In his reading of this chapter, however, Derrida picks up on Rousseau's image of the touch of a finger and suggests that "there is something catastrophic in the movement that brings about the emergence from the state of nature and in the awakening of the imagination" (*Of Grammatology*, 258), arguing that this movement is inextricably associated with the interdiction of incest, the need to prevent, as Rousseau himself puts it, a man and woman from becoming "husband and wife without ceasing to be brother and sister" (45). Only after the festival, Rousseau's image of human community and ritual, did incest become a transgressive act, for prior to that time, Rousseau insists, "instinct held the place of passion, habit held the place of preference" (45).

Not surprisingly, Marx does not approach the question of incest in his "Economic and Philosophic Manuscripts of 1844," but he similarly argues that human history is the story of our origins or beginnings in nature and also of our alienation from it, pointing out, for example, that when we observe that "man's physical and spiritual life is linked to nature," we are really only saying that "nature is linked to itself, for man is a part of nature" (75). Yet, Marx also stresses the fact that human history involves our estrangement from nature: "The nature which comes to be in human history," he writes, "the genesis of human society — is man's *real* nature; hence nature as it comes to be through industry, even though in an *estranged* form, is true *anthropological* nature" (90, emphasis Marx's). We can come into full realization or consciousness, he argues, only in a social community that enables us to realize our "natural" or human capabilities. Transcendence of alienation is brought about not through an attempt to escape or flee from the human, but rather by embracing its possibilities in a society forged through history by men and women. Thus Marx defines "communism" as the "complete return of man to himself as a social (i.e., human) being—a return become conscious, and accomplished within the entire wealth of previous development." It is, he suggests, "the *genuine* resolution of the conflict between man and nature and man and man" (84), a state in which humanism and naturalism are no longer at odds, but rather each is the other's equal.[18]

Dickens, as we might expect, comes at these questions from a different perspective than either Rousseau or Marx, but the questions he poses are strikingly similar.[19] In *Martin Chuzzlewit*'s America, Rousseau's festival becomes the psychic inversion of itself, an abnormal or grotesque celebration of a vision of community that has its origins in Oedipal violence and incestuous desires, even as it attempts to reject the human. There is no resolution, genuine or otherwise, of that conflict between man and nature that Marx speaks of, even though the Americans speak *ad nauseam* of their reintegration back into a natural realm or kingdom. *Martin Chuzzlewit* anticipates various modern and postmodern novels in its fascination with the ways in which psychoanalytic dynamics are textualized in the body politic of a nation; if we wish to understand the ways in which desire and fantasy are inscribed as narrative in America's history, the novel argues, we must regard its language, myths, and legends of its history as symptomatic gestures that disclose a desire whose presence remains repressed. "Longing on a large scale is what makes history," writes DeLillo in *Underworld* (11), and *Martin Chuzzlewit* charts out, as it were, the trajectory of America's longing.

Dickens was fascinated by America's unconscious texts and their articulation in its history, finding such texts in America's legends and traditions, as the Americans do America in many voices, but all telling the same story. Freedom in America is identified with participation in a natural or primeval state, and thus its citizens envision themselves as the children of freedom and the offspring of nature, related to the bears, buffalo, and wolves. In a speech that was apparently given by an Illinois lawyer in defense of his client, making its way east in time for Dickens to read about it during his visit, Elijah Pogram praises his fellow countryman: "He is a true-born child of this free hemisphere! Verdant as the mountains of our country; bright and flowing as our mineral Licks; unspiled by withering conventionalities as air our broad and boundless Perarers! Rough he may be. So air our Barrs. Wild he may be. So air our Buffalers. But he is a child of Natur, and a child of Freedom; and his boastful answer to the Despot and Tyrant is, that his bright home is in the Setting Sun" (460).[20] Hannibal Chollop, the recipient of Pogram's praise, is not a child, however, but a violent and angry adult male, armed with a "brace of revolving pistols in his coat-pocket, with seven barrels apiece," a sword stick he refers to as the "Tickler," and a great knife, the "Ripper," that he uses as "a means of ventilating the stomach of any adversary in a close contest" (448).

The American voices that Martin and Mark hear, however, insist on repeating this tale of natural origin and childlike nature. Attempting to inhabit a world represented as newly born and innocent, the Americans reject any suggestion that their desire for wholeness or unity cannot be realized. What they seek is newness itself, a rebirth that will allow them to be cleansed of the past and to escape the burden of time and history, and, as such, America is a trope, identifying that which cannot be named directly. Jacqueline Rose has spoken of "the link between historic destiny and the fantasies which support and lend to that destiny their shape" (21), and America, Dickens suggests, inhabits its own fantasies about itself, creating a language and set of myths regarding its historic destiny through which it attempts to sustain such fantasies. Language, however, testifies to separation and difference, and, having fallen into speech, Dickens's America, contrary to its own professions, is not Rousseau's pastoral or prefestival landscape. Rather, mid-nineteenth-century America is still reenacting earlier battles with England, battles that were themselves but repetitions of still earlier conflicts, structured along kinship lines and reflecting Oedipal antagonisms and desires that Dickens identifies as early as the novel's first chapter. Repetition, Freud suggests, enables us to remember what would otherwise remain repressed, and the most important narratives of America's history are not those that are publicly celebrated, but rather the repressed narratives of desire that are plotted out along lines of repetition.

One of the Americans in *Martin Chuzzlewit*, Mr. Bevan, remarks that America was born late enough to "escape the ages of bloodshed and cruelty through which other nations have passed" (239), but the novel suggests otherwise, arguing that America perpetuates or repeats the patterns of aggression and violence inscribed in its myths of origin. In its antagonism toward the Old World, and its continued resistance to external change and the forces of acculturation, America in *Martin Chuzzlewit* seems frozen at a particular point in its history, compelled, like the hysteric, to repeat or relive this moment through various substitutive reenactments of it. As such, the various incantations in praise of America's youthfulness and naturalness that we hear within the American dialogue are all versions of the same choric refrain. As emissaries from the Old World, young Martin and Mark bear the brunt of most of this violence and aggression. Such is the case, for example, in the "Le-vee" scene, often criticized for its lack of credibility, in which the Americans see Martin and Mark off to Eden and thus to what the Americans believe will be their certain death. Readers of the novel have observed that it is unlikely that such a gathering would have been held to bid farewell to someone as unknown as Martin, and have accused Dickens of awkwardly inserting his own American experiences into the novel. But realism in Dickens's novels almost always defers to his stronger imaginative impulses, and this ceremonial farewell ritualistically enacts the aggressive tendencies toward Mark and Martin evident throughout much of their stay in America. When Martin and Mark return from Eden, thus repeating in their own way young Bailey's return from the dead, the Americans are not only surprised but disappointed as well: young Martin observes, for example, that "we've come back alive, you see" (463), and Captain Kedgwick replies, "It ain't the right thing I did expect. . . . A man ain't got no right to be a public man, unless he meets the public views. Our fashionable people wouldn't have attended his Le-vee, if they had know'd it" (463). As the narrator remarks, "Nothing mollified the captain, who persisted in taking it very ill that they had not both died in Eden" (463).

I have always been haunted by this image, and during one
period of my life it keep recurring in my dreams: A person finds
himself in a world of children, from which he cannot escape.

And suddenly childhood, which we all lyricize and adore, reveals itself as pure horror.

MILAN KUNDERA, *The Book of Laughter and Forgetting*

In Milan Kundera's *Book of Laughter and Forgetting*, a group of children hound Tamina, one of its central characters, to death; and just as the Americans desire the deaths of Mark and Martin, so too does Dickens's America, compulsively fixed or frozen on images of rebirth and a new childhood, reveal itself as "pure horror." The grotesque in Dickens often assumes the form of something that seems to exist outside of nature and whose misshapen or distorted gestures and appearance reveal a psychic imbalance or disequilibrium. This is particularly the case in Dickens with the adult who has failed to outgrow childhood or who has never known childhood, as, for example, in the Smallweed family in *Bleak House*—"little old men and women there have been, but no child, until Mr. Smallweed's grandmother, now living, became weak in her intellect, and fell (for the first time) into a childish state" (257). But in the American sections, the grotesque is associated not with particular individuals or families, but rather with a whole nation. For if the Americans fantasize themselves as children, Dickens explores the psychic inversion of this myth, locating evidence of this infantile sexuality not only in the excremental vision of the American newspapers, but also in the voracious orality of its citizens.[21]

"What culture consciously prohibits," writes Catherine Clément, "it creates in the form of abnormality" (*The Lives and Legends of Jacques Lacan*, 83), and the abnormal, as gesture and act, discloses the site of interdicted desire in *Martin Chuzzlewit*. One such site is the dining room in Mrs. Pawkins's boarding house: "All the knives and forks were working away at a rate that was quite alarming; very few words were spoken; and everybody seemed to eat his utmost in self-defense, as if a famine were expected to set in before breakfast-time to-morrow morning, and it had become high time to assert the first law of nature" (232). This pre-Darwinian "first law of nature," that of survival, is here taken to its grotesque extreme, stripped of all restraint or facade:

Great heaps of indigestible matter melted away as ice before the sun. It was a solemn and an awful thing to see. Dyspeptic individuals bolted their food in wedges; feeding, not themselves, but broods of nightmares, who were continually standing at livery within them. Spare men, with lank and rigid cheeks, came out unsatisfied from the destruction of heavy dishes, and glared with watchful eyes upon the pastry. What Mrs. Pawkins felt each day at dinner-time is hidden from all human knowledge. (232–33)

Like the "broods of nightmares," situated in the scene and yet not a visible part of it, this passage, like those we saw in *Robinson Crusoe*, seems to be of uncertain or ambiguous origin. Where does it come from and what does it mean? Its language seems excessive, but also peculiarly elusive, making us wonder if Dickens has perhaps finally overdone it—after all, what he is talking about is nothing more than a bunch of people eating dinner in a boardinghouse. But even as we might suspect that this is the case, our suspicions are at the same time rendered uneasy by the sense that we have not said enough, that it is precisely toward the superfluity or excess of this scene that we need to turn our attention.

Rendered along the lines of the grotesque, this particular scene depicts a ritual of bodily exchange and interchange, and, as such, invokes Bakhtin's description of the grotesque body spoken of earlier. In the English episodes, the grotesque body is often an image of life and fecundity, a comic celebration of the noncanonical (Mrs. Gamp, for example, or even Poll Sweedlepipe's epicene gait and gestures). In the American sections, on the other hand, the grotesque is haunted and death-ridden, as in this scene, dominated by its spectral icon of "spare men, with lank and rigid cheeks." All is hidden, except from Mrs. Pawkins, and she remains silent about what she sees. However, not quite all is hidden. To intrude into this dining scene is to enter forbidden realms: "It was," we are told, "a solemn and an awful thing to see." Nature, writes Bataille, participates in "a squandering of living energy and an orgy of annihilation" (61), and, in the midst of this "destructive and implacable frenzy" (62), human nature is that which says "no" to such squandering and destruction. But in this scene, the boundaries between the natural and the human seem to melt, "like ice before the sun." By trying to assert fully "the first law of nature," Dickens's Americans seem to have been absorbed into the natural realm, and in this orgiastic frenzy of feeding, the dynamics of death, violence, and the erotic bleed into one another. Nightmares, like faithful servants, wait on the devourers, and desire, seen in those who "glared with

watchful eyes upon the pastry," leads only to disappointment and unsatisfied appetites. And, as such, desire locates this drama in the realm of the
human rather than the realm of the natural. For the "spare men, with lank
and rigid cheeks" remain unsatiated, we are told, even after "the destruction of heavy dishes." If desire often finds itself articulated through the language of hunger or thirst, it also testifies to the inaccessibility of that which
might satisfy either. Separated from a part of ourselves by language, we cannot recover that which we are missing or lacking, and thus while the child
in Freud's parable of the "fort-da" game may be able to better cope with his
mother's absence through the articulation of language in play, he nevertheless gives voice to an irretrievable loss. Similarly, the diners at Mrs.
Pawkins's table can devour all the "heavy dishes" that are set in front of
them, but it is never enough, for their hunger is still unsatisfied.

Broods of nightmares not only encircle Mrs. Pawkins's table, but are
also seen in Dickens's American landscape, for it too is haunted and specter-
ridden. Such, for example, is the case with Eden: "Their own land was mere
forest. The trees had grown so thick and close that they shouldered one
another out of their places, and the weakest, forced into shapes of strange
distortion, languished like cripples. . . . A jungle deep and dark, with neither earth nor water at its roots, but putrid matter, formed of the pulpy offal
of the two, and of their own corruption" (328). The corpse, Julia Kristeva
notes, is "the most sickening of wastes," for "seen without God and outside
of science, [it] is the utmost of abjection. It is death infecting life" (*Powers
of Horror*, 3). Dickens's language, however, suggests not so much a corpse
as a commingling of fecundity and decay, what the text identifies as "corruption"; this scene would seem to confirm Kristeva's placing of the abject
on the side of the feminine, horror in the presence of signs of sexual difference (71).[22] Eden is at once womb and tomb, for we have come across not
a dissected corpse, but rather a living being that seems open, exposed. We
witness the messy and churning activities in the body cavity, represented by
a language that suggests both fascination and horror at what it sees. For we
have stumbled on a topographic representation of the taboo, the regions of
desire and emotion that assume chthonic shapes, what Robert Polhemus
has referred to as the "murk of nature" in Dickens's novels.[23]

The landscape that Mark and Martin enter is one of generation and
decay: "A marsh on which the good growth of the earth seemed to have

been wrecked and cast away, that from its decomposing ashes vile and ugly things might rise; where the very trees took the aspect of huge weeds, begotten of the slime from which they sprung, by the hot sun that burnt them up; where fatal maladies, seeking whom they might infect, came forth, at night, in misty shapes, and creeping out upon the water, hunted them like specters until day" (325). In its primordial stench and its pulpy fluids, Eden captures the contiguity of growth and corruption, like weeds "begotten of the slime from which they sprung." A land that is at once sensuous and repulsive, it would seem to accommodate within itself all possibilities, all contradictions.

There are few, if any, other such sites in Victorian fiction, but we can locate a comparable one in Freud's *The Interpretation of Dreams,* and more specifically in his centrally important "The Dream of Irma's Injection."[24] I would like to turn to this dream for a moment, for it enables us to better understand, I think, the directions and dynamics of Dickens's language. This particular dream had its origins in Freud's treatment of a young woman who was also a friend of his family. Because his narrative account of this dream is fairly long, I will cite only the section in which Freud dreams of actually looking into Irma's mouth: "I took her to the window and looked down her throat, and she showed signs of recalcitrance, like women with artificial dentures. I thought to myself that there was no need for her to do that. — She then opened her mouth properly and on the right I found a big white patch; at another place I saw extensive whitish grey scabs upon some remarkably curly turbinal structures which were evidently modeled on the turbinal bones of the nose" (*SE,* 6:107).[25] At the end of his commentary on this dream, Freud writes, "I could spend much more time over it, [and] derive further information from it" (121), but confesses that he will not do so: "Considerations which arise in the case of every dream of my own restrain me from pursuing my interpretive work" (121). Lacan picks up on this question of repression or denial in Freud's commentary, and asks why Freud refuses to look any further into his dream. In order to understand why Freud does so, Lacan suggests, we need to distinguish between the Freud who interpreted his dreams and the Freud who dreamt his dreams. In his commentary on the dream, Freud retreats from the dream's "unconscious desire," pushing it away, Lacan suggests, because it "horrifies" him (*Seminar II,* 151). And what it is that "horrifies" him is precisely what he sees when he looks into Irma's mouth, a site that "has all the equivalences in terms of sig-nifications, all the condensations you could want" (154): "The complex, unlocatable form, which also makes it into the primitive object *par excel-lence*, the abyss of the feminine organ from which all life emerges, the gulf of the mouth, in which everything is swallowed up, and no less the image of death in which everything comes to its end" (164). It is, Lacan notes, "a hor-rendous discovery here, that of the flesh one never sees, the foundation of things, the other side of the head, the face" (154). Like Freud's dream, Dick-ens's Eden moves toward something that remains by definition unnamable, "this something," writes Lacan, "faced with which all words cease and all categories fail" (164).

But in the case of *Martin Chuzzlewit*, words do not cease. Invoking images of the female body, Dickens's Eden is regarded with that ambigu-ous mixture of horror and fascination that enshrouds the text's vision of the female. Given the virtual absence of the feminine in the American episodes, the subterranean fears and desires are directed toward nature as trope, toward what Camille Paglia has described as its "female procreativeness," that "blind grinding of subterranean forces, the long slow suck, the murk and ooze" (*Sexual Personae*, 5–6, 12). As such, this particular landscape in America charts out the topography of desire, for it is not so much a land of earth and water as a dream landscape concealing primary desires behind secondary ones. It gives us glimpses of otherwise hidden scenarios and memories, for it seems to contain all opposites within itself, as the images of life and death, form and formlessness, alpha and omega, merge into one another. In the images of orality and excremental activity that we find scattered through the American episodes of *Martin Chuzzlewit*, we can discern evidence of the etiology of disgust, but the symptomatic gestures of disgust, whether regis-tered somatically or linguistically, testify, as Freud points out, to repressed sexual desire.[26] As the construct of a desire, America invokes images of the female body, and, more specifically, the land as the body of the mother.[27] It resembles in striking ways, in fact, one of the three fundamental mother images that Gilles Deleuze has spoken of, namely, "the primitive, uterine, hetaeric, mother, mother of the cloaca and swamp" (*Masochism*, 49).[28] What binds the energies of the American plot together is the desire to become an infant once again, to return to an earlier home, and thus to erase loss or absence. At one point, Freud characterizes love as "a homesickness," arguing, "Whenever a man dreams of a place or country and says to himself, 'I've been here before,' we may interpret the place as being his mother's genitals or her body" (*SE*, 17:245). The Americans know love as such a homesickness, for their collective fantasy is to restore what has been lost, returning to a place they have known before.

America would seem, then, to promise a domain outside of time, one beyond the reaches of the Old World, with its images of patriarchal authority and culture. General Choke tells Martin, "We are a new country, here sir" (299), adding that the United States "are for the regeneration of man" (300). Unlike their European neighbors, General Choke observes, the Americans have not "lapsed in the slow course of time into degenerate practices" (299–300). However, the American in *Martin Chuzzlewit* is not only a child, but a violent and voracious infant. Dickens suggests that the relationship between the Americans and the land is, like everything in the country, defined by violence, and the Americans' desire to regain that which has been lost, to return to that from which they have been expelled, suggests a desperation born of an unacknowledged realization that they cannot have what they want. "Culture first comes to the infant by way of an image," writes Catherine Clément, "its own image, born of a separation" (87). What the Americans vehemently deny is precisely this separation: their invocation of animal imagery (buffaloes, bears, wolves) in characterizing their own condition testifies to their dream of a world prior to weaning, prior to separation or division and thus prior to culture. And yet, of course, the Americans have been born into language and thus into a world that denies them access to such an All. They too know Rousseau's world of loss and separation, and what they want most is precisely what they cannot have.

We shall be compelled to say that "the aim of all life is death."

SIGMUND FREUD, *Beyond the Pleasure Principle*

Desire for Lacan is "the metonymy of the want-to-be" (*Ecrits*, 259), and, since lack, at the heart of the human condition, is expressible only through substitutions, it can be neither fully articulated nor satisfied. Anger and aggression have their origin in our belief that the other, a mirror image of ourselves structured along the path of the imaginary, possesses a fullness or totality that we do not.[29] We find this particular manifestation of desire in the numerous scenarios of aggression and competition that punctuate Dickens's American landscapes. The violence of the Americans, born of a fear that the other may have what they want (in both senses of "want"), is defined not only by an outward aggression or wish to kill, but also by a desire to die. At the heart of the American dream, then, is a desire to repeat the experiences of an imagined past, or, in other words, to return to the beginning. Freud points out that the repetition compulsion has its origin in a desire for death, a wish to return once more to an inanimate state: "The compulsion to repeat must be ascribed to the unconscious repressed," he writes, arising from "an urge inherent in organic life to restore an earlier state of things" (*SE*, 18:14, 36). America in *Martin Chuzzlewit*, like its landscape of Eden, is a place constructed by fantasies of both beginning and end, for the American desire for rebirth is in fact the desire for a new death.

Dickens's characters are often haunted by death, drawn toward darkened landscapes of cessation and ease. The narrator observes of Anthony Chuzzlewit, for example, that "it was frightening to see how the principle of life shut up within his withered frame, fought like a strong devil, mad to be released, and rent its ancient prison house" (263), and Montague Tigg similarly moves in a dreamlike trance toward his own death as he takes part in an unconscious script acted out in the silent realms on the other side of language. But Freud suggests that our self-love or ego instincts most often prevent us from short-circuiting our own particular narrative or destiny, and *Martin Chuzzlewit* similarly suggests that we must defer the wish for death, not attempting to delete the middle of our histories. At one point, the text explores the relationship between America's violence and its refusal to defer such desires. The scene begins with Elijah Pogram claiming that young Martin's criticism of Hannibal Chollop's violence is simply another example of "the settled opposition to our Institution which pervades the British mind" (460). Martin responds by asking Elijah: "Are Mr. Chollop and the class he represents, an Institution here? Are pistols with revolving-barrels, swordsticks, bowie knives, and such things, Institutions on which you pride yourselves? Are bloody duels, brutal combats, savage assaults, shootings down and stabbings in the street, your Institutions!" (460). This dialogue between the Old World (Martin) and the new (Elijah) concerns nothing less than the structure of society itself, what Elijah refers to as American "institutions," the laws and codes governing human behavior and relationships. Martin tells Elijah, "You may make anything an Institution if you like" (461), but he also points out that most of Elijah's so-called institutions are in fact crimes or transgressions against institutions. Such lawlessness is not, Martin goes on, a matter of Americans' returning to nature, but rather of their stopping short of or failing at the minimum rituals and ceremonies that define the human community: "It's a question of losing the natural politeness of a savage, and that instinctive good-breeding which admonishes one man not to offend and disgust another" (462). Martin continues: "The mass of your country-men begin by stubbornly neglecting little social observances, which have nothing to do with gentility, custom, usage, government, or country, but are acts of common, decent, natural, human politeness. . . . From disregarding small obligations they come in regular course to disregard great ones; and so refuse to pay their debts" (462).

Young Martin's reference to the refusal of the Americans to "pay their debts" is crucial here, and I will return to it. As readers such as Barbara Hardy and Stuart Curran point out, young Martin grows up during his stay in America, for the trials he undergoes there chasten him and teach him to be less self-centered, more compassionate toward the needs and pains of others.[30] But other things seem to be going on as well. For the most part, the drift of young Martin's argument is fairly clear, as he attempts to distinguish between false or artificial forms on one hand and those that are deeply inscribed in culture or society on the other. Martin suspects that there is something wrong about America, and, in struggling to define it, he speaks of the refusal on the part of the Americans to acknowledge the debts that they owe: "What they may do, or what they refuse to do next, I don't know; but any man may see if he will, that it will be something following in nat-ural succession, and a part of one great growth, which is rotten at the root" (462). If his language is a bit stiff, even stuffy, it is because, having previ-ously spoken only with the voice of the son, he now seems uncomfortable with the newly acquired voice of the father—or, more precisely, with Lacan's Name-of-the-Father, the name that the child learns to speak and to take as its own through the resolution of the Oedipus complex.[31] It is, Lacan argues, this Name-of-the-Father that speaks with the voice of the Law that "superimposes the kingdom of culture on that of a nature abandoned to the laws of mating" (*Ecrits*, 66).

As Lacan points out, this new identity is "essentially a function of symbolic identification" (*Ecrits*, 67), our inscription in the human community and its laws. Lacan, like young Martin, talks of the debts that we must pay in order to inhabit this symbolic network of community and laws. Young Martin's voice is strange and his argument awkward because he must try to articulate the ambiguous and tentative questions of succession and kinship structures that are raised as early as the novel's introductory sections. But he seems quite clear about the question of debts, the conditions owed by us by virtue of our entrance into culture and its symbolic structures. The Americans, in young Martin's words, have refused to pay their debt, for in their fantasies of returning to nature, and thus escaping separation and loss, they have attempted to deny their entry into human culture. Suffering from a collective cultural neurosis, America seems frozen at a particular moment in its history and forced to repeat this moment through substitutive reenactments.

Nature in America's myth of its own origin and creation not only occupies an antagonistic relationship to the human community and its institutions, but also testifies as trope to the absence of community among those who pursue it so desperately. As such, it is a metaphor for loss, for the fragmented, scattered sense of self trying to restore itself to wholeness or unity once again. Eden, with its own particular iconography, stands forth as both ironic reminder of loss and emblem of America's central dream. In speaking of the "fetish character of the object of human desire," Lacan points out that the "object of the fantasy . . . is that other element that takes the place of what the subject is symbolically deprived of," and in this respect, America is a fetish, an attempt to find a replacement for that which has been lost or that from which one has been separated, namely a wholeness or unity that cannot be restored or regained.[32] The repetitive insistence on that unity in the signifying chain of American myth and language is nothing less than the function of the obsession of an impossible desire.

Although the collective American voice has rejected the Old World as home, it has not yet created its own home, and thus it still seeks in nature to alleviate that homesickness that cannot be cured. In their flight from time and the inherited experiences of the past, and in their refusal to pay the debts that they owe, the Americans, like William Blake's Thel, have transformed the pastoral landscape of their dreams into the specter-ridden swamps of nightmares. Having failed to accept their insertion as subjects into the symbolic realm, with its subsequent sacrifice and debt, America's citizens pursue a kingdom of nature rather than a kingdom of culture. They thus engage, the novel suggests, in a cycle of repetition and return that is death-ridden and death-haunted, born in violence and destined to have violence written into all aspects of the country's history, past and future.

2

Exile and Desire in Thackeray's *Notes of a Journey from Cornhill to Grand Cairo*

> The pathos of exile resides in the loss of contact with the solidity
> and satisfactions of earth. That is why exiles look at non-exiles
> with a certain resentment: *What is it like to be born in a place*
> *and to live there more or less forever, to know that you are of it?*
>
> EDWARD W. SAID, "The Mind of Winter: Reflections on
> Life in Exile"

As befits a document that provides us with glimpses into the nature and origin of the imperialistic imagination, Thackeray's *Notes of a Journey from Cornhill to Grand Cairo* was conceived of in the Reform Club of London, one of those patriarchal centers of wealth and power out of which radiated the heady impulses of Victorian England's political and economic energies. During a dinner held there on August 20, 1844, Thackeray was invited to accompany James Emerson Tennent and his family on their tour of the East. When Thackeray discovered that all of his expenses were to be paid by Tennent's friends, the directors of the Peninsular and Orient Company, he accepted the invitation immediately, and within three days he had embarked on his voyage.

He published his account of the journey in 1846, having written it in order to persuade some skeptical friends that he had indeed taken such a trip. Thackeray would later characterize this trip as an "easy . . . [and] charming" journey that left him with "a store of pleasant recollections for after days."[1] Thackeray's biographer, Gordon N. Ray, notes that the work was well received and describes the piece as "a light-hearted narrative, which testifies to Thackeray's having contrived to remain on good terms with everyone, even with himself, during the whole of the voyage out" (*Thackeray*, 316). Ray does point out, however, that Thomas Carlyle took exception to the trip, likening Thackeray's acceptance of such an offer to "the practice of a blind fiddler going to and fro on a penny ferry-boat in Scotland, and playing tunes to the passengers for halfpence" (301).

It is not surprising that the initial reviews of Thackeray's essay were favorable, for *Notes of a Journey from Cornhill to Grand Cairo* seems to affirm the collective myths and impressions of the Orient to which much of the Victorian age subscribed, and it does so through a voice already familiar to Thackeray's readers, that of Michael Angelo Titmarsh, an overweight, slightly jaded, and opinionated humorist and observer of human nature. But modern readers also regard the essay as generally untroubled. Patrick Brantlinger, for example, writes that "Titmarsh-Thackeray indulges happily in many of the sensual pleasures of the East" (*Rules of Darkness*, 135), and Deborah Thomas similarly notes that "Thackeray's response was generally positive to the non-Western culture he encountered in his 1844 journey" (*Thackeray and Slavery*, 43). Thackeray's essay itself, however, seems to challenge such characterizations, for it is a complex and often troubling narrative, reflecting unresolved and, indeed, often unacknowledged conflicts on Thackeray's part. Its voice is variously aggressive, sensitive, self-denigrating, racist, and insightful and moving, depending on when and where we happen to listen. As a document, it testifies to power, but in doing so, it also confesses to weakness and enervation; and even as it professes the presence of community, it does so with a language whose futile attempts to bridge distances call attention to the loneliness and alienation on which they are grounded.

Edward Said makes only a passing reference to Thackeray's essay in his *Orientalism*, describing it as "moderately amusing" (195). Nevertheless,

Thackeray was a member of that "cultural hegemony" that Said argues gave Orientalism its strength and durability, and throughout his essay, Thackeray assumes strategies and rhetorical positions that enable him to maintain, albeit uneasily, that Western "positional superiority" spoken of by Said (7). But even after we acknowledge the presence of such impulses or dynamics in the essay, we are still left with residues of meaning—conflicts and tensions generated by Thackeray's language and the images it invokes—that call our attention to an internal discontinuity in the text, to something other than the story of an easy or charming journey. I want to focus on these residues of meaning, considering their possible origins as well as their dynamics. I am interested not only in what Thackeray saw, but also in how he saw what he saw—in the relationship, in other words, often strained and ambiguous, between himself as perceiving subject and the varied and multiple objects of his attention. "Unconscious desire has its own history," writes Peter Brooks, "a history unavailable to the conscious subject but persistently repeating its thrust and drive in present symbolic formations" (278), and this chapter focuses on how unconscious desire is written into Thackeray's essay.[2]

I also approach the question of colonialism differently than some of Thackeray's earlier readers.[3] Although Thackeray would later create in the character of Jo Sedley in *Vanity Fair* a devastating satirical portrait of the English presence in India, a reader of *Notes of a Journey from Cornhill to Grand Cairo* could have little doubt that Thackeray subscribed to many of the beliefs and prejudices of his age. At one point, for example, he speaks admiringly of "the excellent book, *Eothen*" (1844) by Alexander William Kinglake:

> We were lodged at Pera at "Misseri's Hotel," the host of which has been made famous ere this time by the excellent book, "Eothen,"—a work for which all the passengers on board our ship had been battling, and which had charmed all—from our great statesman, our polished lawyer, our young Oxonian, who sighed over certain passengers he feared were wicked, down to the writer of this, who, after perusing it with delight, laid it down with wonder, exclaiming, "Aut Diabolus aut." (406)[4]

Kinglake's book was immensely popular, but it was also, as Said points out, "a pathetic catalogue of pompous ethnocentrisms" filled with "anti-Semitism,

xenophobia, and general all-purpose race prejudice" (193). Thackeray read
Eothen with delight and wonder because he shared a good number of these
attitudes in common with Kinglake, and, indeed, we can find them expressed
throughout his essay. But while I acknowledge their presence, not much
would be served, it seems to me, by belaboring the obvious.

Rather, I am interested in exploring the dynamics that play back and
forth between Thackeray as tourist or traveler and the various objects of his
attention. Throughout Thackeray's journey, he looks in at (or rather attempts
to look in at) scenes and activities from which he remains excluded. Perceiving himself as an outsider, an "interesting stranger" (505), he gazes, often
from a distance, at hidden and secret spaces that remain inaccessible, yet
compellingly attractive. During his travels through the Orient, Thackeray
visits strange or alien lands that nevertheless remind him by virtue of their
unity and wholeness (whether imaginary or real does not matter) of a completeness or wholeness that he too once possessed, or at least remembers or
imagines himself as having once possessed. The intensity of Thackeray's
gaze as tourist derives from a sense of lack or absence, a desire on his part to
retrieve a remembered or lost unity and to expand a self that has become
enervated or diminished. Speaking of admittedly different forms of Western
appropriation or control, Claude Lévi-Strauss identifies impulses similar to
those we find in Thackeray's essay, when, toward the end of *Tristes Tropiques*,
he reflects on the origin and nature of Western anthropology: "If the West has
produced anthropologists, it is because it was so tormented by remorse that it
had to compare its own image with that of other societies, in the hope that
they would either display the same shortcomings or help the West to explain
how these defects could have come into being" (388). The narrative impulses
in Thackeray's essay and his travels through the East seem to have their origin in remorse as well, deriving their directions and energies from a sense of
lack, something very like the "shortcomings" and "defects" that Lévi-Strauss
suggests compel the West to seek out something other than its own image.

As Thackeray observes, within the space of several months, he was able to
see as many cities as Ulysses saw in ten years, recording his impressions of such
cities as Vigo, Cadiz, Malta, Athens, Smyrna, Constantinople, Jerusalem,
Alexandria, and finally Cairo. By providing his readers with "faithful transcripts of everyday Oriental life" (400), he hopes to move beyond the standard
images of the East presented by earlier Western artists. "I wonder," he writes,

"that no painter has given us familiar views of the East: not processions, grand sultans, or magnificent landscapes; but faithful transcripts of every-day Oriental life, such as each street will supply to him" (400). But while Thackeray wants to capture the "real" East—its coffeehouses, merchants, plane trees, and minstrels, its bartering of goods—the language with which he attempts to do so is often distanced and monochromatic:

> There was under the plane-trees a little coffee-house, shaded by a trellis-work, covered over with a vine, and ornamented with many rows of shining pots and water-pipes. . . . Hard by the coffee-house were a garden and a bub-bling marble-fountain, and over the stream was a broken summer-house, to which amateurs may ascend, for the purpose of examining the river. . . . The master of the house, dressed in a white turban and light blue pelisse, lolled under the coffee-house awning; the slave in white with a crimson striped jacket, his face as black as ebony, brought us pipes and lemonade. (400)

Thackeray's prose seems tired, unimaginative, without that specificity of detail that he evokes elsewhere in his writings. The coffeehouse, the garden, and the summerhouse—none of these images impress themselves on our mind's eye, for we have only a vague sense of their particularity of form, structure, and design. The whole passage, in fact, is characterized by easy phrase and lazy construction, from the "bubbling marble-fountain" and the master, "lolling under the coffee-house," to the slave, "his face as black as ebony."

Even as he tries to record his first images of the East, then, Thackeray diminishes the multiplicity and opaqueness of its life, emptying the land-scapes and cityscapes of whatever potential they might have to reduce the distances separating them from himself. In the course of his journey, he confesses to the poverty of his own imagination by turning away from the landscapes themselves and toward Western icons of the East, and, like so many of his contemporaries, he invokes literary sources, especially the *Arabian Nights*. Such is the case, for example, when he describes his first sight of the East—appropriately enough, seen from the ship through a telescope, and thus a vision characterized by both distance and silence:

> There lay the town [of Smyrna] with minarets and cypresses, domes and castles; great guns were firing off, and the blood-red flag of the Sultan

flaring over the fort ever since sunrise; woods and mountains came down to the gulf's edge, and as you looked at them with the telescope, there peeped out of the general mass a score of pleasant episodes of Eastern life—there were cottages with quaint roofs; silent cool kiosks, where the chief of the eunuch brings down ladies of the harem. I saw Hassan, the fisherman, getting his nets; and Ali Baba going off with his donkey to the great forest for wood. (395)

Thackeray initially gazes on the city itself, but then moves quickly toward a language that again is general ("there peeped out of the general mass a score of pleasant episodes of Eastern life"), and heavily allusive and abstract (moving from the cityscape to literary figures such as Hassan and even to literary vignettes, such as "Ali Baba going off with his donkey to the great forest for wood"). Thackeray's language flattens his gestures of response, stripping his perceptions of depth and substance, for while he gives us details of the everyday, they are seen from the outside and from a distance. Nevertheless, even as his focus tends to glance off specific sights and move toward abstract or generalized literary images, such moments are still able to invoke intensely personal responses from him. The first sight of the East, he tells us, is fatal to the imagination, and subsequent sights of it only remind us of glories that have passed, of wonders that we desire, but can no longer enjoy. "The first day in the East is like that. After that there is nothing. The wonder is gone, and the thrill of that delightful shock, which so seldom touches the nerves of the plain men of the world, though they seek for it everywhere" (395). Such a sight, when seen for the first time, constitutes a Coleridgean miracle of rare device, in which the literary icons of the imagination and the shapes and forms of the substantial world merge momentarily in a scene of visionary unity. "A man only sees the miracle once," Thackeray reflects; "though you yearn after it ever so, it won't come again. I saw nothing of Ali Baba and Hassan the next time we came to Smyrna" (395–96). Thackeray's dreams and memories are betrayed by the sights he sees, and thus he recommends that those who wish to understand Smyrna and who have "loved the 'Arabian Nights' in their youth" should land for a maximum of two hours and never return again, for only this initial sight, what Thackeray refers to as "one *dip* into Constantinople or Smyrna" (396), can stand up against the memories of the scenes that we have carried with us from our youth.[5] Although his "dip" into Constantinople is a bit murkier, more unsettling, than his first view of Smyrna, Thackeray once again draws on art, but in this case the theater rather than the *Arabian Nights*:

> When we rose at sunrise to see the famous entry to Constantinople, we found, in the place of the city and the sun, a bright white fog, which hid both from sight, and which only disappeared as the vessel advanced towards the Golden Horn. There the fog cleared off as it were by flakes, and as you see gauze curtains lifted away, one by one, before a great fairy scene at the theatre. This will give idea enough of the fog; the difficulty is to describe the scene afterwards, which was in truth the great fairy scene, than which it is impossible to conceive anything more brilliant and magnificent. I can't go to any more romantic place than Drury Lane, to draw my similes from Drury Lane, such as we used to see it in our youth . . . the view of Constantinople is as fine as any of Stanfield's best theatrical pictures, seen at the best period of youth, when fancy had all the bloom on her. (403)

This particular sight, Thackeray writes, "caused a thrill of pleasure, and awakened an innocent fulness of sensual enjoyment that is only given to boys," no small accomplishment given Thackeray's conviction that "the enjoyments of boyish fancy are the most intense and delicious in the world" (403).

"What does man find in metonymy," asks Lacan, "if not the power to circumvent the obstacles of social censure" (*Ecrits*, 158). Thackeray's language, like that of Christina Rossetti's "Goblin Market," registers *jouissance* as intensity, even as it denies it or calls it by another name. Thackeray's language is rich, sensual, and erotic. If "the enjoyments of boyish fancy are the most intense and delicious in the world" (403), Constantinople, or at least one's first sight of it, can capture once again such enjoyments. The analytic process, Lacan argues, attempts to free the subject's speech by introducing "him into the language of his desire," thus making it possible for the subject to move toward a "primary language in which, beyond what he tells us of himself, he is already talking to us unknown to himself" (*Ecrits*, 81). In moments such as the sighting of Constantinople, Thackeray talks to us, as it were, even while "unknown to himself," for we catch glimpses of "the language of his desire" as the trajectory of his narrative moves away from the cityscapes toward sites of reflection and reverie, his ineffectual disclaimers notwithstanding. When he writes of the "thrill of pleasure" or the "fulness of sensual enjoyment," he speaks of a pleasure that is perhaps boyish, but not innocent. Or, more precisely, although such "sensual enjoyment" may have been innocent—that is to say, not understood—when it was first experienced in boyhood, the language that the adult narrator draws on in seeking to recover it suggests its essentially erotic basis. In *I Lost It at the Movies*, the film critic Pauline Kael explores various forms of theatrical ravishment; Thackeray might have called his account *I Lost It at the Playhouse, but Found It Again Overseas*, for he warns his reader that unless he— Thackeray's implied reader is almost always male—has been "ravished at the play-house" (403) as a youth, he will be unable to imaginatively participate in the experiences described.

The directions of Thackeray's essay at this point are complex, rich, conflicted. On one hand, like his Romantic predecessors, he would seem to be arguing for what Theodor Adorno has described as Proust's "faith with the childhood potential for unimpaired experience" ("On Proust," 315), suggesting that the sights seen during his travels may make it possible for him to feel once again what he felt then, "when fancy had all the bloom on her" (403). On the other hand, the language that he invokes in recalling or remembering such moments reminds us that our deepest fantasies and desires are often masturbatory in nature. Passages such as the description of Constantinople, glancing off the scenes being described, give us a glimpse of the desires and impulses that lie behind the shape and directions of Thackeray's narrative.

Thackeray is also concerned with his readers' desires, suggesting, in fact, that by reading his accounts, they too might come to experience sensual enjoyment once again. "Some men may read this who are in want of a sensation" (396), he writes, and they too might be able to rediscover sensations they thought they had lost or had forgotten. If he writes well enough and powerfully enough, he hopes, he might enable his readers to be excited as he was excited, to feel what he felt.[6] When Thackeray speaks of "sensations," or of that "shock, which so seldom touches the nerves of plain men" (395), we need to take him at his word, making the connection, as his language certainly does, between his project and those of sensation novelists such as Elizabeth Braddon and Wilkie Collins. As D. A. Miller points out, such literature "offers us one of the first instances of modern literature to address itself primarily to the sympathetic nervous system, where it grounds its adrenaline effects: accelerated heart rate and respiration, increased blood pressure, the pallor resulting from vasoconstriction, and so on" ("Cage aux Folles," 146). But as he also notes, a "silence" has fallen "over the question of sensation" (147), for even while writing of sensational fiction, critics have ignored or repressed sensation, "an overnice literary criticism" assuring us that such novels are "beneath notice" (147). The implication of such criticism, Miller observes, is that "sensation is felt to occupy a natural site entirely outside meaning, as though in the breathless body signification expired" (147). Thackeray, however, knows better, and seeks through his narrative to uncover repositories in the body of forgotten or repressed memories that can be retrieved and felt once again as "sensations," not only by Thackeray, but by his readers as well.

What is especially striking about these scenes in Thackeray is their evanescent nature, the way they are structured along the lines of encounter and loss. Like Robinson Crusoe's first sight of the foundering ship, they are characterized by a fleeting glimpse of something that immediately opens up a recognition that is experienced or registered as loss. "There is nothing," he writes, "the wonder is gone" (395), or, "A man only sees the miracle once [and] though you yearn after it ever so, it won't come again" (395–96). Confirming what we have already known, while at the same time reminding us of what we have lost, such experiences, tenuously and momentarily apprehended, are gone almost as soon as they appear. The nature or origin of these sensations would seem to be among the central questions raised by Thackeray's essay, and, on certain matters, the text seems fairly clear. For example, the experiences he speaks of seem to have their origin in a remote past, and are sought by those who wish to retrieve this past, or, more precisely, to once again experience the "sensations" buried within it. Thackeray's voyage is important, in other words, because it enables him (and, he hopes, his readers as well) to rediscover lost sensations, to be ravished once again.

The passages charting out the complex and ambiguous dynamics between Thackeray's past and present contain some of his most powerful and evocative writing, moments in which his sense of loss and, indeed, of pain is often almost palpable. But the passages nevertheless remain elusive, their meaning or directions hard to fix or stabilize. We hear, for example, that "the wonder is gone" and of "the thrill of that delightful shock, which so seldom touches the nerves of plain men of the world, though they seek for it everywhere" (395). But what is this shock, the nature of the thrill it evokes, and the characteristics of the delightful sensations it registers? How does this shock touch "the nerves of plain men," and why so seldom, and what compels these men to "seek for it everywhere"? These questions, and there are others as well, arise not because of sloppy or careless writing on Thackeray's part—on the contrary, his language at such moments is precise and careful—but rather because the answers to such questions remain as elusive for Thackeray as they are for us.

However, Freud's essay on the uncanny, concerned in large part with precisely how and why psychic shock is registered, can, I think, help open up Thackeray's text. The uncanny, Freud tells us, is "something which ought to have remained hidden but has come to light" (SE, 17:241), the "secretly famil-iar" (heimlich-heimisch) that has undergone repression and then returned from it (17:245). One characteristic of literature of the uncanny is the recur-rence of certain patterns, what Freud describes as "the constant recurrence of the same thing—the repetition of the same features or character—traits or vicissitudes" (17:234). Such patterns, arising when recollection itself is blocked by resistance, and thus often constituting a form of remembering, are at the heart of Thackeray's essay, for throughout it juxtaposes the present, namely, the sights and sounds experienced in the East, and the past, specifi-cally, his memories of his childhood and the experiences associated with that period of time. And this past recurs, as Thackeray's narrative reminds us, in a present whose intensity derives from its capacity not only to accommodate such repetitions, but also to actually initiate them. In other words, what Thackeray seeks as he travels as an adult through the East is a world capable of invoking the sensations aroused by the splendor of the playhouse; he wants to experience once again the thrills and shocks of his youth. But, at the same time, his experiences in the East are possible only because repressed or for-gotten memories, once reawakened, invest them with a sense of loss. In other words, just as the present would seem to recover the past, so too does the past give shape to the present and help to actualize it.

Categories of cause and effect, and even past and future, here become unstable, undecidable, and, as such, these experiences in the East participate in the dynamics that Freud characterizes as "deferred action," or *Nachträglichkeit,* most famously explored by him in his case history of the Wolf Man.[7] In describing the dynamics and characteristics of deferred action, Freud is especially careful with his language, anxious not to be misunderstood. Discussing, for example, the relationship between the primal scene, when, at the age of one and a half, the Wolf Man apparently witnessed his parents making love *a tergo,* and his later shattering dream, when he was four years old, of the wolves in the tree outside of his bedroom window, Freud speaks of what he calls the "activation" of the earlier scene, emphasizing, "I purposely avoid the word 'recollection'" (SE, 17: 44). He also notes that although "the effects of the [first] scene were deferred," it is important to realize that "it had lost none of its freshness" (17:44). The first or primal scene, then, is not remembered or recollected, as such, but rather "activated," brought out of the past, as fresh or potent as ever, into the present by the dream, even while it is in turn responsible for helping shape the dream and making it possible. In speaking of the primal scene and its inscription in the Wolf Man's painful and convoluted history of obsessions and hysterical symptoms, Freud confesses that we can never determine for certain whether he actually at the age of one and a half awoke from his nap to see his parents making love, or whether this scene was later imagined by him, but it finally does not matter: "It is also a matter of indifference in this connection," writes Freud, "whether we choose to regard it as a primal *scene* or as a primal *phantasy*" (SE, 17:120, emphasis Freud's).

Similarly, we can never know whether the thrills and shocks Thackeray describes actually happened, or whether he later imagined or fantasized them, for such moments in Thackeray's narrative occupy a site that Ned Lukacher, revising Freud's concept of the "primal scene," describes as "an ontologically undecidable intertextual event that is situated in the differential space between historical memory and imaginative construction, between archival verification and interpretive free play" (24).[8] What matters most is not whether such scenes are remembered or reconstructed, but rather their presence and the significance of the space they occupy. And they are indeed significant.

Thackeray's voyage to the East becomes a desire-driven quest to recover sensations from a past that has been repressed but not forgotten. He gazes on a world that seems to possess something that he is missing, something that he wants. Lacan argues, "The gaze I encounter . . . is not a seen gaze, but a gaze imagined by me in the field of the Other" (*Concepts*, 84), and, as such, it exists within "the function of desire" (85). In other words, we gaze at that which we want but no longer have.[9] But what do we want that we no longer have, or, more specifically, what does Thackeray want that he no longer has? What is he looking for, and why does he seem to find it, only to see it slip away again?

I approach these questions by turning to Thackeray's description of a harem. In his account of the glories of Stanfield's panorama, visited by him during "the best period of youth, when fancy had all the bloom on her" (403), he remembers "when all the heroines who danced before the scene appeared as ravishing beauties." While he is certain that the harem also contains "wondrous beauties," he cannot see them, for they are concealed by "barred and filigreed windows." Their very inaccessibility, however, whets his desire to see them, making them even more present in his fantasies and daydreams: "We passed a long row of barred and filigreed windows, looking on the water, [and] when we were told that those were the apartments of his Highness's ladies, and actually heard them whispering and laughing behind the bars—a strange feeling of curiosity came over some ill-regulated minds—just to have *one* peep, one look at all those wondrous beauties" (412–13, emphasis Thackeray's). Freud reminds us that "visual impressions remain the most frequent pathway along which libidinal excitation is aroused" (*SE*, 7:156), adding that "the progressive concealment of the body which goes along with civilization keeps sexual curiosity awake" (156). Sexual curiosity is fully awake here, as Thackeray tells of hearing "the whispering and laughing behind the bars," and of his eagerness to "have *one* peep, one look at all those wondrous beauties." Thackeray's "strange feeling of curiosity" is experienced by those with "ill-regulated minds," namely, those, such as himself, who have momentarily escaped or evaded the dynamics of repression or regulation. This "strange feeling" continues as Thackeray recalls having heard about a particular trapdoor in this harem, located above a river into which "some luckless beauty is plunged occasionally, and the trap-door is shut." After such moments, he observes, "the dancing and singing, and the smoking and the laughing go on as before" (413). He has heard that "it is death to pick up any of the sacks [containing the bodies of such "luckless" women] thereabouts, if a stray one should float by you," but adds that "there were none any day when I passed, *at least, on the surface of the water*" (413, emphasis Thackeray's).

In some respects, this passage testifies to a fairly common identification in the Western mind of the Orient with sexuality.[10] Thackeray is fascinated, however, not only by what Said has described as the "sexual promise (and threat)" of the Orient, but also, or especially, by the ambivalent layers and levels of concealment created by the harem's architectural structure. What he finds, or rather what he imagines he would find, since he is not allowed access into the inner structures, is a design that calls attention to its own inner spaces or chambers, and to the promises and threats they contain. For these interiors are concealed not only by walls, but also by doors that would seem to invite entrance, but actually promise death or destruction to any unauthorized person who might enter them. Thackeray momentarily envisions a dangerously eroticized world uninhibited by restraint; the harem that he gazes on from the outside, imagining its interior chambers, is the metaphor for a desire that is enclosed but not concealed. Spatial design here is pregnant with meaning, from the barred and filigreed windows of the harem to its subterranean passages concealed by a treacherous surface containing hidden trapdoors. The violated female body that Thackeray speaks of, the luckless beauty who has in the midst of celebration and dance plunged to her death through a trapdoor, is inscribed with an eroticized language disturbed by sadistic impulses. And although he tells us that no such bodies were found on any of the days that he happened to pass, he almost immediately qualifies his assertion, confessing that this was true, "*at least, on the surface of the water*" (413). Such a disclaimer not only tends to belie the assertion it follows but also reminds us that Thackeray is always more interested in depths than in surfaces.

Such depths continue to compel Thackeray's attention as he tells of a passage in his guidebook hinting at the punishment that would "befall a stranger caught prying in the mysterious *first* court of the palace" (420). "I have read 'Bluebeard,'" Thackeray writes, "and don't care for peeping into forbidden doors; so the second court was quite enough for me" (420). But it is the first court, and not the second, that continues to hold power over him, for he confesses in the very next sentence to his fascination with the "forbidden." He imagines "the pleasure of beholding it [the first court] being heightened, as it were, by the notion of the invisible danger sitting next door, with uplifted scimitar ready to fall on you—present though not seen" (420). In this image of a "mysterious *first* court" (emphasis Thackeray's) protected by "forbidden doors" and containing mysterious and wondrous beauties guarded by an "uplifted scimitar ready to fall," we can find, in its Oedipal echoes of threatened castration and the interdiction of desire, an emblem of the defensive structures and patterns of Thackeray's narrative itself.

If, on one hand, Thackeray's text testifies to the insistent presence of a desire that will not be silenced and cannot be satisfied, it also points to equally insistent pressures that will not allow that desire to appear as such. The text of Thackeray's travel guide mirrors his own ambivalent desires, for while it informs him of the existence of forbidden interiors, it also warns against trying to gain access to them. These forbidden spaces are compelling, but also protected by threatening prohibitions against their being entered or penetrated. The dynamics of this particular fantasy operate in the realms of both anticipated pleasure and death, and, indeed, the text suggests that the intensity or *jouissance* of the daydream is intensified by the proximity of danger. As Thackeray gazes at the walls and doors that conceal but also invite, he imagines an interior world that promises the fulfillment of desire.

This particular moment has many of the elements of a daydream or fantasy, as Thackeray, his curiosity stimulated by the thoughts of "all those wondrous beauties" and the sounds of their "whispering and laughing behind the bars" (10), imagines various scenarios or possibilities, hinting at them vaguely enough to perhaps implicate his readers in the filling in of the blank spaces of what might be seen if that "one peep" could be managed. I speak of "a daydream or fantasy," but Freud makes no distinction between them, noting, for example, that "the best known productions of phantasy are the so-called 'day-dreams,'" for "the essence of the happiness of phantasy—making the obtaining of pleasure free once more from the assent of reality—is shown in them unmistakably" (SE, 16:372). As Laplanche and Pontalis note in their article "Fantasy and the Origins of Sexuality" Freud, "when studying the metapsychology of dreams, discovers the same relationship between the deepest unconscious fantasy and the daydream; the fantasy is present at both extremities of the process of dreaming" (12). "The daydream," they observe, "is a shadow play, utilizing its kaleidoscopic material drawn from all quarters of human experience, but involving the original fantasy, whose dramatis personae, the court cards, receive their notation from a family legend which is mutilated, disordered, and misunderstood. Its structure is the primal fantasy in which the Oedipus configuration can be easily distinguished" (13). The daydream is multivalenced, drawing on a wide range of experiences, and structured along the lines of the primal fantasy. Primal fantasies, as Freud describes them, are concerned with questions of origin or beginning, with the emergence of the human being into subjectivity, and include, for example, "fantasies of seduction, the origin and upsurge of sexuality; fantasies of castration, the origin of the differences between the sexes" (11).[11]

The women inside the harem, those invisible but wondrous beauties who laugh and sing, somehow cease to be the primary object of Thackeray's desire, for what he seems to seek in the passage is the sustaining of desire itself, as he moves around and toward the exploration of something that both authorizes and is denied by the structured prohibition of access to the interior, the uplifted scimitar ready to fall. Like some of the other scenes we have looked at, but more so, this scene is disturbed, agitated, by masturbatory impulses intensified by the possibility of danger and even death attached to such thoughts or fantasies. The first court is that which remains forever lost, denied, prohibited, insofar as it promises the erasure of difference, the disappearance of Ghosh's "border between oneself and one's image in the mirror." As Peter Brooks notes, "desire is inherently unsatisfied and unsatisfiable since it is linked to memory traces and seeks its realization in the hallucinatory reproduction of indestructible signs of infantile satisfaction" (55). But while desire may be unsatisfied and unsatisfiable, it is also timeless, constant; and thus, because this first court promises us a love that cannot be anymore, it is one that "plain men of the world" seek everywhere.

"There are . . . good reasons," writes Freud, "why a child sucking at his mother's breast has become the prototype of every relation of love. The finding of an object is in fact a refinding of it" (*SE*, 7:222). But the refinding of such a love (or rather the attempt to refind it), as Freud also notes, becomes messier as we grow older, complicated and riven by the various impulses and desires that he describes as "sexual aberrations" in his *Three Essays on Sexuality*, including, as we see in Thackeray, those of sadism and masochism. In a section entitled "Transformations of Puberty," Freud speaks specifically of "adolescent boys," the same boys Thackeray describes as having been ravished in the playhouse and having known the "fulness of sensual enjoyment" and the "intense and delicious" enjoyments of boyish fancy. Returning to his central notion that the finding of an object of desire is the refinding of it, Freud tells us that in the case of adolescent boys, the choice of an object is limited almost exclusively to "the world of ideas." For even though "infantile tendencies invariably emerge once more," social pressures and taboos dictate that "the sexual life of maturing youth is almost entirely restricted to indulging in phantasies" (SE, 7:226–27). In their fantasies and dreams, maturing youths invoke once again the "infantile tendencies" that alone promise love, the memory traces Peter Brooks speaks of, but now such desire is complicated or troubled, as Freud tells us, by "intensified pressure from somatic sources," or by what Thackeray remembers as *jouissance*, the "intense and delicious" shocks of moments like the ravishing ones in the playhouse.[12] *Jouissance*, as Bruce Fink notes, "is what comes to substitute for the lost 'mother child unity'" ("The Subject and the Other's Desire," 87), but, as we have seen in the various impulses that agitate Thackeray's fantasies about the harem, such *jouissance* can assume strange and disturbing forms. Fink notes: "This pleasure, this excitation due to sex, vision, and/or violence, whether positively or negatively connoted by conscience, whether considered innocently pleasurable or disgustingly repulsive, is termed *jouissance*, and that is what the subject orchestrates for himself or herself in fantasy" (87). Through such fantasies, the boy who enjoyed images of completeness or wholeness—as well as the man who wants to enjoy them once again (and to enable other men to enjoy them)—may seek to recover them, but the wound of separation cannot be erased or healed, for the unity being sought is "a chimerical, unrealizable moment" (82), requiring nothing less than the impossible foregoing of subjectivity itself.[13] Desire, then, must remain unsatisfied, the scarred site of loss and lack.

There is a point, Freud tells us, at which every dream descends into mystery and the unknown, the "omphalos" or navel of a dream, and the presence of such a site makes any dream uninterpretable in any final sense; for we can never trace it back to its origins or beginnings. In trying to understand the heavily layered and elusive nature of Thackeray's narrative, we get the sense that at times we are in the presence of such a site, as the narrator pursues the recovery of fantasies and shocks that themselves register even more deeply hidden or obscured fictional scenarios of sensual pleasure and completeness from an infantile past. And as Thackeray listens to the whispering and laughing of female voices behind the barred windows of the harem, he imagines the sounds of an impossible dream, for these fantasized interiors, the locus of both fear and desire, testify to the desire to return to a state prior to the pain of isolation and individualization.

> The wistful yearning towards home, in absence from it, as the shadows of evening deepened, and he followed in thought what was doing there from hour to hour, interpreted to him much of a yearning and regret he experienced afterwards, towards he knew not what, out of strange ways of feeling and thought in which, from time to time, his spirit found itself alone.

WALTER PATER, *The Child in the House*

Walter Pater's *The Child in the House*, perhaps the most Wordsworthian of all his writings, begins when his central figure, Florian Deleal, meets by chance on the road "a poor aged man," who just happens to mention the name of the place where Florian grew up (1,469). That night Florian is visited by a dream vision of his childhood home, and it in turn leads him to reflect on "that process of brain-building by which we are, each one of us, what we are" (1,469). *The Child in the House* is a wonderfully rich and haunting piece, but I consider briefly only its conclusion, the site of the above epigraph. In the conclusion, we are given access to Florian's remembrance of anxiously returning, as a twelve-year-old boy, to retrieve a caged bird he had inadvertently left behind during his family's move from the house where he had lived for most of his life. Florian "had never left his home before, and anticipating much from this change, had long dreamed over it" (1,477), but he now goes back to the house in distress, imagining the creature as "one left by others to perish of hunger in a closed house" (1,478). But although the bird itself is in good health, Florian finds a house emptied of furniture and belongings, its rooms filled, as Pater tells us, "with a look of meekness in their denudation" (1,478). And as he wanders through the empty and now strange house, young Florian knows that he has suffered a loss or wound whose pain will continue to torment him long after this day is over: "The aspect of the place touched him like the face of one dead; and a clinging back towards it came over him, so intense that he knew it would last long, and spoiling all his pleasure in the realisation of a thing so eagerly anticipated. And so, with the bird found, but himself in an agony of home-sickness, thus capriciously sprung up within him, he was driven quickly away, far into the rural distance, so fondly speculated on, of that favorite country road" (1,478).

This moment hits Florian with an almost visceral force, as the "aspect of the place," resembling "the face of one dead" mirrors a death as separation or loss that Florian too has experienced. And as "a clinging back towards it came over him, so intense that he knew it would last long," Florian knows that "it" is no longer there, and will never be there again. Thus, he experiences an "agony of homesickness" as he is driven away, toward a "rural distance" that cannot silence or erase the impossible desire he seeks as he glances backward toward a space that will long haunt him, even as he haunts it. Thackeray's essay is also a wounded narrative that glances backward, similarly haunted by images of distance that cannot be narrowed or closed, driven by images of loss—of a world that has been denuded and emptied. This sense of lack or absence gives rise to conflicts and tensions evident in the multivocality of Thackeray's essay, with its often disturbing cultural and ideological biases. At one point, for example, in claiming that all people, bound together by virtue of their mortality, should feel compassion for one another, Thackeray suggests that "the Maker has linked the whole race of man with this chain of love" and that "the whole family of Adam" should be tied together by "kindly feelings" (385). Juxtaposed, however, to this vision of a universal family are other images, more disturbingly presented. One such image, an almost perfect icon of nineteenth-century British imperialism—Britannia's enormous weight and majesty being supported, as it were, by the dark races of her empire—is seen when Thackeray tells of some British ladies who were, in his words, "scared and astonished by the naked savage brutes, who were shouldering the poor things to and fro" as they were carried from their ship to land (444). Also disturbing is Thackeray's description of Jews on board the ship that carried him to Jaffa. Thackeray observes that "the dirt of these children of captivity exceeds all possibility of description," just before he describes it in detail: "The profusion of stinks which they raised, the grease of their venerable garments and faces, the horrible messes cooked in the filthy pots, and devoured with the nasty fingers, the squalor of mats, pots, old bedding, and foul carpets of our Hebrew friends, could hardly be painted by Swift, in his dirtiest mood, and cannot be, of course, attempted by my timid and genteel pen" (423).

Said observes that the general attitudes found in nineteenth-century European racial theories were reinforced by "the appeal of linguistics, anthropology, and biology"—by what he, drawing on the work of Foucault, refers to as "discourses." These disciplines and systems of thought provided the age with "empirical evidence" to support racist attitudes (*Orientalism*, 232, 231), and one of the effects of these discourses was the assimilation or blurring of all differences. Thus, as Said puts it, "no Semite could ever shake loose the pastoral, desert environment of his tent and tribe," and "every manifestation of actual 'Semitic' life could be, and ought to be, referred back to the primitive explanatory category of 'the Semitic'" (234). Such an attitude is evident in Thackeray's description of some Jewish pilgrims he observes in Rhodes:

> There was our venerable Rabbi, who, robed in white and silver, and bending over his book . . . looked like a patriarch, and whom I saw chaffering about a fowl with a brother Rhodian Israelite. How they fought over the body of that lean animal! The street swarmed with Jews: goggling eyes looked out from the old carved casements—hooked noses issued from the low antique doors—Jew boys driving donkeys, Hebrew mothers nursing children, dusky, tawdry, ragged young beauties and most venerable gray-bearded fathers were all gathered round about the affair of the hen! (425)

Thackeray asks us to "think of the centuries during which these wonderful people have remained unchanged; and how, from the days of Jacob downwards, they have believed and swindled!" (425). And yet, we find in his description a vibrant community of men, women, and children, bending, chaffering, fighting, driving, nursing, and gathering. Such images stand in sharp contrast to those of enervation and, indeed, of death and apathy that Thackeray uses to characterize himself and his fellow travelers. As in the earlier passages in which Thackeray is isolated from the city scenes of

Smyrna and Constantinople, capable of witnessing them only from a distance and as a solitary outsider, the intensity of his language here testifies to a recognition—never fully evaded, I think, by verbal irony—of a sense of loss. Images of lassitude or weariness are associated with the English tourist at large, as Thackeray tries to conceal the specific in the general, the particularity of his own responses in those of "the Englishman, with his hands in his pockets, [who] has been seen all the world over: staring down the crater of Vesuvius, or into a Hottentot kraal—or at a pyramid, or a Parisian coffee-house, or an Esquimaux hut—with the same insolent calmness of demeanour" (466–67).

Soon after this passage, Thackeray's irony attempts to deflect this image of someone dead to wonder and joy by suggesting a kind of practical or hard-nosed English "scorn, bewilderment, and shame" at such "strange rites and ceremonies" as the English tourist might find abroad. But at the center of this vignette, we find once again "the English stranger [who] looks on the scene" from a distance (469)—as he stares at pilgrims on the way to the Church of the Holy Sepulchre and walks into the church and "gazes round easily at the place, in which people of every other nation in the world are in tears, or in rapture, or wonder" (467). Whether it is the Church of the Holy Sepulchre or the Pyramids of Egypt, the relationship between Thackeray and the object of his attention is one of distance and separation, of barriers that cannot be broken down and of an insolence and rudeness that only partially defend the narrator against fears of a failure not only of will, but of love and the imagination as well. The various voices and narrative postures erected by Thackeray in order to protect himself against such fears serve instead to call such fears to our attention.

The sights that he sees and tries to appropriate or capture remain silent and monochromatic, disconcertingly both close and distant, provoking the narrative voice into an anxiety inadequately concealed by irony and self-deprecating humor. "I had been preparing myself overnight," he writes, "with the help of a cigar and a moonlight contemplation on deck, for sensations on landing in Egypt. I was ready to yield myself up with solemnity to the mystic grandeur of the scene of initiation" (480). But such an opportunity does not occur; the scene of initiation is postponed indefinitely, and we find a language that is flat, empty, and strikingly sad: "There they [the Pyramids] lay, rosy and solemn in the distance—those old, majestic, mystical, familiar edifices. Several of us tried to be impressed" (488). Toward the end of his essay, Thackeray describes walking through Cairo late at night and passing by an insane asylum: "As you pass the mad-house, there is one poor fellow still talking to the moon—no sleep for him. He howls and sings there all the night—quite cheerfully, however. He has not lost his vanity with his reason; he is a Prince in spite of the bars and the straw." And on the streets surrounding this solitary singer are "mysterious people . . . curled up and sleeping in the porches," and lanterns that "redouble the darkness in the solitary, echoing street" (509).

The various faces of madness haunted the nineteenth-century artist, testifying to the silent and unbridgeable chasm between the isolated madman or madwoman and the outside world, with all of its multitudinous impulses and energies. Several years later, in *Vanity Fair*, Thackeray would describe George Gaunt, the younger son of Lord Steyne. Once George begins to act strangely, he is "sent off" to Brazil: "But people knew better; he never returned from that Brazil expedition—never died there—never lived there—never was there at all. He was nowhere: he was gone out altogether" (456). The fear of madness in Thackeray's work springs from the fear of an isolation that cannot be diminished, of the solitary figure cut off from sources of love, energy, and joy; the various images of madness, death, and isolation blend into one another in the kaleidoscopic icons of fragmentation and separation that emanate from the age. The image of the mad "Prince" singing happily in his cell, however, stands in sharp and expressive contrast to Thackeray's own voice, eminently sane and exceedingly lonely, born of separation or isolation and telling a story that remains singularly free of celebration or of song.

At one point Thackeray suggests, "It is worth while to have made the journey for this pleasure: to have walked the deck on long nights, and have thought of home. You have no leisure to do so in the city" (482). As the essay closes, he returns once again to this image of home, observing that "the happiest and best of all the recollections . . . are those of the hours passed at night on the deck . . . and your thoughts were fixed upon home far away" (514). The passage from Edward Said that serves as the epigraph for this chapter speaks eloquently of the nature of home and exile, and also helps to amplify or illuminate the impulses that seem to be behind Thackeray's *Journey from Cornhill to Grand Cairo*. For while Thackeray's thoughts in his narrative often turn to "home," home, as Said points out, is the place in which one is born to live there more or less forever, knowing that one is of it; and such a place does not exist for Thackeray, who knows all too well Pater's "agony of homesickness." Or rather, it exists only as his "home far away," a site characterized by absence as well as presence, experienced by Thackeray as that which was known once but is now lost.

3

Death, Desire, and the Site of the Prostitute in Elizabeth Gaskell's *Ruth*

> "When I covered sports, I used to get together with the other writers on the road. Hotel rooms, planes, taxis, restaurants. There was only one topic of conversation. Sex and death."
> "That's two topics."
> "You're right, Jack."
> "I would hate to believe they are inextricably linked."
>
> DON DELILLO, *White Noise*

When Freud listened to his patients talk, he heard in their stumbles, hesitations, and denials evidence of the unconscious making itself known. Semantic stuttering, Freud realized, was often performative, as significant and revealing as the narrative it interrupted or disfigured. In literary texts as well, narrative hiccups or disruptions often alert us to unconscious articulations, and in the case of Elizabeth Gaskell's *Ruth* in particular, a number of readers have detected textual discontinuities or glitches. Jenny Uglow reads *Ruth* as a novel that possesses "an imbalance, a distress which makes one question the deep motive beneath the writing" (*Elizabeth Gaskell*,337), and traces the source of the distress to Gaskell's "private identification, not altogether acknowledged" (337) with Ruth and Jemima's repression and punishment by the world and God. Felicia Bonaparte, less "concerned with Gaskell's fiction as works of literature" than with the way in which it enables us "to explore Elizabeth Gaskell's inner existence" (*The Gypsy-Bachelor of Manchester*, 1), locates the site of the text's disruption in what she characterizes as Gaskell's demon, an inner struggle or drama that wrote itself out in her fictions. Rosemarie Bodenheimer, on the other hand, argues in *The Politics of Story in Victorian Social Fiction* that the tensions between the pastoral and social arguments of the text make for "a discontinuity in the novel" (153), and Hilary Schor similarly sees *Ruth* as "a divided and contradictory work" ("The Plot of the Beautiful Ignoramus," 46) and finds evidence in its narrative tensions of "one woman's attempt to rewrite romanticism, and write the woman's story into the tradition" (46).[1]

I too look at the narrative tensions and evidence of distress that we find in *Ruth*, but I want to approach them somewhat differently. What I find especially intriguing about *Ruth* is precisely what it does not say, but what is nevertheless, in Macherey's terms, acted out by the elaboration of certain utterances in it.[2] Although Schor's reading of *Ruth* is often a compelling one, I am not persuaded by her argument that "the specific literary heritage the novel invokes and criticizes is the Romantic project Gaskell claimed as the inspiration for her earliest attempts at writing" (47). Rather, I would argue that *Ruth* returns to one of the questions at the heart of the Romantic project, namely, an exploration of the psychoanalytic dynamics inherent in the relationship between death and sexuality. Like DeLillo in the epigraph from *White Noise*, Gaskell seems to be suggesting that sex and death are not two separate topics, but rather are "inextricably linked."

The question of how sex and death are related is raised by earlier Romantics, such as Coleridge in "Christabel" and Keats in "The Eve of St. Agnes," but Gaskell pursues it along her own paths, or, to be more precise, *Ruth* pursues it along its own lines, for the text knows more than and goes places other than where the author had in mind. Some time ago (1908), Anne Thackeray Ritchie pointed out that while some writers "create their characters and rule over this dream-world of theirs as Prospero did in his island," others "seem to be rather the servants of their imagination, and to be governed by their fantasies" ("Mrs. Gaskell," 217–18). Significantly enough, Ritchie includes Gaskell in this latter group, and, indeed, Gaskell herself was familiar with such "fantasies"—at one point, for example, characterizing Charlotte Brontë (to whom she often refers when reflecting on her own art) as a writer whose fictions "give one the idea of creative power carried to the verge of insanity" (*Letters*, 398). *Ruth* is a polysemic text, destabilized not only by its ambiguous genealogy or origins, but also by the turbulent presence of erotic desires in it. Coral Lansbury points out that "few writers have conveyed the intricacies of sexual passion with such perception as Gaskell" (*Elizabeth Gaskell*, 29), and Felicia Bonaparte similarly remarks that "Gaskell was not just extremely sensual, she was also extremely sexual. She had a healthy interest in sex, as her fiction clearly shows, and a healthy appreciation of the power of sexual passion" (87).

But while Gaskell's appreciation of sexual passion might very well have been "healthy," such language, at least as far as *Ruth* is concerned, tends to blur some rather important issues, for it is not only a sexy novel, it is also a death-haunted novel—just as its eponymous central figure is an intensely passionate woman around whom an aura of death and dissolution lingers. If we are to understand the relationship between these two impulses in the novel, we must do so in part, at least, by exploring the ways in which the erotic is invested with death along the lines identified by Bataille. But we need to follow other avenues of inquiry as well. Hilary Schor has suggested that "one way to approach the complexities of a novel like *Ruth* is through the broader social history of which it is a part, the cultural discourse surrounding women in the 1850s, particularly the figure of the prostitute" (47–48), arguing that both the novel and such cultural debates circle "around the observation of the woman" (48). Schor, however, focuses her attention not on the figure of the prostitute, but rather on the ways in which Gaskell's text constitutes a problematic Victorian revision (woman empowered by a voice, enabled to write and narrate) of the Romantic inheritance (woman as seen, observed, silent), and thus on the inconsistencies in the text generated by the tensions between its social and literary impulses. *Ruth* is a Romantic text, albeit a conflicted one, marking its heroine's body as the site of the prostitute and later in the novel as the site of the corpse and thus of contagion. Sarah Webster Goodwin suggests, "The prostitute haunts the romantic text," and "is akin to the corpse in the ways in which she inspires fears of—and desire for—contagion" ("Romanticism," 152–53). As Goodwin also observes, however, such fears and desires are most often repressed, emerging through "association and implication rather than by overt statement" (153).

At times Gaskell seemed uncomfortable with the fact that her novels seemed to conceal or disguise the woman who wrote them. "The difference between Miss Brontë and me," she observes, "is that she puts all her naughtiness into her books, and I put all my goodness," adding that "my books are so far better than I am that I often feel ashamed of having written them and as if I were a hypocrite" (*Letters*, 228). "Naughty" and "naughtiness" are important semantic markers for Gaskell, and frequently identify sexual transgression or excess. The young boy who slaps Ruth early in the novel, for example, calls her "a bad naughty girl," and Farquhar later tries to "put the naughty, wilful, plaguing Jemima Bradshaw out of his head" (71, 229). Jenny Uglow suggests that "*Ruth* is a study of repression which is itself repressed" (327), but Gaskell seemed anxious about it, suspecting that it was not repressed enough, that she had not succeeded in writing all the naughtiness out of her text: "I . . . cd not get over the hard things people said of Ruth," she writes to Eliza Fox, "I mean I was just in that feverish way when I could not get them out of my head by thinking of anything else but dreamt about them and all that. I think I must be an improper woman without knowing it, I do so manage to shock people" (*Letters*, 222–23). Just as Ruth tries unsuccessfully to pass herself off as something she is not—namely, a widowed wife and mother—Gaskell fears that she may be something other than what she seems to be, that *Ruth*, like an errant fantasy or disturbing dream, discloses a hidden authorial self ("an improper woman") guilty of a sexual impropriety or transgression that has somehow thus far escaped her detection.

In "George Eliot and *Daniel Deronda*," an essay examining the conjunction of gender and authorship in the nineteenth-century British novel, Catherine Gallagher suggests ways in which we might understand better, I think, the nature or origin of the apprehensions or uneasiness on Gaskell's part regarding *Ruth*. Arguing that one of the factors structuring this conjunction was the "specific historical associations confronting professional woman writers in the nineteenth-century, when the metaphor of the author as whore was commonplace" (41), Gallagher examines the historical and social reasons for this particular metaphor. She points out that "the last half of the eighteenth century is the period both when the identity of text and self begin to be strongly asserted and when the legal basis for commodifying texts (as distinct from books) comes into being in copyright law. This combination puts writers in the marketplace in the position of selling themselves, like whores" (43). To sell oneself, whether as prostitute or writer, meant exposure to the marketplace and the voices in it. As Gallagher notes, "Both the woman writer and the prostitute . . . are established in the sphere of exchange that excludes natural generation and substitutes for it an excruciatingly dangerous love affair with a multitude" (55). Gaskell's letters indicate that she is quite aware of this multitude, anxious as a professional writer to get her material published, yet also tormented by a fear of public exposure. Given the fact, or Gaskell's belief, that her other novels were so much "better" than Gaskell herself, they did not cause her to hear the loud clamor of the public voices or to feel the intensity of the public's gaze, but with *Ruth*, all of this seems to have changed.

If in part the conflicts involved in the writing of *Ruth* involved Gaskell's own ambivalent feelings toward a profession to which she was also deeply committed, as well as her own anxieties about what this novel in particular revealed (or concealed) about herself as woman and writer, they undoubtedly arose also from the subject matter of *Ruth*.[3] In mid-nineteenth-century England, any novelist, and most certainly a woman, had to be uneasy about creating as the central figure of her novel a "fallen woman" who gives birth to a son out of wedlock and then attempts to move both herself and her child back into "respectable" society by concealing her past. In *Ruth*, Gaskell's uneasiness also stems from the fact that the novel is haunted by the figure of the prostitute, not only marking the site of Ruth's body but also shaping the patterns and directions of the novel's plot. It is not that Ruth believes herself to be a prostitute or that any of her acquaintances believe she is one, or that Gaskell feels that she is, or, for that matter, that I do. Rather, the text itself believes it, giving voice to this belief in a number of ways. For now, I give two brief examples.

The first example involves a dream that Ruth has early in the novel. This dream has its origins in Ruth's reflections about her young son, which in turn lead her to think about the weaknesses of his father, Bellingham, and his "selfish, worldly nature" (163). As Gaskell describes this scene, Ruth's reflections become "a compelling presence that had taken possession of her" (163), and she soon tires, falling into "a kind of feverish slumber" (163).

It is at this point that the dream itself begins:

> She dreamt that the innocent babe that lay by her side in soft ruddy slumber had started up into man's growth, and . . . he was a repetition of his father; and, like him, had lured some maiden (who in her dream seemed strangely like herself, only more utterly sad and desolate even than she) into sin, and left her there to even a worse fate than that of suicide. For Ruth believed there was a worse. She dreamt she saw the girl, wandering, lost; and that she saw her son in high places, prosperous—but with more than blood on his soul. She saw her son dragged down by the clinging girl into some pit of horrors into which she dared not look, but from whence his father's voice was heard. (163)

Gillian Beer has noted that dreams in the nineteenth-century British novel "are messengers from beyond the self. Yet they tally with the self's deepest needs. They endorse the unconscious" (*Darwin's Plots*, 45–46). Ruth's dream is such a messenger, testifying to truths beyond the conscious self of Ruth. Although she dares not look into that Hell or "pit of horrors" from which the father's voice comes, her dream reveals that Ruth has seen it nevertheless, for she dreams that the girl abandoned into sin and prostitution "seemed strangely like herself, only more utterly sad and desolate even than she." Exemplifying what Freud refers to as the dream technique of condensation, the figures of the mother and father become "strangely" mingled or merged in the dream with those of the son and the maiden/prostitute, as all four are caught up in the repetitive patterns of a sexually charged drama of sin and damnation, in which the roles and even the identities of the players flow into one another.

The second example of the text's belief that Ruth is a prostitute is more subtly introduced and more pervasively felt throughout the novel. Ever since its publication, one of the more problematic aspects of *Ruth* has been its apparent exaggeration of its central figure's guilt. Critics have been perplexed by Ruth's combination of innocence on one hand and excessive penance and guilt on the other. As Hilary Schor remarks, "Critics, even contemporaries of Gaskell, have seen this as a flaw in the novel: she carefully creates Ruth's innocence but spends the rest of the novel insisting on her guilt in order to work out her repentance" (66).[4] This insistence has alienated modern readers in large part because of its exaggerated religiosity, but Gaskell's contemporaries also saw it as exorbitant or overwrought, and thus when Angus Easson remarks that "in pleading a case, Gaskell overstates it" (*Elizabeth Gaskell*, 125), he echoes George Eliot's remarks as well as those of a number of other readers both before and after him.[5]

And yet it is possible that the text knows better than its readers, even better than Gaskell herself. In speaking of the melancholic in "Mourning and Melancholia," Freud argues that we must take the man's self-reproaches of guilt and unworthiness seriously, for such a person, Freud points out, "reproaches himself, vilifies himself and expects to be cast out and punished."[6] It is futile to contradict such a person or try to talk him out of his self-accusations, Freud adds, for he "must surely be right in some way and be describing something that is as it seems to him to be" (*SE*, 14:246). This "something," however, operates at an unconscious level, and thus what is important is not whether "the melancholic's self-denigration is correct, in the sense that his self-criticism agrees with the opinion of other people" (247), but rather that it gives a "correct description of his psychological situation" (247). The melancholic, Freud writes, "has a keener eye for the truth than other people who are not melancholic" (246). *Ruth* too has this keener eye, insofar as Gaskell's text, like Freud's melancholic, testifies to unconscious guilt and self-hatred, as it identifies Ruth's body as that of the prostitute, the site of both fear and desire. The extreme pronouncements and gestures of guilt and self-reproach on Ruth's part may indeed be disproportionate to what Ruth should feel, but nevertheless accurately register a psychological truth. And, again, while other factors also undoubtedly feed into Ruth's self-hatred—such as the age's stigma against sex out of wedlock, its attitudes toward the fallen woman, and perhaps even her own excessive gullibility or naïveté—they do not in and of themselves account for the ways in which the novel moves toward its troubling closure. But before looking at the closure, I look at several other aspects of the novel.

The directions of my argument in this chapter will, in fact, be fourfold. First of all, I consider the relationship between lack and desire in *Ruth*, especially the ways in which Gaskell explores the death of the mother as the creation of a tear, as it were, in the fabric of Ruth's being, a Lacanian emptiness that Ruth tries to fill in by various means, all of them finally unsuccessful. This lack and the desire born out of it appear in compulsive patterns on

Ruth's part that are inextricably connected with the aura of death that pervades this novel, as she tries to return to or recuperate a sense of wholeness or fullness that she remembers or imagines herself once having experienced. In the second section of this chapter, I look at the ways in which Ruth seeks wholeness through the erotic as Bataille characterizes it, namely, an attempt to break down the discontinuities and ruptures of being that constitute human subjectivity. In doing so, I will be looking at two scenes in particular, both involving Ruth and Bellingham. The first, set in Wales and occurring early in the novel, is an intensely erotic moment that not only affirms the body and its pleasures but also provides evidence of a *jouissance* on Ruth's part that exists outside the consciousness of either Ruth or the narrative voice. The second scene occurs later in the novel at Abermouth, when Ruth recognizes Bellingham (now going by the name of Donne) before he realizes who she is. In this scene, the unconscious of the text finds partial articulation in the interior meditations of Bellingham, when the still unrecognized governess at the breakfast table in front of him triggers memories of Ruth, who he imagines has by now turned to prostitution. Here the representation of the female body becomes more problematic and unsettling, leading to the third section of my argument, in which I will explore the ways in which Ruth's erotic body becomes a sustained object of both fear and desire, insofar as it is identified with the prostitute as well as with death and contagion.

And finally I will turn my attention to the closure of *Ruth*, in which Ruth comes to inhabit a zone between life and death, associated as prostitute with the diseased nature of urban society itself. Empowered precisely to the extent that she inhabits the realm of the taboo—her body eroticized by the aura of death and dissolution that surrounds it—she can redeem or help cleanse society only insofar as she loses her own body, absorbing society's disease and contagion within herself and thus moving toward a death that finally has very little to do with Bellingham. Suggesting in disturbing ways the possibility that sex and death might in fact be one topic rather than two—that they are, at least in this novel, inextricably linked—Ruth's death is represented as an eroticized experience, breaking down the walls of separation and discontinuity that haunt Ruth, as the maternal becomes invested, as it is earlier in the novel, with ominous and mysterious overtones.[7]

> Demand in itself bears on something other than the satisfaction it
> calls for. It is demand of a presence or absence—which is what is
> manifested in the primordial relation to the mother.
>
> LACAN, *Ecrits*

Margaret Homans has suggested that Gaskell comes the closest of all
nineteenth-century writers "to Woolf's sense of the possibility and desir-
ability of articulating a nonsymbolic mother-daughter language" (*Bearing
the Word*, 21), but in Gaskell, as in Woolf, we also see the darker side of this
language.[8] The dead mother figures prominently in *Ruth*, identifying a
desire born out of lack or separation, associated throughout the text with
Ruth's desire to return to or recover a time prior to lack or separation. As
such, the mother's figural presence in the metonymic signifying chain identifies a site of absence or want, a hole that Ruth attempts to fill in her search
for love in other places.[9] In her essay "Freud's Mnemonic: Screen Memories and Feminist Nostalgia," Mary Jacobus argues against writers such as
Adrienne Rich (*Of Woman Born*, 1976) and Phyllis Chesler (*Women and
Madness*, 1973) who would locate in the mother-daughter relationship "the
possibility of a utopian state in which our relations to the body could be
unalienated, and our psychic state whole" (16). Drawing in part on Jane Gallop's *Reading Lacan*, Jacobus reminds us that such a nostalgia, one that Gallop relates specifically to the feminine, is in fact "rooted in the desire to forget
the irretrievability of 'the mother as mother'" (20). "The mother," as Jacobus
observes, "is not only always lost but never possessed, always a sign of alienation" (20). She also notes, "No violent separation can be envisaged without
an aura of pathos, because separation is inscribed from the start" (18). We
find evidence of this pathos and alienation inscribed in Ruth's narrative, as
she dreams, for example, of her mother, "coming, as she used to do, to see if
I were asleep and comfortable; and when I tried to take hold of her, she went
away and left me alone—I don't know where; so strange!" (9).[10] Such nostalgia drives her to other strange sites, as she seeks out the coldest and darkest corner in Mrs. Mason's house, because the faded floral-patterned panels

remind her "of other sister-flowers that grew and blossomed, and withered away in her early home" (7). Love, Gaskell writes, "was very precious to Ruth now, as of old time . . . [and] lonely as the impressible years of her youth had been—without parents, without brother or sister—it was, perhaps, no wonder that she clung tenaciously to every symptom of regard" (248). Ruth's life moves from one "symptom of regard" to another, interspersed with moments and days of emptiness and loneliness, dreary and empty Sundays with their "monotonous idleness" and "dull length of day" (35), and the months in the Benson household after her past is discovered, in which "few events broke the monotony of their lives, and those events were of a depressing kind" (377).

Lacan identifies our primordial sense of loss with the mother, but he also suggests, as Barbara Johnson points out, that "the mother addressed is somehow a personification, not a person, a personification of presence or absence, of Otherness itself" ("Apostrophe, Animation, and Abortion," 38). Desire, Lacan adds, "annuls the particularity of everything that can be granted by transmuting it into a proof of love," and, therefore, desire is often characterized by a "paradoxical, deviant, erratic, eccentric, even scandalous character" (*Ecrits*, 286). In *Ruth*, Gaskell explores the eccentricity of desire, often by peeling away the layers of realism that hide the truth about its "scandalous character." Such, for example, is the case when Ruth sees Thurstan Benson just after she has been deserted by Bellingham. Exhausted from chasing the receding carriage carrying Bellingham and his mother away from her, Ruth feels separated from all love and care. "There's a hole in the sky, where God used to be," Willie Nelson tells us in "Heartland," and Ruth too experiences the presence of such a hole, as she "doubted God," felt that there "was no pity anywhere," and her cries seemed to Benson "the wildest, dreariest crying ever mortal cried" (96). At this moment, a "shadow" falls across Ruth's garments and she looks up, seeing Benson, "the deformed gentleman she had twice before seen" (95), and then, in one of the finest examples of the uncanny in Victorian fiction, Ruth sees in him or hears in his words something else, or rather feels something else: "She regarded him fixedly in a dreamy way, as if they struck some chord in her heart, and she were listening to its echo, and so it was. His pitiful look, or his words, reminded her of the childish days when she knelt at her mother's knee, and she was only conscious of a straining, longing desire to recall it all" (96).

This passage seems at once incredibly accessible and elusive, slippery. We are told that Benson's presence, his voice, or perhaps even just his expression—what Gaskell refers to as his "pitiful look"—reminds Ruth of her mother, or rather, to be precise, those "childish days when she knelt at her mother's knee." This moment, grounded in a profound sense of separation on Ruth's part, not only from Bellingham but from God as well, ends with what Gaskell describes as Ruth's sudden "straining, longing desire to recall it all." What precisely "it all" refers to in this context remains unclear, but it seems Ruth is pursuing more the echo of a particular chord, to use the language of the passage, than any specific event or moment that can be retrieved or remembered. For as much as any other scene in the novel, this scene discloses that Gaskell was intrigued by the mysterious and complex dynamics of human memory—by the way, for example, particular fragrances or aromas can trigger long-forgotten memories.

If, writes Walter Benjamin, "the recognition of a scent is more privileged to provide consolation than any other recollection, this may be so because it deeply drugs the sense of time. A scent may drown years in the odor it recalls" (*Illuminations*, 184).[11] Gaskell too knew of the way a scent could drown years, writing to a friend in 1848, for example, "I have just been up to our room. There is a fire in it, and a smell of baking, and oddly enough the feelings and recollections of 3 years ago come over me so strongly—when I used to sit up in the room so often in the evenings reading by the fire, and watching my darling *darling* Willie, who now sleeps sounder still in the dull, dreary chapel-yard at Warrington" (*Letters*, 57, emphasis Gaskell's). Describing in *Ruth* how "the bush of sweetbrier, underneath the rear window, scented the place, and the delicious fragrance reminded [Ruth] of her old home," Gaskell remarks, "I think scents affect and quicken the memory more than either sights or sounds" (60). Gaskell was fascinated by experiences that lie just beyond the edge of conscious recall, what Proust would later identify as *mémoire involontaire*, moments that have not been explicitly or consciously experienced.[12] At one point, for example, as Ruth watches Sally's movements, Gaskell writes, "All these particulars sank unconsciously into Ruth's mind; but they did not rise to the surface, and become perceptible, for a length of time" (137). And just before she sees Benson, Ruth throws herself by the side of the road, apparently conscious of nothing except the fact that Bellingham "was gone" (94). But

Gaskell tells us that this is not quite so, that "afterwards, long afterwards, she remembered the exact motion of a bright green beetle busily meandering among the wild thyme near her, and she recalled the musical, balanced, wavering drop of a skylark into her nest near the heather-bed where she lay" (94).

The movements of a bright beetle, the descent of a skylark into her nest, or the everyday gestures of a woman can sink unconsciously into us, emerging later to make themselves felt. During this particular moment when she looks at Benson, the mysterious memory that Ruth longs or strains to recall resembles in its elusiveness George Eliot's twentieth echo of an echo; but whatever it might be—and we never find out—its effects are unmistakably clear. "But suddenly she startled him, as she herself was startled into a keen sense of the suffering of the present; she sprang up and pushed him aside, and went rapidly towards the gate of the field" (96), intending to drown herself in the fast-moving waters she had seen earlier. What is striking about this moment is not its unexpectedness, although we, like Benson and perhaps even Ruth herself, are initially startled by it, but rather the various ways in which the text prepares us for it. Thurstan's presence, Ruth's memory of her mother and her straining and longing to "recall it all," to invoke once again those echoes in her heart—all precede her attempt to crash through separation and distance, to free herself from loss by violently breaking through it to some kind of unity or wholeness. The repetition compulsion, as Freud notes in *Beyond the Pleasure Principle*, is "something that seems more primitive, more elementary, more instinctual, than the pleasure principle which it overrides" (17). In this scene, the pleasure principle, or the urge toward self-preservation, is overpowered by something else, an elementary and instinctual urge on Ruth's part toward a death that remains throughout inexorably linked with images of a maternal love.

Even Ruth's relationship with the natural world, often interpreted as Gaskell's attempt to depict Ruth as a daughter of nature and thus to soften or screen her heroine's sexuality, has an aura of death around it, and perhaps nowhere more so than in the scenes in which Ruth wanders in the magnificence of the "Alpine country."[13] The scene presents Ruth as a child of nature, filled with both delight and silent awe in the presence of such natural splendor: "It was most true enjoyment to Ruth. It was opening a new sense; vast ideas of beauty and grandeur filled her mind at the sight of the mountains. . . . She was almost overpowered by the vague and solemn delight" (65). Ruth, Gaskell writes, "knew not if she moved or stood still, for the grandeur of this beautiful earth absorbed all idea of separate and individual existence" (65); and, as she continues to gaze on nature, "the open air, that kind soothing balm which gentle mother Nature offers to us all in our seasons of depression, relieved her" (66). This moment exemplifies the Romantic sublime, but, as Bonaparte notes, Gaskell's prose in *Ruth* often seems dead (80), and if it is not dead here, it is certainly moribund. Gaskell's language, with its "gentle Mother Nature" and "soothing balm" seems tired, her tropes shopworn, but we must not allow them to deaden our critical ear, for the passage is also an unsettling one, almost ominous, as if its clichés were calling attention to their own inadequacy. In his essay on the sublime, Edmund Burke locates terror at its center—terror, he tells us, "is in all cases whatsoever, either more openly or latently the ruling principle of the sublime" (*Philosophical Enquiry*, 58). And in an essay entitled "The Principle of Reason: The University in the Eyes of its Pupils," Derrida, drawing on Burke's essay, similarly argues that terror is the gorge or abyss over which the sublime is suspended, suggesting that the Romantic sublime leads our thoughts not only toward sites of grandeur, but also in the direction of solitude and destruction, toward death itself. Gaskell's invocation of the Romantic sublime draws on a similar topography, as Ruth's thoughts wander in the direction of dissolution and death, compelled by a desire for her identity or individuality to be erased by "the grandeur of this beautiful earth [that] absorbed all idea of separate and individual existence" (65). Erotic experiences, however, can also diminish or absorb the painful notion of a "separate and individual existence," and it is to such experiences in *Ruth* that I now turn.

In the moments before he pulled her over again, her greed now answering his urgency, she felt, "Oh, I am dying," and understood one of the oldest metaphors.

A. S. BYATT, *Still Life*

Gaskell's *Ruth* is, in part at least, an extended meditation on A. S. Byatt's metaphor. Ruth's circuitous journey toward the end is punctuated by erotic moments that affirm the pleasures of the body and thus would seem to stand in sharp contrast to incidents we have seen in which the text is death haunted, attracted to images of annihilation. Yet Gaskell realizes that, as Bataille puts it, "the urge towards love, pushed to its limits, is an urge towards death" (*Erotism*, 42), and in *Ruth*, these two urges are intimately and yet ambiguously entangled. "Bodies in Gaskell have a life of their own," Felicia Bonaparte notes (88), and in *Ruth*, the discourse of the body extends beyond narrative commentary and understanding. Often, in fact, the erotic dynamics of particular scenes and their language of the body not only escape narrative commentary, but also are presented in such a way as to screen what is being said or to deflect our attention from it.

Coral Lansbury, for example, suggests that although Gaskell's Ruth possesses the face and body of a Greek goddess, she also has "the mind of an untutored child. Stupidity defines her character" (23). While there have undoubtedly been British heroines more cerebral than Ruth Hilton, I am not sure if she does in fact have the mind of "an untutored child"—but we can nevertheless appreciate Lansbury's remark, for the narrative voice frequently calls our attention to Ruth's childlike nature and naïveté. If we take the narrative voice at its word, as a number of readers have, we buy into the innocence of Ruth and into a convenient and too easy theory of victimization that nicely glosses over the truth that the text itself discloses; for if Gaskell's narrative voice represses this truth, the text written by "an improper woman" does not.[14]

This truth, in which Ruth's "hidden sexuality" comes out of hiding, disclosing itself to be vigorous and passionate, is particularly evident in the first scene I examine.[15] Hilary Schor has found in this moment evidence of "aesthetic prostitution" and of "trafficking in women," suggesting that Ruth is a "sexual victim" (67) who becomes a sexual "piece" for Bellingham (64). Let's look at what is going in the scene. It occurs during Ruth and Bellingham's stay in Wales, in a "green" away from town when Bellingham arranges a "coronet" of flowers in Ruth's hair. As he does so, Ruth basks in his pleasure, knowing, Gaskell writes, "that he was pleased from his manner, which had the joyousness of a child playing with a new toy, and she did not think twice

of his occupation. It was pleasant to forget everything except his pleasure"
(74). When Bellingham asks Ruth to look at her reflection in the pond, she

> obeyed, and could not help seeing her own loveliness; it gave her a sense
> of satisfaction for an instant, as the sight of any other beautiful object
> would have done, but she never thought of associating it with herself. She
> knew she was beautiful; but that seemed abstract, and removed from her-
> self. Her existence was in feeling, and thinking, and loving.
>
> Down in that green hollow they were quite in harmony. Her beauty
> was all that Mr. Bellingham cared for, and it was supreme. It was all he
> recognized of her, and he was proud of it. She stood in her white dress
> against the trees which grew around; her face was flushed into a brilliancy
> of colour which resembled that of a rose in June; the great heavy white
> flowers drooped on either side of her beautiful head, and if her brown hair
> was a little disordered, the very disorder only seemed to add a grace. She
> pleased him more by looking so lovely than by all her tender endeavours
> to fall in with his varying humour. (74–75)

I have cited the passage in its entirety because only in this way can we
see the conflicting narrative impulses operating in it. We have, on one
hand, the scene itself and, on the other, Gaskell's narrative commentary
on it. The former shows us a Ruth deriving pleasure and giving pleasure,
while the latter speaks of Ruth's abstractedness from the scene itself and
from Bellingham's attitudes toward Ruth. Here, as elsewhere in the novel,
Bellingham is genuinely astounded, indeed startled, by Ruth's beauty, but
it is only fair to add that he might also regard her as a "piece," since, as
Hélène Cixous notes, "It is men who like to play dolls. As we have known
since Pygmalion" ("Sorties," 66). However, if we are wholly taken in by the
commentary, including its remarks about Bellingham, we misread the
scene by reducing its ambiguity, and especially Ruth's role in it.

Schor, for example, remarks that the flowers for Bellingham are "pleasant embellishments to his toy," while for Gaskell "they are a part of that
'thinking, and feeling, and loving' [*sic*] that are Ruth's true beauty, and that
make her a perfect observer of nature" (64). Similarly, her description of
Ruth—"surrounded by white flowers, her face itself is like 'a rose in June,'

the 'disorder only seem[ing] to add a grace'" (64)—suggests that the grace alluded to is only an illusion, something that the disorder only "seemed" to add. In the specific passage Schor has in mind, Gaskell writes, "the great heavy white flowers drooped on either side of her beautiful head, and if her brown hair was a little disordered, the very disorder only seemed to add a grace" (74–75). Depending, however, on whether we choose to give emphasis to the "only" or the "seemed" of the independent clause of Gaskell's observation, we arrive at two very different interpretations. If we emphasize the "only," the passage is arguing that Ruth's "disorder," like that "sweet disorder in the dresse" of Herrick's lady in "Delight in Disorder," does in fact bestow grace on her appearance. On the other hand, if we emphasize the "seemed," we arrive at a reading much closer to Schor's. All of this is, of course, as it should be, for the figural dimensions of language prevent us from finding a single ground or center for our reading. Gaskell's text, rich and multilayered, refuses to grant us the ability to arrive at a fixed or absolute meaning.

We have in this scene two Ruths, then, Bellingham's and Gaskell's—one a toy, a plaything, a piece, a doll, the other a creature of "true beauty," a "perfect observer of nature." But there is, I would suggest, a third Ruth, existing in the hollows between these two formulaic images of woman, eluding both of these easy appropriations. This Ruth is not, as some of her readers seem to want her to be, either victim or toy doll, but rather a sexual being who is capable of experiencing erotic pleasure, at times by giving pleasure to others. Gaskell is a sensitive and subtle student of human gestures, and the act of giving for her is no simple matter. At several points in the novel, in fact, she explores the nature of gifts and the implications of receiving or bestowing them, disclosing, as she does so, Ruth's feelings regarding such matters. In a scene I will return to later, Ruth refuses Mr. Bradshaw's gift of muslin because he has no right to give it to her: "I only knew that Mr. Bradshaw's giving me a present hurt me, instead of making me glad" (157), she tells Thurstan. And, similarly, when Bellingham's mother sends her some money, Ruth again refuses the gift, telling Faith Benson why she does so: "While he [Bellingham] . . . loved me, he gave me many things—my watch—oh, so many things; and I took them from him gladly and thankfully because he loved me—for, I would have given him anything—and I thought of them as signs of love. But this money pains my heart" (127).[16]

In the scene with Bellingham in the green hollow, the giving and receiving of pleasure are not Schor's acts of "aesthetic prostitution," but rather another "sign of love." To adorn another with flowers or to allow oneself to be adorned with them is a gesture of celebration and love, an ancient and recurrent act that affirms the erotic body and its capacity for pleasure and love, and it is precisely such a gesture that we find in Gaskell's text. "The lived body affectively bathes in language," suggests Ellie Ragland-Sullivan (*Jacques Lacan and the Philosophy of Psychoanalysis*, 108), and we must read the language of the lived body carefully. Gaskell writes that Ruth's "face was flushed into a brilliancy of colour which resembled that of a rose in June" (74). This image of the rose, with its iconic invocation of female sexuality, calls to mind not only William Blake's "The Sick Rose," with its "bed of crimson joy" being destroyed by the "dark secret love" of the phallic "invisible worm / That flies in the night" (*Poetry and Prose*, 23), but also Emily Dickinson's striking invocation of the flower when she describes

> Depths of Ruby, undrained,
> Hid, Lip, for Thee —
> Play it were a Humming Bird —
> And just sipped — me —
> (*Complete Poems*, 334, 158)

In Edith Wharton's unpublished "Fragment of Beatrice Palmato," we find her too drawing on such images: "Suddenly his head bent lower, and with a deeper thrill she felt his lips pressed upon that quivering invisible bud, and then the delicate firm thrust of his tongue, so full and yet so infinitely subtle, pressing apart the close petals, and forcing itself in deeper and deeper through the passage that glowed."[17]

We err, as Edith Wharton's glowing imagery indicates, if we confuse the erotogenic body with the organic one, for the former is "a sort of magic place," to use Monique David-Ménard's phrase, in which everything is played out for the subject and always is "a space of *jouissance*" (42). Bodies in Gaskell are frequently "a sort of magic place," inaccessible to either the conscious subject or the narrative voice. Ruth's body especially is such a site — not only the flushed brilliance of her skin, but also her gestures and the very ways in which she inhabits space.[18] "She stood in her white dress,"

we hear, "against the trees which grew around" (75)—her body is inscribed
with a repressed or elided history otherwise concealed from us, in particular, the history occupying the silent spaces between the fourth and fifth
chapters, from the time we see her get into the carriage with Bellingham
and leave for London until the time we find her in Wales. This particular
narrative silence, however, makes its presence felt, for the history contained
in these blank spaces is later written through the birth of a son conceived
during this time, and also through the ways in which narratives of guilt and
desire are textualized by Ruth's body.[19]

It is its repressed history that her body, as both theater and instrument,
acts out through its pantomimes of pleasure, as well as through the discourse
of its other movements and gestures.[20] Ruth does indeed possess what Jenny
Uglow aptly describes as "a languorous wildness" (330) that disturbs and dis-
rupts male equanimity, and her disheveled hair in this scene functions as a
floating signifier, identifying that mysterious animality or "wildness" of which
Bataille writes: "The image of the desirable woman at first imagined would
be insipid and unprovocative if it did not at the same time also promise or
reveal a mysterious animal aspect, more momentously suggestive" (143).[21]
What is suggested, Bataille notes, are the female genitals, already conveyed
by Gaskell through the imagery of the scene's setting, aptly described by
Uglow as "a sexualized landscape of a deep pool in a mountain cleft, fringed
with green trees" (330). If Bellingham finds pleasure in Ruth, his presence is
finally almost ancillary, his delight compared to the "joyousness" of a child
with a new toy, although it is possible that both Ruth and Gaskell underestimate the pleasure children can find in new toys. Ruth seems to understand
the origins of Bellingham's "joyousness" and is not terribly disturbed by it, in
fact "did not think twice about his occupation" (74). In any case, the primary
site of *jouissance* in this passage is Ruth's body itself, not Ruth's or Bellingham's consciousness of it. Metaphor, Lacan suggests, contains a surplus of
meaning, the result of the pressure of the occulted term making itself felt:
"The creative spark of the metaphor," he writes, "flashes between two signifiers one of which has taken the place of the other in the signifying chain, the
occulted signifier remaining present through its (metonymic) connexion with
the rest of the chain" (*Ecrits*, 157). And the fullness and languor of the "great
heavy white flowers" that "drooped on either side of [Ruth's] beautiful head"
suggest, when read alongside her disordered brown hair and her brilliantly

flushed skin, a surplus of meaning as the occulted term makes itself known, giving us a body that identifies itself as the site of postorgasmic pleasure.

In speaking of *Ruth*, Jeanette Shumaker observes that the "pleasure associated with desire is felt most intensely in the absence of sexual behavior" ("Gaskell's *Ruth* and Hardy's *Tess*," 153), but Gaskell's text argues otherwise. This scene relies on neither a male gaze, nor a female narrative voice momentarily occupying the site of the male gaze; instead it draws on a figural language whose presence destabilizes any attempt on our part to identify its point of origin or to thematize the scene along binary lines (or even to demarcate the boundaries of textuality itself, since we too are implicated in the gaze). Pleasure for Ruth is often polymorphous and perverse, almost always associated with her body, and especially her hair, as a site of erotic pleasure that is experienced but cannot be articulated. Ruth experiences what Lacan characterizes as "a *jouissance* of the body" proper to woman, "of which she herself may know nothing, except that she experiences it—that much she does know" ("God," 145).

The next scene I look at also involves the gaze, but differs in two respects from the earlier scene—most certainly in the control and power that Ruth exercises in it, but also in being agitated by unsettling or disturbing impulses. This particular vignette occurs fairly late in the novel, when Bellingham, running for Parliament under the name of Donne, visits the Bradshaw residence at Abermouth. Although Ruth immediately recognizes him, she must suppress her feelings and memories:

> Her great desire was to hold quiet till she was alone. Quietness it was not—it was rigidity; but she succeeded in being rigid in look and movement, and went through her duties . . . with wooden precision. But her heart felt at times like ice, at times like burning fire; always a heavy, heavy weight within her. . . . Ruth's sense of hearing was quickened to miserable intensity as she stood before the chimney-piece, grasping it tight with both hands—gazing into the dying fire, but seeing—not the dead grey embers . . . but an old farm-house, and climbing winding road, and a little golden breezy common, with a rural inn on the hill-top, far, far away. (271)

Finding in the dying fire rekindled memories of the "far, far away" days that she and Bellingham spent together in the Welsh country inn, Ruth is torn between her resurgent feelings of love for Bellingham—"Oh, darling love! am I talking against you?" she asks herself (273)—and a need to conceal her desire. "Torn and perplexed" (273), she seeks refuge in the privacy of her own room, and the choreography of her gestures, as Gaskell explicitly describes them, testifies to the sexual nature of Ruth's anguish: "She fastened her door, and threw open the window, cold and threatening as was the night. She tore off her gown; she put her hair back from her heated face" (272). Soon after this moment, Gaskell once again focuses her attention on Ruth's body and especially her hair as "a space of *jouissance*" (David-Ménard, 42), as Ruth tries to quench the fires burning in her by immersing herself in a turbulence outside of herself. Experiencing a resurgent desire for Bellingham that cannot be repressed ("I love him; I cannot forget—I cannot!" [274]), Ruth, we are told, "threw her body half out of the window into the cold night air." The storm, Gaskell writes, "did her good," for "the blast-driven rain came on her again, and drenched her hair through and through" (274). One wonders if Flaubert perhaps took lessons from Gaskell in the depiction of female sexual desire, for three years later in *Madame Bovary*, he describes a strikingly similar moment involving Emma's desire for Léon: "Consumed more ardently than ever by that inner flame to which adultery added fuel, panting, tremulous, all desire, she threw open the window, breathed in the cold air, shook loose in the wind her masses of hair, too heavy, and, gazing upon the stars, longed for some princely love" (204). Although Flaubert's language is more explicit, he and Gaskell are talking about the same thing. Gaskell, however, draws on the proverbial "cold shower" often recommended as a sure cure for overheated sexual passion, as she drenches her heroine with a "blast-driven rain," assuring us that it "did her good."

The next morning, Ruth joins the rest of the household for breakfast, knowing that Bellingham will be there and that he has not yet recognized her. As Ruth enters the room, she feels "almost a strange exultant sense of *power* over herself" (276, emphasis mine), and even as Bellingham comes into the room, this power, though temporarily threatened, remains in place: "Ruth felt as if that moment was like death. She had a kind of desire to make some sharp sound, to relieve a choking sensation, but it was over in an instant, and she sat on very composed and silent—to all outward appearance, the very model of a governess who knew her place" (276). "And by and by," the passage continues, Ruth "felt strangely at ease in her sense of *power*" (276, emphasis mine). Schor suggests that "what Ruth's love of beauty excludes is any understanding of power" (60), but while this might be so in the case of the early Ruth, it is certainly not true of the woman we see in this scene. The central dynamics of this episode involve, in fact, the exercise and pleasure of power, and Gaskell locates the site of such power in the body and its gestures. As in the earlier scene, we are taken to sites beyond narrative commentary, and in Ruth's momentary "desire to make some sharp sound, to relieve a choking sensation" (276), we find a discourse being played out in the body—the hysteric body as the field of unconscious desire that finds articulation not only in the choking sensation, but in the movements, states, and positions of the body. That love and desire which cannot be given voice except in the solitude of the bedroom must be swallowed, repressed, causing a painful choking sensation that in turn invokes the desire to "make some sharp sound" to relieve it.

But Ruth, still not recognized by Bellingham, watches him and begins, after a momentary setback, to inhabit a site characterized by power and control: "Suddenly Ruth felt that his attention was caught by her. Until now, seeing his short-sightedness, she had believed herself safe; now her face flushed with a painful, miserable blush. But in an instant, she was strong and quiet. She looked up straight at his face; and, as if this action took him aback, he began eating away with great diligence. She had seen him" (277). Bellingham is so discomfited, in fact, by Ruth's behavior that he drops his eyeglass, "perplexed by the straightforward brave look she had sent right at him" (277–78). In part, at least, this is a wonderful comic moment, and Gaskell, I think, means it to be read as such, but it is also something more. Several levels of discomfort are registered by Bellingham as he looks at the "governess," comparing her to Ruth and seeing similarities in the two women, although the governess's hair, he decides, is "darker," and she has "less colour" than the Ruth he knew and is "altogether a more-refined looking person" (278). And then, as Bellingham thinks about the less-refined and darker-skinned Ruth, another source of discomfort is disclosed: "Poor Ruth! and, for the first time for several years, he wondered what had become of her; though, of course, there was but one thing that could have happened, and perhaps it was as well he did not know her end, for most likely it would have made him very uncomfortable" (278).

The "one thing that could have happened" is, of course, that Ruth turned to prostitution, for Bellingham imagines that she would have had little choice but to take to the streets once he deserted her.[22] But what is most interesting about this scene is not so much what is said as what is not said, for if Bellingham's initial discomfort, provoked by the governess's unsettling stare, leads him to think, with yet more discomfort, of Ruth and his imagined scenario of her history, his associations work in places other than on the conscious level. Bellingham's discomfort—and the above passage makes it clear that he is uncomfortable already, not that he might have been had he known the details of Ruth's "fate"—is registered through sensations of the body, like Ruth's "choking sensation" (276), as the beauty of one woman immediately leads him to think of yet another, constructing a narrative history she occupies primarily in sexual terms. In "Visual Pleasure and Narrative Cinema," Laura Mulvey points out that the female figure in films is situated in an ambiguous field for the male viewer, for while, on one hand, she is an object of erotic fantasies, she also "connotes something that the look continually circles around but disavows: her lack of a penis, implying a threat of castration and hence unpleasure" (13). Here too the source of Bellingham's discomfort is situated between the fear of castration on one hand, as the unnerving power of Ruth's look "unmans" him, forcing him to avert his gaze from her, and sexual arousal on the other, as he bathes both Ruth and the governess in his eroticized fantasies or reveries.

In this particular case, however—and in this respect this scene is radically different from the earlier one—the figure of the prostitute is deeply encoded in the passage, an object of both illicit desire and fear. Bellingham does not essentially misinterpret Ruth's "straightforward brave look" (Gaskell's tired language only half-heartedly conceals what Ruth's look really conveys) but in fact he understands it on levels deeper than the narrative voice, and most certainly deeper than either he or Ruth can acknowledge. Drawing on Freud's discovery of "a psychological domain . . . [whose] dynamics are characterized by a sublimity that simultaneously baffles representation and insists on being known" (*Making a Social Body*, 147), Mary Poovey notes that Gaskell in *Mary Barton* "begins to delineate a domain that does not precisely coincide with the social domain her domestic narrative supposedly illuminates" (147). Poovey's remark is also applicable to

Ruth, for this particular scene between Ruth and Bellingham presents us with a moment that similarly baffles traditional representation, in that neither Ruth nor Bellingham can acknowledge or even recognize what is happening, but the scene leaves no doubt that the moment insists on making itself felt. The power that Ruth exercises and enjoys exercising is indeed given sexual overtones, and as she basks in it, her pleasure in such a position is only too evident. Insofar as she exercises such power, enjoying the feeling that she derives from it, and enjoying Bellingham's discomfort, she is in fact the prostitute Bellingham imagines Ruth to have become. She is not the Dickensian prostitute filled with remorse and self-hatred, but the prostitute as she was constructed by and in turn inhabited the imagination of the nineteenth century, namely, a woman who actually enjoys the exercise of sexual power and control.

But, and this point is crucial, Ruth is not only a prostitute insofar as she inhabits such a realm in Bellingham's erotic fantasies, but is in fact a prostitute in the imaginative construction of the novel as well, a signifier identifying, as it were, the textual unconscious of *Ruth*. In other words, the eroticized fantasies that Bellingham entertains also operate in the text as a whole, helping to structure it and establish its teleology, enabling us to understand better, for example, the problematics raised by its closure. Gaskell's text, or at least its unconscious, not only explores the dynamics of eroticism but exemplifies such erotics insofar as it violates images of Ruth as innocent, virtuous, and finally redeemed—images, in other words, that the narrative voice wishes for us to carry away from the novel.

A destabilizing presence in the nineteenth century, the prostitute shatters comfortable patriarchal hierarchies, but she also undermines or threatens the age's image of woman. "The prostitute," as Sarah Webster Goodwin notes, "figures forth repressed and illicit desire, 'depraved' sexuality, the woman's 'unchaste' body, the animal that is on the margin of the human being" (158). As such, she haunts not only Bellingham's thoughts, but also Gaskell's text, as the primary signifier of the repressed. Her presence in *Ruth* is often ambiguous and overdetermined, inscribed variously in the novel as a signifier of financial transactions and commodification, as a signifier of sexual pleasure and the eroticized body, and, especially later in the novel, as an agent of death and contagion. In this particular scene between Ruth and Bellingham, however, the dynamics of the conscious exercise of female erotic pleasure and power prevail, although destabilized by the occulted figure of the prostitute. For the text makes it clear not only that Ruth is fully aware of her control of the situation, but that she revels in it, taking particular pleasure in the obvious discomfort she evokes in Bellingham/Donne. And in her "straightforward brave look," we find the gaze of Medusa, associated, as we will see in the next chapter, with castration anxiety; and in the association Bellingham draws between the woman who causes him to feel discomfort and the prostitute he imagines Ruth to have become, his thoughts wander in the direction of Bataille's mysterious realm or region, that which is below the surface and unseen, metonymically figured forth in the gaze.

Woman is the opposite of the dandy. Therefore she must inspire horror . . . Woman is *natural*, that is to say abominable.

CHARLES-PIERRE BAUDELAIRE, "Mon Coeur mis à nu"

Bellingham, however, is not the only one to acknowledge this power or to become unsettled by it. Like old Martin Chuzzlewit, Mr. Bradshaw is an imposing figure: "Every moral error or delinquency came under his unsparing comment" (210), writes Gaskell, although he was "stained by no vice himself," at least in "his own eyes or in that of any human being who cared to judge him" (210). He also resembles old Martin in that he too is a grotesque version of the law and of patriarchal control, reigning through terror and condescension dispensed in equal portions. Having succeeded in "training" his wife in such ways that Jemima no longer dares confide in her mother, Bradshaw has also virtually emasculated his son, Richard, a young man in possession of a weak mouth and cowardly behavior who lives in constant terror of his father.[23] Like Dickens, Gaskell explores the Oedipal dynamics of the familial structure through her representation of the father-son relationship, but Gaskell also explores what Foucault has identified as "a complicated network" of "mobile sexualities" present in the nineteenth-century family structure. For while the nineteenth-century family might have been in part "a monogamic and conjugal cell," it was also, as Foucault points out, "a network of pleasures and powers linked together at multiple points and according to transformable relationships" (*The History of Sexuality*, 46). The family, he adds, "even when brought down to its smallest dimensions, [was] a complicated network, saturated with multiple, fragmentary, and mobile sexualities" (46).

It is into such a complicated network that Ruth enters, stirring up the sexual tensions and "mobile sexualities" even more. In a scene alluded to earlier, Bradshaw offers Ruth a piece of "very fine muslin" (156) that she insists on sending back, telling Thurstan Benson that Bradshaw "had no right to offer it to me" (156), and although she tells Benson that she "never reasoned why I felt as I did," that she knew only that "Mr. Bradshaw's giving me a present hurt me, instead of making me glad" (157), she concurs with Benson's observation that a gift received from a person one neither esteems nor loves only "takes its place among your property as so much money's worth" (157). Ruth sees but cannot articulate what it is that Benson sees, namely, that if she had accepted Bradshaw's gift, it would have established a relationship in which a required response of gratitude and obligation on her part would be structured along economic lines, thus inserting her into a position similar to that identified by the young boy early in the novel when he calls her a "bad, naughty girl" (71). In writing of the nineteenth-century prostitute, Alain Corbin points out that one of the age's images of the prostitute "integrates the prostitute with that chain of resigned female bodies in the lower classes" ("Commercial Sexuality in Nineteenth-Century France," 213), and while Corbin has in mind primarily the women "bound to the instinctive physical needs of upper-class males" (213), such as the nursery maid or the female servant, Ruth's presence in the household, even though a governess to Bradshaw's daughters, is also linked to such a chain, and, as such, associated with the figure of the prostitute even before Bradshaw finds out about her past.

"Modern society," Foucault suggests, "is perverse . . . it is in actual fact, and directly, perverse" (*History of Sexuality*, 47), and, especially toward the later sections of Gaskell's novel, the figure of Ruth is overdetermined, mobile, multiple, and also the focus or center of this perversity. Ruth resists Bradshaw's overtures of a gift precisely because she knows what he wants—a want operating in places unknown to Bradshaw, and screened by not necessarily hypocritical overtures of Christian charity or generosity. And even though Ruth rejects Bradshaw's favors, she nevertheless "found favor with him" (159), and soon enters his household, a resident object of erotic fantasies that are translated into language only after the unconscious becomes conscious—namely, after Ruth's past is discovered. "His face was almost purple with suppressed agitation" (336), we read, and Bradshaw's response to Ruth's uncovered history seems hysterical, as he warns his family that Ruth's presence will pollute the household, possibly infecting his daughters, transmitting to them whatever it is that she possesses—"When such a woman came into my family," he says, "there is no wonder at any corruption—any evil—any defilement" (338). As Jill Matus notes, once Ruth's status as fallen governess is discovered, she becomes a "moral contaminant [who] conjures up fears by her mere presence of an invisible but deadly miasma of corruption" (*Unstable Bodies*, 126). "Look at that woman," Bradshaw tells Jemima, "corrupt long before she was your age—hypocrite for years! If ever you, or any child of mine, cared for her, shake her off from you, as St. Paul shook off the viper—even into the fire" (338). But Bradshaw shares his hysteria in common with his age. The prostitute "is the *putain* (whore), whose body smells bad," writes Corbin (211), and Bradshaw's language, filled with images of disease and corruption that identify Ruth as evil and defiling, suggests that hers is the body of the prostitute. This body, however, is an object not only of repulsion, but of danger-laden desire as well, and Bradshaw's hysteric reaction when he discovers Ruth's sexual history discloses a tumultuous commingling of fear and desire.

Even more than her father's, however, Jemima's response to Ruth's past enables us to see that Ruth's power is associated not only with feminine sexuality, but more specifically with the age's image of the prostitute. Gaskell's depiction of feminine sexuality, like her text itself, is split or bifurcated, exalting in the power and pleasure it represents while at the same time harboring a profound distrust, even hostility, toward it. However, it is possible that Gaskell's ambivalence, admittedly the source of much of the novel's power and inner conflict, arises not only from her "private identification, not altogether acknowledged, with Ruth and Jemima's repression and punishment by the world and God," as Jenny Uglow suggests (337), but also from her own identification with the figure of the prostitute. Arguing along lines similar to those pursued by Gallagher, Goodwin observes that while "it may be something of a truism that the male romantic artist suspected he was prostituting himself," the situation for the female writer was even more problematic, for she saw in the prostitute, her "uncanny double," not only a body she did not know as her own, but also someone inhabiting "a prescribed role that haunts her as the predictable consequence of acts that challenge the code of propriety. Writing—especially writing for a large and popular audience—was one of them" (159–60). Goodwin points out that the figure of the prostitute is "a mobile figure," identified overtly with "the mother, the daughter, the maidservant, the fiancée, and even the man" (155), and although her presence in Gaskell is not quite so refracted, it is nevertheless a mobile one. Jemima, for example, understands precisely the ways in which her body, like the prostitute's, is a commodity to be bought or sold. One passage in particular makes this connection clear, suggesting as well that "piece" had many of the same sexual connotations for Gaskell's age as it has for ours: "She even wished that they [her family] might not go through the form of pretending to try to gain her consent to the marriage, if it involved all this premeditated action and speech-making—such moving about of every one into their right places, like pieces at chess. She felt as if she would rather be bought openly, like an Oriental daughter, where no one is degraded in their own eyes by being parties to such a contract" (240–41).

Desire in Gaskell's text is no simple matter, involving not only impulses of aggression and violence (for example, the eroticized scene in which Sally crops Ruth's hair) but also relationships in which the dynamics of transference and identification figure prominently.[24] Jemima is an extraordinary figure of power and passion such as only Gaskell can draw, capable of hate, love, anger, jealousy, at once painfully inhibited and fascinated by her own sexual urges and impulses.[25] Through Jemima, Gaskell explores what Bataille

identifies as the profoundly religious sense of the erotic. "The inner experience of eroticism," he writes, "demands from the subject sensitiveness to the
anguish at the heart of the taboo no less great than the desire which leads him
to infringe it. This is religious sensibility and it always links desire closely with
terror, intense pleasure and anguish" (38–39). And, he adds in a passage that
might serve as a gloss to Gaskell's text, "Anyone who does not feel or feels
only furtively the anguish, nausea and horror commonly felt by young girls
in the last century is not susceptible to these emotions" (39). Jemima experiences such "anguish, nausea and horror": "The very foundations of
Jemima's belief in her mind were shaken," Gaskell writes, as Jemima wonders, "Who was true? Who was not? Who was good and pure? Who was
not?" (326). Ruth has given her "a terrible glimpse into the dark lurid gulf—
the capability for evil, in her heart" (245). "O God," cries Jemima, "help
me! I did not know I was so wicked" (245). If eroticism, in Bataille's words,
is characterized by the shattering of "an ordered, parsimonious, and shut-
tered reality" (104)—the creation of a wound or rupture that will not heal
of its own accord—then Jemima's world has indeed been shattered by the
erotic, as she responds with a "shrinking, shuddering recoil" (324) when
she learns that Ruth "had been stained with that evil most repugnant to
[Jemima's] womanly modesty" (324).

The language of the daughter in this case bears a striking resemblance
to that of the father, for both identify Ruth with the diseased and corrupted
body of the prostitute. For Jemima, the prostitute is the uncanny double,
bearing a body that is and is not her own, insofar as she identifies with Ruth
and yet represses the identification. The particular nature and site of this
stain of the fallen woman and the text on which it is written are more fully
disclosed in an amazing passage whose sustained trope registers the degree
of Jemima's shock:

> She was stunned by the shock she had received. The diver, leaving
> the green sward, smooth and known, where his friends stand with their
> smiling faces, admiring his glad bravery—the diver, down in an instant in
> the horrid depths of the sea, close to some strange, ghastly, lidless-eyed
> monster, can hardly more feel his blood curdle at the near terror than did
> Jemima now. Two hours ago . . . she had never imagined that she should

ever come in contact with anyone who had committed open sin; she had never shaped her conviction into words, but still it was *there*, that all the respectable, all the family and religious circumstances of her life, would hedge her in, and guard her from ever encountering the great shock of coming face to face with vice. (323, emphasis Gaskell's)

Woman, Elisabeth Bronfen observes, is "construed as a symptom of death's presence, precisely because she is the site where the repressed anxiety about death re-emerges in a displaced, disfigured form" (*Over Her Dead Body*, 215), and in this passage, the repressed textual anxieties in regard to both the female body and death converge, displaced and disfigured, in a mysterious watery site deep beneath the green sward. In Gaskell's sexually gendered trope, the diver leaving the safety and familiarity of the "green sward, smooth and known" and descending into "the horrid depths of the sea" where he confronts "some strange, ghastly, lidless-eyed monster" (323), encounters a vividly imagined female sexuality, a murky womb world of procreation that threatens to destroy the forces of order and respectability that are supposed to guard or "hedge" us in from such sights.

Jemima is wracked throughout the novel by repressed desires and emotions inscribed as text on an increasingly neurasthenic body—Ruth is struck by the change in Jemima's looks, how "the large eyes, so brilliant once, were dim and clouded; the complexion sallow and colourless" (227). Jemima confronts in Ruth a narrative of transgression in which she finds an important aspect of her own unconscious history. But finally, the form of the social novel itself and Jemima's own retreat back into a known and familiar world dictate that she will not travel where Ruth has been, that she will emerge out of the dangerous and horrid depths and return to the world of her father and Farquhar, succumbing by the end to the cultural pressures and forces—what she alludes to earlier as "management" (238)—initially resisted by her. Stripped of her anger and smoldering outrage and inhabiting a fading body whose disappearance prefigures that literal death soon to be experienced by Ruth, Jemima internalizes the rules and strictures that initially offended her and is thus transformed into a young woman capable of living in and helping to insure the stability of a social order that tolerates transgressive behavior for only so long.

As putrid body and emunctory/sewer, the prostitute maintains complex relations with the corpse in the symbolic imagination of these
times.

ALAIN CORBIN

Along with *Wuthering Heights* and *Jude the Obscure, Ruth* is one of the
nineteenth-century's most love-haunted and death-ridden novels. From the
opening pages, with the death of Ruth's mother, whose absence is felt as a
physical pain or presence, to the charnel-house landscape of the novel's
closing sections, with its topography of disease and death, Ruth's desires for
love and death are often difficult to distinguish from each other. Both permeate the text, disturbing the apparent clarity and purposiveness of its
social and religious themes. The double urges of love and death, woven
together throughout the novel, are deeply implicated in the directions of its
closure. On one hand, *Ruth* continues to explore the nature of lack as well
as the desire born out of it. In Lacanian terms, Ruth participates in the
tragedy of the human condition itself, for what she most desires is to be
desired, to be recognized by the mother, but the object of desire, as Lacan
points out, is "irremediably separated" from us. As he puts it in the epigraph
to this study, "It is in the nature of desire to be radically torn. The very
image of man brings in here a mediation which is always imaginary, always
problematic, and which is therefore never completely fulfilled" (*Seminar
II*, 166). In Gaskell's novel, this drama assumes an intensely personal narrative, as the death of Ruth's mother and Ruth's subsequent feeling of separation or aloneness are repeated in a number of different imaginary or
specular scenarios in which she seeks ways of diminishing or erasing this
lack. Moving beyond any easy ideological casting of Ruth as innocent victim in a predatory world, Gaskell depicts her as seeking a love that neither
the world itself nor any other person can give her, haunted by images of
wholeness that constitute the object of her gaze and desire.

This lack is also behind the Lacanian death drive, "the traumatic
knowledge," as Ellie Ragland describes it, that "we all possess but have not
assimilated in memory, fantasy, or dreams" ("Lacan, the Death Drive, and

the Dream of the Burning Child," 86), originating in the separations that she suggests "give birth to desire by enforcing myriad cuts and interventions in the seemingly continuous space of space itself" (92). Ruth's life is filled with such cuts and interventions, the spaces of her history deeply punctuated by separations and other traumatic marks, and yet, as Sally points out to Ruth on a number of occasions, the lives of most human beings are similarly scarred. In order to appreciate the strength of Ruth's death drive, even after the birth of her son and her apparent social redemption, we need to pay attention to the ways in which the text identifies her with the prostitute/corpse. Similarly, if we are to understand why Ruth turns to Bellingham and death at the end of the novel, when the doctor's admonition to her that she is virtually committing suicide echoes our own frustration and knowledge, we need to look at the ways in which she is written into the unconscious of the text. For if Ruth's history tells, in part, of the translation of her own unconscious desires into a personal narrative, her history is also written by a textual unconscious that situates her body in the text as an object not only of desire and repulsion, but also of corruption and disease. Toward the end of *Ruth*, the maternal, the erotic, and contagion or death merge in a complex and often ambiguous pattern, and running through this weave is Ruth's strange and haunting presence as a prostitute and corpse.

What is most striking about the conclusion of *Ruth* is not Ruth's resolute movement toward death—after all, she moves toward it even before her flight toward the rushing waters is interrupted by Thurstan Benson's fall—but rather that even in the novel's final pages, she is invested with the taboo. Her body in the end does not radiate a languorous sensuality, as it does earlier in the novel, but instead is surrounded by and itself gives off an eroticized aura of death and dying. Ruth, like Anne Catherick or Laura Fairlie in *The Woman in White*, becomes one of the "dead-alive," but in rather unique ways. If she is associated earlier with the taboo by virtue of her sexual history, she is later associated with it through what the text refers to as her "connexion with death." As she moves in the town, making contact with the sick and dying, she becomes a figure of awe. "The roughest boys of the rough populace" would "make way for her when she passed along the streets" (391–92), Gaskell observes, remarking that Ruth "was so often in connexion with death that something of the superstitious awe with which the dead were regarded by those rough boys in the midst of their strong life surrounded her" (392). If the young boy at the beginning of the novel knew

Ruth to be "a bad, naughty girl" (71) only because he had heard his mother say so, these "rough boys," as Gaskell's text makes clear, sense that somehow Ruth's relationship with death extends beyond that of her role as nurse or caretaker, and they are thus uneasy in her presence, much as they would be uneasy in the presence of a corpse.

In moving through the plague-ridden town, apparently impervious to the death and dying around her, Ruth seems to move toward apotheosis or sanctification, and, indeed, public discourse about her suggests she achieves such status, that she has become virtue personified.[26] But this movement is possible only because she already occupies, as the street boys intuitively know, the figural space of corruption and disease. Like Alain Corbin's prostitute, Ruth occupies an ambiguous status in Gaskell's text, for she is "at once menace and remedy, agent of putrefaction and drain" (212). Although public discourse interprets Ruth's gestures as evidence of her goodness and holiness, performed "for the love of God, and of the blessed Jesus" (429) — and the narrative voice clearly intends for us to assent to such interpretations — she is, insofar as she is associated with the corpse, already dead. She is a metonymic presence in a diseased and death-ridden city that reflects her own condition writ large and whose contagion she will absorb into herself, thus becoming instrumental in cleansing the city of its corruption.

Gaskell's description of the genealogy and site of the contagion suggests the degree to which the nineteenth-century imagination linked prostitution and the diseased city: "There came creeping, creeping, in hidden, slimy courses, the terrible fever — that fever which is never utterly banished from the sad haunts of vice and misery, but lives in such darkness like a wild beast in the recesses of his den" (424).[27] The disease, as Gaskell describes it, has an etiology both economic and moral, beginning in the "low Irish lodging-houses" (424), where it was "so common it excited little attention" (424), and then spreading out to more affluent neighborhoods, where it excited a good deal of attention: "It had, like the blaze of a fire which had long smouldered, burst forth in many places at once — not merely among the loose-living and vicious, but among the decently poor — nay, even among the well-to-do and respectable" (424). Although "the terrible fever" Gaskell has in mind is cholera, her language resembles that of nineteenth-century delineations of venereal diseases such as syphilis and gonorrhea, which, as Judith Walkowitz points out, "conformed to medical and social theories that looked upon disease as a result of 'sin' as well of bodily imbalance and excess" (*Prostitution*, 56). Mid-Victorian England feared, as Walkowitz observes, that "an epidemic of venereal disease was sweeping the nation" (50), and Gaskell's passages reveal similar anxieties, telling of how the disease moved beyond "sad haunts of vice and misery," inhabited by "the loose and vicious," and made itself felt "even among the well-to-do and respectable" (424). The images of invasion and contagion associated with the disease-infected city are also reminiscent of Bradshaw's account of how Ruth "invaded" his house, threatening to spread her contagion and corruption in it: "How deep is the corruption this wanton has spread in my family" (339), he exclaims, fooling all by means of her "sickly hypocritical face" (337).

Ruth's movement toward death at the end of the novel is in this respect the final progression of a diseased condition with which she has earlier been identified. We find at the end a strange mingling of the erotic and death, not the images of a postorgasmic languidness on Ruth's part evident in some of the earlier scenes, but similar images of pleasure, such as her rose-colored "gently parted lips," a quietly rendered *jouissance* of death. Benson notes that "he had never seen her face so fair and gentle as it was now, when she was living in the midst of disease and woe" (428), also observing that although "she seemed a little paler," her "eyes were as full of spiritual light, the gently parted lips as rosy, and the smile, if more rare, yet as sweet as ever" (431). The final pages of the novel also stress that "continuity of being" that Bataille identifies as an essential feature of the erotic (16), as we hear that Ruth "did not feel much change from the earliest Ruth she could remember. Everything seemed to change but herself. . . . She and the distant hills that she saw from her chamber window, seemed the only things which were the same as when she first came to Eccleston" (392). Just as, in the earlier Alpine scene, "the grandeur of this beautiful earth absorbed all idea of separate and individual existence" (65), here too nature provides the specular image of a continuity. Ruth finds in this image a reflection of a similar changelessness on her part, while at the same time locating in the "other"—in this case, her neighbor and his daughter—the realities of aging and maturing, what the narrator refers to as "the lapse of life and time" (392).[28] But Ruth's own lapses "of life and time"—her childhood, her seduction, her betrayal and pregnancy, and even the birth of her son—have been forgotten or repressed, buried in places inaccessible to the Ruth we now see.

The groundswell of song and public voices on Ruth's behalf toward the end of the novel does not muffle the unsettling images and gestures that constitute Ruth's final days. Her return to Bellingham finally has little to do with him, for he becomes no more than an occasion enabling Ruth to complete her circuitous journey. And as she does so, the maternal becomes entangled with images of death and cessation, as Ruth moves toward a condition that involves nothing less than her own abdication of motherhood, an oblivion encompassing her own son as well: "She could not remember the present time, or where she was. All times of her earliest youth—the days of her childhood—were in her memory with a minuteness and fulness of detail which was miserable; for all along she felt that she had no real grasp on the scenes that were passing through her mind—that somehow, they were long gone by, and gone by for ever—and yet she could not remember who she was now, nor where she was" (444). Ruth's memory of the days of childhood interposes itself between Ruth and the immediate world around her, and we find a totalizing isolation that wears the face of madness: "She never looked at anyone with the slightest glimpse of memory or intelligence in her face; no, not even at Leonard" (448).[29]

In speaking of *Oedipus at Colonus*, Lacan suggests that "life doesn't want to be healed," that "the life we're captive of, this essentially alienated life, ex-sisting, this life in the other, is as such joined to death, it always returns to death, and is only drawn into increasingly large and more roundabout circuits by what Freud calls the elements of the world" (*Seminar II*, 233). Oedipus, Lacan argues, "lives a life which is dead, which is that death which is precisely there under life" (232), and Ruth too lives such a life, momentarily immersed in the "elements of the world," her return to death deferred, but only momentarily. At the end *Ruth* presents us with a Lacanian image of existence, as Ruth's "life in the other" is joined to death, returning, as it must, to death. Desire in *Ruth* is finally not the desire for man, God, or mother, but for that which cannot be said, the unnamable itself. And if Ruth herself as prostitute/corpse is also situated in the text as the unnamable, both by virtue of her own desires and as an object of illicit desire and repulsion, at the end she is absorbed in the unnamable, becoming a name as she is translated into the language of legends and folklore.

4

Entangled Desire

Wanting and Narrative Structure in Wilkie Collins's The Woman in White

> We tell ourselves stories in order to live. . . . We look for the sermon in the suicide, for the social or moral lesson in the murder of five. We interpret what we see, select the most workable of the multiple choices. We live entirely, especially if we are writers, by the imposition of a narrative line upon disparate images, by the "ideas" with which we have learned to freeze the shifting phantasmagoria which is our actual experience.
>
> JOAN DIDION, *The White Album*

The Woman in White is a text haunted by the urge to write or narrate, by the need to interpose language between ourselves and the terror of existence, Didion's "shifting phantasmagoria." Marian at one point writes in her journal, "In the perilous uncertainty of our present situation, it is hard to say what future interests may not depend upon the regularity of the entries in my journal" (307). But at the same time *The Woman in White* is a text riddled with silences and omissions. "Silence itself—the things one declines to say, or is forbidden to name," writes Foucault, "is less the absolute limit of discourse . . . than an element which functions alongside the things said" (*History of Sexuality*, 27), and although *The Woman in White* proclaims its own completeness, silence does in fact surround the things that its narrators decline to say or are forbidden to name. "I must suppress nothing from beginning to end of the terrible story that I now stand committed to reveal" (106), writes Walter, only to later confess that he has in fact concealed the whole of his first week in London with Marian and Laura.[1] His suppressions, in fact, even spill over into the text's margins, as one of his footnotes informs us of "careful suppressions and alterations" regarding Pesca's history (594). Similarly, although Walter refuses to wear a disguise, finding, as he puts it, "something so repellent to me in the idea, something so meanly like the common herd of spies and informers" (433), at the same time he lives in a world of pseudonyms and masks. "We are numbered no longer with the people whose lives are open and known" he observes (433), telling us later that the whole story has been told "under feigned names" (563).

Walter's tale, in fact, is the narrative equivalent of "Button, button, who's got the button"; but we are never certain who has the button or even, for that matter, whether a button actually exists. Inviting us to participate in the solution of a mystery (Who is the woman in white and what is she doing?), the text leads us into a labyrinth in which the nature of both the mystery and the solution becomes obscure.[2] The text withholds information from us almost at will and frequently calls attention to the inadequacy of its own narrative voices, suggesting that we need to look beneath the surface. "Any narrative," Paul de Man suggests, "is primarily the allegory of its own reading" (*Allegories of Reading*, 76), and *The Woman in White* at several points provides us with an allegory of its reading. Watchful and suspicious, Walter listens carefully to Mrs. Clements's story: "There was one point in the narrative which made me doubt the propriety of accepting it unreservedly, and which suggested the idea of something hidden below the surface" (491). Marian similarly asserts, "My own convictions led me to believe that the hidden contents of the parchment [belonging to Percival Glyde] concealed a transaction of the meanest and the most fraudulent kind" (274).[3]

Given the various ways in which *The Woman in White* seems to be in conflict with its own stated purposes and designs, one can understand why

Laurie Langbauer suggests that a "textual unconscious" seems to operate in it ("Women in White, Men in Feminism," 222). And as Freud often reminds us, the unconscious makes itself heard and known through narrative patterns and structures. At the beginning of his case history of Dora, for example, Freud expresses his amazement that some analysts can "produce such smooth and precise histories in cases of hysteria," when, in fact, the narratives as recounted by the patients themselves are often confused and jumbled, resembling "an unnavigable river whose stream is at one moment choked by masses of rock and at another divided and lost among shallows and sandbanks."[4] The inability on the part of patients "to give an ordered account of their life" possesses "great theoretical significance," he points out, since their disordered or jumbled narratives, no less than other hysteric symptoms, disclose a story that needs to be heard (SE, 7:16). In fact, Freud tells us, a "smooth and precise" narrative might very well distort or misrepresent the history it intends to convey and should alert us to the possibility of repression or resistance. Narratives that have no loose ends, or pretend to have none, that deny the presence of any uncertainties or confusions, are likely to be hiding something, attempting to throw us off the trail of that which they are attempting to repress.

Like Freud's analysts, Walter suggests that he is presenting us with a "smooth and precise" history: "I shall relate both narratives," he writes of Laura's and Marian's narratives, "not in the words (often interrupted, often inevitably confused) of the speakers themselves, but in the words of the brief, plain, studiously simple abstract which I committed to writing for my own guidance" (435). Yet Walter's narrative is in fact broken, fragmented, and interrupted, resembling, in fact, the hysterical accounts he associates with the feminine narratives of Marian and Laura. Charles Bernheimer points out that while Freud admits "that his own text is fragmentary, full of detours, gaps, and omissions," he nevertheless insists "on its differences from Dora's hysterically disjunctive and incoherent narratives" (*In Dora's Case*, 18), and Walter too insists on the differences between his narrative and those he is retelling in his own fashion. His insistence on these differences is a crucial part of his narrative, insofar as his desire to create a smooth and precise narrative testifies to the presence of another history that emerges in spite of resistances against it. I would like to turn to that other (his)story now.

"If there is no longer a Father, why tell stories?" asks Roland Barthes. "Isn't storytelling always a way of searching for one's origin, speaking one's conflicts with the Law, entering into the dialectic of tenderness and hatred?" (47). Nowhere is this story of law, tenderness, and perhaps even hatred more in evidence than in Walter's early account of how he happened to come to his position at Limmeridge House. For if the moment of Anne Catherick's touch constitutes, as D. A. Miller suggests, a primal scene that Walter returns to throughout the course of his narrative, Walter's story also suggests other origins or beginnings. Winifred Hughes has said of *The Woman in White* that in it, "as in any novel by Wilkie Collins, victory belongs to rationality, defeat to the failure of reason" (*The Maniac in the Cellar*, 142), but while Walter may at times believe that this is so, rationality in *The Woman in White* is but a paltry thing when compared to the desires and fears that haunt its characters. Like *Martin Chuzzlewit, The Woman in White* is concerned with questions of succession and kinship structures and with the dynamics of desire and conflict in the family. Well before Anne Catherick's initial appearance, we find out that although Walter's father has been dead for some years (3), he is still present in the conflicts and dynamics sketched out by the novel's opening pages. Walter has no childhood, or at least none registered by the text, and thus the Oedipal struggles often explicit in Dickens (such as the famous biting scene in *David Copperfield*) are repressed in Collins's novel, acted out in different ways. Tamar Heller finds in Walter's early narrative evidence of an initial powerlessness and even of the "symbolic emasculation of the male artist" (*Dead Secrets*, 117) who is forced to exist on the outer margins of economic gentility, but I would like to suggest that this economic struggle screens more powerful and primitive conflicts.

Through a particularly rich and multilayered discourse, this early narrative discloses Walter's conflicted attitudes toward the heritage prepared for him by his dead father and the feelings of guilt and confusion created by such conflict. Walter's inexplicable resistance to the imprecations of his family and Pesca to accept the teaching position that has been offered to him, for example, manifests itself in aggressive forms, as he attempts to make sure that his dead father will not be inadvertently empowered through his own repetition of his father's career or his acceptance of connections that have been forged by his father. But just as Tom Pinch's "killing" of Pecksniff by denying his existence serves only to give Pecksniff yet more power, so too do Walter's various gestures of resistance and denial acknowledge the power that the dead father still wields.[5] What is most striking about this early narrative is not what is said, but rather *how what is said is said*, for it is punctuated by moments of discomfort, confusion, and bewilderment, by what Walter refers to as the "jarring" of his emotions. Collins's novels often direct our attention to conflicts being acted out beneath the surface—such as the theft of the diamond from Rachael's room in *The Moonstone*, with its overtones of rape and violation—and this early narrative in *The Woman in White* takes place on similar levels, serving not as a prelude to Anne Catherick's appearance, but rather as a censored chapter that Walter will in the course of the novel rewrite or reenact in various ways.[6] We have the impression that we are hearing a story other than the one Walter thinks he is telling, that another history, albeit an unconscious one, is being told.

What is especially strange about Walter's behavior is not that he is uncomfortable about accepting the position Pesca has located for him—although that is peculiar enough—but rather that he can offer no reasons for his discomfort, actually speaking of his "unaccountable perversity" (45), his "unreasonable disinclination," and his "own complete discomfiture": "Neither my mother's evident astonishment at my behaviour, nor Pesca's fervid enumeration of the advantages offered to me by my new employment, had any effect in shaking my unreasonable disinclination to go to Limmeridge House" (44). Unable to understand why he wants to decline such a lucrative and attractive offer, Walter confesses that his objections are feeble and his continued resistance to the Limmeridge House position willful and perverse. Although he seems confused or bewildered, however, his language is precise and careful. He says, for example, that he "succeeded to his [father's] connection and had every reason to feel grateful for the prospect that awaited me at my starting in life" (34–35), but as the construction of his confession emphasizes, having "every reason to feel grateful" is not necessarily the same as feeling gratitude. Walter's gestures of resistance and denial attempt to keep his father buried, to still his voice and presence by rejecting the economic connections and social structures most closely identified with him. Desire, Lacan, tells us, is the wish to reunite with the mother

beyond the father's name, and the death of the father is symbolically necessary, often registered in terms of socially subversive acts or gestures. Walter's
resistance assumes the form of social subversion; he is unwilling to move
into the filial spaces created for him by his father, and his persistent deafness
to his family's pleas to accept the teaching position demonstrates his wish to
keep his father dead through a series of "perverse" denials or refusals.

Desire or human motive in Collins's texts is never a simple matter, however, and if Walter is reluctant to succeed to his father's connections and
thus to the patriarchal power and prestige embodied by these structures,
his misgivings also arise from Pesca's ambiguous presence in the Hartright
household. At one point, Pesca observes that his boots would "creak like
the golden Papa's" (44) if he were able to earn the salary of four guineas a
week that awaits Walter at Limmeridge House, and although Pesca has been
unable to fill the boots of Walter's dead Papa, both Walter and his sister seem
to fear that Pesca would not mind trying. Walter tells us, for example, that
Pesca was one of Walter's mother's "especial favourites": "His wildest eccen-
tricities were always pardonable in her eyes . . . from the first moment when
she found out that the little Professor was deeply and gratefully attached to
her son, she opened her heart to him unreservedly, and took all his puzzling
foreign peculiarities for granted" (37). And some of Walter's other remarks,
encoded in the language of the nineteenth-century novel, also suggest the
barely sublimated eroticism of the relationship between his mother and
Pesca, as when Walter observes, for example, "I never saw my mother and sister together in Pesca's society, without finding my mother much the younger
woman of the two" (38), or when he confesses, "We of the young generation
are nothing like so hearty and so impulsive as some of our elders" (38).

Although more benign and less explicitly sexual than Dickens's Quilp,
the equally diminutive Pesca is nevertheless filled with similar libidinal exuberance. Walter's sister, we hear, was troubled by this relationship, "always
more or less undisguisedly astonished," we read, "at her mother's familiarity with the eccentric little foreigner" (38), and although Philip O'Neil
argues that "it is a sense of propriety, insular propriety, which causes Sarah
to take exception to Pesca" (102), the energy and indeed turbulence created
by this relationship suggest that something other, or more, than insular propriety is behind Sarah's anxiety. It is she, after all, who must pick up the
wreckage that Pesca's exuberance leaves behind: "very provoking: it spoils

the Set" (38), Sarah notes at one point when Pesca, in his excitement, breaks a teacup, warning her mother that "the next thing [Pesca] will break . . . will be the back of the best armchair" (39). The household "set" has indeed been broken or disrupted by Pesca's presence, and the "connections" once enjoyed by his father cannot be Walter's, since they have already been appropriated by "the eccentric little foreigner" (38).

Heller sees in Walter's reluctance to accept the position at Limmeridge House yet more evidence of what she refers to as a "language of impotence" (118), but Walter's narrative suggests otherwise. What compels Walter to want to stay at home perhaps has something to do with frugality, but has even more to do with his unwillingness to yield any sooner than necessary his place in a family setting that has already been altered by Pesca's presence. "Every manifestation of the father in a text is a refinding of the absent father," Robert Con Davis observes in *The Fictional Father* (3), and Walter refinds the absent father in Pesca, to whom, ironically enough, Walter himself has given life in rescuing him from drowning. Pesca not only is instrumental in attempting to move Walter out of his own house, insofar as he has moved into a position of familiarity with the mother, but he also speaks to Walter with the voice of the father when he attempts to persuade Walter to pursue the rewards of wealth and power: "When your sun shines in Cumberland (English proverb), in the name of heaven make your hay. Marry one of the two young Misses; become Honourable Hartright, M.P.; and when you are on top of the ladder remember that Pesca, at the bottom, has done it all!" (46). After this animated speech by a rather buoyant Pesca about making hay and marrying, however, Walter not only fails to laugh, but finds Pesca's words to be especially painful: "I tried to laugh with my little friend over his parting jest, but my spirits were not to be commanded. Something jarred in me almost painfully while he was speaking his light farewell words" (46). The diminutive Pesca threatens to become Freud's "little thing" in the Hartright household, occupying the space vacated by Walter's dead father, and thus it is not surprising that something should "jar" in Walter as Pesca seems to be hurrying him, as it were, out his own front door.[7]

When Walter finally does accept the position at Limmeridge House, he discovers there as well the power wielded by the dead father. This particular section of the novel follows close on the heels of Walter's earlier resistance against patriarchal presences—both of his dead father and of Pesca. Walter still feels all of the guilt and ambivalence evoked by this resistance; his transgressions against the voice and interdictions of the dead father are cumulative, assuming finally the magnitude of a crime whose expiation requires nothing less than his exile from society as cultural outlaw. In order to understand the nature of these transgressions, however, we need to look carefully at what happens in Limmeridge House itself.

Anne Catherick's entrance into the novel is, of course, striking and memorable. "Moira had power now, she'd been set loose, she'd set herself loose. She was now a loose woman," writes Margaret Atwood in *The Handmaid's Tale* (172), and Anne Catherick, empowered by the taboo that surrounds her, enters this novel as a "loose woman," a woman on the loose. In *Totem and Taboo*, Freud writes that the *délire du toucher*, the touching phobia, is associated with the taboo, and its reach extends beyond physical contact itself: "Anything that directs the patient's thoughts to the forbidden object, anything that brings him into intellectual contact with it, is just as much prohibited as direct physical contact. This same extension also occurs in case of taboo" (*SE*, 13:27). Situated in a field of emotional ambivalence, the taboo has its origin in "a prohibited action, for performing which a strong inclination exists in the unconscious" (32), and thus Collins's characters want to look, but dare not; they want to touch, but must restrain their hands.[8] Anne Catherick, however, fails to control her hands, and when she touches Walter's shoulder, her gesture lingers, its presence marking the site of the forbidden.[9] If I might draw on Margaret Atwood's *The Handmaid's Tale* once more, it is there that Offred, the narrator, confesses, "I hunger to commit the act of touch" (14). Anne Catherick too knows such hunger: "I was obliged to steal after you and touch you," she tells Walter (49), and like a magical incantation, her words summon echoing responses from Walter: "Steal after me and touch me?" he asks, "Why not call to me? Strange, to say the least of it" (49). Like the sight of the dead, Anne's touch immobilizes its object: "Every drop of blood," Walter tells us, "in my body was brought to a stop by a touch of the hand laid lightly and suddenly on my shoulder from behind me" (47).

Laura's first appearance in the novel may not be as dramatic or memorable as Anne Catherick's, but a similar taboo or *délire du toucher* also surrounds her. "Labyrinth," John Ruskin tells us, "properly means 'rope-walk' or 'coil-of-rope-walk,' its first syllable being probably the same as our English name, 'Laura'" (*Fors Clavigera*, 408), and although Ruskin's etymology is perhaps questionable, his remark is nevertheless a fruitful one, for it links Laura by name as well as by destiny to the labyrinthine patterns that permeate *The Woman in White*. It is not Anne Catherick's sensational emergence in the novel, but Laura's deferred entrance, that is most striking. Soon after arriving at Limmeridge House, Walter is told by Marian that Laura is confined to her room and "nursing that essential feminine malady, a slight headache" (59), and that he thus must wait to meet her. Marian's reference to Laura's "malady" is peculiarly phrased, even in a household as neurasthenic as Limmeridge House—it may, like the walls that separate Laura and Walter, hide that which is not to be spoken or seen. As we have seen, Lacan argues that metaphor always contains a surplus of meaning, the result of the pressure of the occulted term making itself felt. Given the various fields of desire that surround Laura throughout much of the novel, the "malady" identified by Marian possibly refers not to a headache, but rather to the occulted signifier of menstruation, not only a more "essential feminine malady," but also a malady that marks, as Lynda Boose points out in "The Father's House and the Daughter in It," "the daughter's entrance into the margins of desire" (35).[10] And since, as Freud points out, the taboo is associated not only with the dead, but with what he refers to as "exceptional states," such as "the physical states of menstruation, puberty or birth" (22), Laura, like Anne, enters the novel surrounded by the *délire du toucher*. Laura remains in this field throughout much of the novel—as when, for example, Walter is giving her a drawing lesson: "The more attentively she watched every movement of my brush, the more closely I was breathing the perfume of her hair, and the warm fragrance of her breath. It was part of my service to live in the very light of her eyes—at one time to be bending over her, so close to her bosom as to tremble at the thought of touching it" (88). Some readers have characterized Walter as a kind of economic eunuch, what Jenny Bourne Taylor, in her *In the Secret Theatre of Home*, describes as "a male governess figure, drained of social and sexual meaning or effectiveness" (108). In her feminist reading of the novel, for example, Anne Cvetkovich argues that "rather than being forbidden or repressed by social

restrictions, desire or sensation does not even appear when the social configuration is inappropriate" (*Mixed Feelings*, 78). It is, however, virtually impossible to reconcile Cvetkovich's remarks with the above passage, and such
misreadings may have come about because readers have taken Walter too
much at his own word, or have somehow overlooked or ignored the strong
presence of testosterone in scenes such as the above. Walter writes, for
example, "I had trained myself to leave all the sympathies natural to my age
in my employer's outer hall, as coolly as I left my umbrella before I went
upstairs" (89). But those who have to suppress their temper are typically
those most inclined to fight, and it does not really matter whether we read
Walter's remarks about his coolness as sincere, self-serving, or simply mis-
taken, for as he bends over the seated Laura, "in that dangerous intimacy of
teacher and pupil" (88), breathing in "the perfume of her hair, and the
warm fragrance of her breath," trembling at the thought of touching her
breasts, but nevertheless wanting to do so, it is pretty clear that he is anything but cool, and that he has not left his "sympathies" or, for that matter,
anything else of his in the outer hall.

But if Walter and Laura's relationship is regarded as transgressive or
illicit—and the novel makes it clear that it is—the question remains why it
should be so. Not only do we have Marian's strident and sustained opposition
to what she sees happening, but the anxiety felt by Walter and Marian themselves seems excessive, hard to account for strictly in terms of economic (poor
boy/rich girl) or pedagogical (teacher/pupil) restraints. An appropriate allegory for reading this section might be the scene in which Laura bungles the
playing of the Mozart melody, when her "fingers wavered on the piano," as
she struck "a false note, [and] confused herself in trying to set it right" (145),
for just as the ruptures or breaks in the musical text alert us to repressed desire,
the exaggerated or excessive responses, the wavering or confusion found in
this section of the narrative similarly disclose various sites of repression.

And in order to understand their presence, we need to pay attention
once again to the dead father, in this case, to Mr. Fairlie. Laura's history is
in large part the history of patriarchal demands and exacted promises.[11]
Marian, for example, tells Gilmore that Laura "entered on this engagement
[with Sir Percival Glyde] at the beginning of her father's fatal illness" (162),
and that her engagement to Sir Percival, "an engagement of honour, not of
love," was sanctioned by her father "on his deathbed, two years since" (97);

and Laura similarly informs Marian that she will not ask to be released from her engagement, not wanting "to add the remembrance that I have broken my promise and forgotten my father's dying words" (186). It is also Laura who tells Percival, "My father's influence and advice has mainly decided me to give you my promise. I was guided by my father, because I had always found him the truest of all advisers, the best and fondest of all protectors and friends. . . . I believe . . . that he knew what was best, and that his hopes and wishes ought to be my hopes and wishes too" (190).

The voice of the father, repeated and reinforced through the daughter's obedience, cannot prohibit desire, but it can attempt to control the directions of that desire. The wedding ceremony, Boose observes, is not about "the union of bride and groom . . . but the separation of daughter from father" (68), who thus becomes "the dispossessed actor of the script" (69). But in this case, it is precisely the presence of the absent father that causes separation and thus dispossession itself to be deferred. Speaking from the center of these entangled dynamics, the voice of the dead father forbids Walter, already ambiguously situated in the household as teacher, lover, and brother, from entering into an intimate relationship with Laura. But while the illicit nature of their desire would seem to arise from the fact that it does not correspond to the structure of exchange Laura's father envisioned, the intensity of their restraint (and desire) is overdetermined, its incestuous overtones later finding a less displaced representation behind a series of disguises when Walter and Laura live together as brother and sister in a setting that has become even more entangled by Marian's presence.[12] Here, as in the case of Tom and Ruth Pinch, that which is behind the speech cannot be spoken, but approached only indirectly or obliquely, and thus we find a series of verbal quadrilles in which whatever cannot be said directly must be circled around, alluded to, but not specifically called by its name. It remains "the other subject" (571), or, as Marian describes it to Walter, "that subject which must not be mentioned between us yet" (571). But because it is repressed, it remains very much present: as Walter himself notes, it "was rather kept alive in them by the restraint which we had imposed upon ourselves" (571).

Laura is surrounded by taboo for much of the novel; after she escapes from the asylum, she is associated not with sexual power or illicit desire, but rather with Anne Catherick and the dead who have escaped the repression of the grave. "The shuddering of an unutterable dread crept over me from head to foot" (431), Walter writes of the moment when he first sees Laura after she escapes from the asylum. Laura's enervating incarceration and extended illness finally remove her from the realm of the taboo and the demonic, but only through a corresponding loss of power. *The Woman in White* is a powerful feminist text and never more so than in its representation of Laura's fate.[13] If we first meet her as a confined (and concealed) young woman, incapacitated by an "essential feminine malady," at the end of the novel, she is still suffering from a feminine malady, but a rather different one than that which earlier confined her. For she is now daughter/prisoner/wife, wearing the marks of "sorrow and suffering" on her face (454) and wracked not so much by bad memories as by the lack of them.

Like Dora (Dickens's, not Freud's), Laura is at once mother/child, or child/mother, and the "stain" associated throughout *The Woman in White* with female sexuality (Mrs. Catherick, for example, asks Percival Glyde to "clear my character of a stain on it which you know I don't deserve" [552–53]) is finally removed. "A body is docile that may be subjected, used, transformed, and improved," suggests Foucault (*Discipline and Punish*, 136), and Marian and Walter "guard" in every sense of the word the docile body of Laura, who ultimately ends up once again as Daddy's girl, with Walter as both husband and father. As D. A. Miller notes, Walter's passion for Laura by the end of the novel is "part-parental, part pedophilic condescension" ("Cage aux Folles," 175), and Laura herself, in Cvetkovich's words, is "reduced to a state of childlike dependence once her memory and identity are stripped away by trauma" (91). If her earlier false note while playing the Mozart melody eloquently expresses the history of desire in a woman denied her own narrative, by the end, Laura's voice has not been erased so much as radically transformed, made all the more frightening because its cadences and patterns testify to happiness and well-being. In speaking of nineteenth-century psychology concerning madness and the mad, Jenny Bourne Taylor notes that "the madwoman of every class is cured through learning to be a middle-class gentlewoman; yet the key sign of that social identity is now receptivity—self-possession merges into being possessed in 'propriety'" (*Secret Theatre*, 38). Such too is the nature of the possession that Laura comes to inhabit.

Walter journeys into a landscape of the dead vividly captured by Marian's prescient dreams, and his self-imposed exile as cultural outlaw is not simply a stock piece of Victorian melodrama on Collins's part, but rather the requisite gesture, in psychoanalytic terms, of an errant son who has transgressed against paternal laws and interdictions. It is as a response to the unconscious crimes he has committed, not his conscious attraction toward Laura or his subsequent disappointment, that Walter's exile must be understood, for it is a symptomatic gesture commensurate with the desires that lie behind it. Like young Martin Chuzzlewit's voyage into Eden or Jonas Chuzzlewit's suicide, Walter's exile is his way of seeking expiation not so much for transgressions committed as for illicit desires frustrated by paternal interdiction. Thus Walter, as a wayward son with errant wishes, must join the legions of the dead as his experiences—again, like young Martin Chuzzlewit's—reenact patterns of life, death, and rebirth. Through such ordeals Walter earns, like Theseus, the mythical hero Walter often invokes, the right to reenter the culture from which he has been exiled. After returning from his travels, Walter no longer speaks with the voice of the son, but rather speaks with that of the father, as he strives to articulate and legitimize kinship structure and filiation by exposing those, like Fosco and Percival Glyde, who have attempted to falsify or erase such lines.

However, at the same time that Collins invokes the Theseus myth, he also significantly rewrites it, for at the end of Theseus' quest, he returns home to be recognized by Aegeus, as Hélène Cixous puts it, in a "splendid moment . . . in which the mystery of filiation is revealed: father and son recognize each other by the signs of their order" (76). There are no swords or sandals in *The Woman in White*, no such splendid moments. Walter is introduced not as a son to his father, as was Theseus, but rather as a father to his son during a brief ceremony conducted by Marian: "Let me make two eminent personages known to one another: Mr. Walter Hartright—the Heir of Limmeridge" (646). This moment and ceremony establish and legitimize lines of kinship, while they are characterized by displacement and signal Walter's movement toward silence and absence. For even as his son moves toward center stage as "the Heir of Limmeridge," Walter moves toward the silence of the end of his narrative. "To be signified is to be absent," Thomas Hanzo points out, adding that "kinship structures mark absences. If I am to be a father, I am not yet a father; if I am a father, my child will replace me" ("Paternity and the Subject in *Bleak House*," 35). If Walter's narrative begins by charting the unconscious dynamics of conflict with an absent father, it ends with his own movement toward the silence of absent fatherhood.

> But there's a Tree, of many, one,
> A single Field which I have looked upon,
> Both of them speak of something that is gone.
>
> WILLIAM WORDSWORTH, "Ode: Intimations of Immortality"

Other kinds of absences or loss also haunt this novel. Associated throughout with the taboo or forbidden (except by Anne Catherick, who utters the phrase as a child might, innocent of its meaning or references but aware of its power to provoke a reaction), "the secret" of *The Woman in White* involves questions of kinship, paternity, and patriarchal desire. Thus various answers to the nature of the secret are sought in historical and genealogical texts and documents—the archival letters of Mrs. Fairlie; Laura's "death certificate," as well as the tombstone inscribed with the dates of her birth, "death," and genealogy; and, of course, the two registers of Percival Glyde's birth. In another sense, however, the "secret" of *The Woman in White* is situated not in one specific act or desire, but rather in the nature of human subjectivity itself. "The primordial separation drama creates a repressed void in being which never ceases to echo," suggests Ellie Ragland-Sullivan (270), and this echo is heard throughout *The Woman in White,* manifested in what Walter describes as "wanting."

Walter first alludes to this wanting when he sees Laura, as he records his impression that she "suggested to me the idea of something wanting" (76). What he literally notes, of course, is the resemblance between Anne and Laura, even though he cannot yet put his finger on it, but Walter's language, tentative and yet again wonderfully precise, suggests that this wanting has more than a single origin.[14] "At one time," he writes, "it seemed like something wanting in *her*: at another, like something wanting in myself" (76, emphasis Collins's). He was, he adds, "most troubled by the sense of incompleteness which it was impossible to discover," unable to situate its origin and nature—"something wanting, something wanting—and where it was, and what it was, I could not say," he admits (76–77). Immediately prior to this moment, Walter draws upon the final lines of Wordsworth's "Intimations Ode" ("To me the meanest flower that blows can give / Thoughts that do often lie too deep for tears" [*Poetical Works*, 463]) when he speaks of how the beauty of woman can touch "sympathies that lie too deep for words, too deep almost for thoughts" (76).

In order to examine more fully the drift of Collins's remarks here—namely, why Walter, in speaking of wanting and the beauty of a woman, should invoke the famous closing lines of Wordsworth's great ode—I turn briefly to George Eliot's *Adam Bede* (1859), published just a year before *The Woman in White*. In it, George Eliot also ponders the nature of a woman's beauty, as she speaks of the "*impersonal* expression in beauty" (400, emphasis Eliot's), arguing that such "beauty has an expression beyond and far above the one woman's soul that it clothes" (400). She continues, suggesting that "it is more than a woman's love that moves us in a woman's eyes—it seems to be a far-off mighty love that has come near to us, and made speech for itself there" (400). Such love, Eliot argues, has finally very little to do with the individuals in question—in this case, Adam Bede's love for the beautiful but shallow Hetty Sorrel—but rather seems to have its origin in our own sense of lack or emptiness, for the voice or "speech" of this "far-off mighty love" both identifies and lessens our sense of loneliness or aloneness, muffling or easing that separation anxiety that characterizes human subjectivity itself. Lacan, Ragland-Sullivan points out, portrays "the unconscious as that memory space created by human language in compensation for separation from the mother and reinforced at the behest of the father" (57). Both Eliot and Collins seem to argue that the beauty of a woman can at moments reach far beyond the woman (or man) in question, disturbing the unconscious—the site of this memory space—and, in doing so, awakening shadowy recollections or fantasies of a time prior to separation and loss. For in arguing that the sympathies invoked by a woman's beauty call forth, as he puts it, "words" and "thoughts" that lie too deep to be known as such, Collins too explores this impersonal expression of beauty, and the sense of wanting or lack that it both identifies and addresses. His invocation of Wordsworth is, in this respect, especially apt, for Wordsworth's poem explores, among other things, the ways in which our sense of loss arises not from nature, but rather from a consciousness suddenly thrown into an awareness of its separation from the things of this earth. The Wordsworthian echoes that reverberate through Walter's voice anticipate not only the sense of wanting that haunts

Collins's text, but also the wounded quality that Collins, as well as Lacan, finds to be constitutive of our relation to the world.

If the beauty of a woman reaches far beyond itself, awakening or agitating deeply buried memories or fantasies, so too does the wounded or inflicted body in Collins's texts carry implications far beyond its own surfaces or boundaries, for the body, especially the scarred or pained body, is at the center of Collins's thinking. As other readers have noted, the female body figures prominently in Collins's fiction as a cipher or text of political discourse and ideology—Laura's bruised arm, for example, tell us as much about the ideology of Collins's discourse in *The Woman in White* as the barbarian girl's scarred body tells us about J. M. Coetzee's in *Waiting for the Barbarians*.[15] But Collins's sense of the "wounded" nature of human experience is often inscribed on the maimed and scarred male body as well, and, indeed, for the most part, the masculine body in *The Woman in White* is a grotesque body, whether inhabited by the epicene Fredric Fairlie or by the obese and protophallic Fosco, who dominates his wife by means of a rod of iron which, we are told, "is a private rod and is always kept upstairs" (244).[16] The male body is diseased or pained, wracked with coughs and pain, disfigured, scarred, mutilated, veering toward loss of control. Pesca can tell of his happiness bursting through his pores like perspiration, but Frederick Fairlie is less comfortable with his secretions: "I cannot see the interest of a secretion from a sentimental point of view. Perhaps my own secretions being all wrong together, I am a little prejudiced on the subject" (363). We first hear of Percival Glyde as a man with a cough, and Anne Catherick's letter to Laura about Percival Glyde warns her to "inquire into the past life of that man with a scar on his hand" (104). When we, along with Laura, inquire into this past life, and as its secrets (and secretions) are finally uncovered, we discover that although his inheritance of Blackwater Park is based on false claims, his title has not been previously challenged, largely because of a reclusiveness on his father's part. The father's reclusiveness has its origin in a "morbid sense of his own personal deformity" (477); he has "suffered from his birth under a painful and incurable deformity and had shunned all society from his earliest year" (476).[17]

Fosco's grotesqueness testifies to the subversive and noncanonical shapes that the eroticized body can assume. As his large and naked body is brought forth for public display in the morgue, the choric praise that surrounds it—"the chattering Frenchwomen about me," writes Walter, "lifted their hands in admiration, and cried in shrill chorus, 'Ah, what a handsome man,'" (643)—is reminiscent of the traditional cries of praise—"oh, what a pretty (big, handsome, etc.) baby"—heard in the birth room, where, we might assume, Fosco's naked body was first exposed to a quasi-public and mostly feminine scrutiny. Fosco, unlike Walter, gladly wears disguises, but nevertheless fails to fool the scar-faced stranger who will rewrite Fosco's body, obliterating Fosco's tattoo, or mark of the Brotherhood, with his own text (*Traditorre*), a gesture that reenacts Walter's erasure and correction of the false narrative of the tombstone. Just as the gaps in the narrative of *The Woman in White* belie Collins's characterization of his text as smooth, so too does the representation of the male body in *The Woman in White* subvert the patriarchal structures that the text would seem to privilege, for the masculine body is inscribed with a lack or incompleteness registered in symptomatic wounds, scars, coughs, and disfigurements. Heller points out that "the intersection, and indeed the collision, of the male and female plots of the novel" give it "its aesthetic and ideological complexity" (112). The male body in Collins's text figures prominently in this collision, but its presence points in other directions as well, toward Lacan's image of the *corps morcelé*, the fragmented or wounded body that is a part of the human condition itself.

This particular image both haunts and empowers the scene in which Walter first sees Marian Halcombe. Although this striking scene has been often alluded to, it is rich enough to warrant being cited in full again:

> I looked from the table to the window farthest from me, and saw a lady standing at it, with her back turned towards me. The instant my eyes rested on her, I was struck by the rare beauty of her form, and by the unaffected grace of her attitude. Her figure was tall, yet not too tall; comely and well-developed, yet not fat; her head set on her shoulders with an easy, pliant firmness; her waist, perfection in the eyes of a man, for it occupied its natural place, it filled out its natural circle, it was visibly and delightfully undeformed by stays. She had not heard my entrance into the room; and I allowed myself the luxury of admiring her for a few moments, before I moved one of the chairs near me, as the least embarrassing means of attracting her attention. She turned toward me immediately. The easy elegance of every movement of her limbs and body as soon as she began to advance from the far end of the room, set me in a flutter of expectation

to see her face clearly. She left the window—and I said to myself, The lady is dark. She moved forward a few steps—and I said to myself, The lady is young. She approached nearer—and I said to myself (with a sense of surprise which words fail me to express), The lady is ugly! (58)

The authors of *Corrupt Relations* suggest that "Hartright lingers agog over it as though it were the most significant item in the strange mystery he is recounting" (Barickman, MacDonald, and Stark, 37). But whatever it is that he is "agog" over—and that question is by no means clear—there is little doubt that Walter was disturbed by this moment when it first occurred and that it unsettles him even now as he tells about it. His language would seem to suggest that he is speaking of more than simply the sight of an ugly face on a beautiful body or a masculine face on a feminine body, for the stereotypic images that we find in this scene resemble certain images of contemporary fashion, in that they contain a disturbing and haunting fusing of the phantasmatic and real, or rather images in which the real below the real assumes phantasmatic forms. In his influential reading of this scene, which he sees as rehearsing the origins of "male nervousness in female contagion" (152), D. A. Miller points out that it develops "all the rhetorical suspense of a striptease, in which, as Barthes has written, 'the entire excitement takes refuge in the hope of seeing the sexual organ'" (176). As Miller notes, however, the place of the genitals—what should be the locus of Walter's "flutter of expectation"—is "strangely occupied by Marian's head and face."

It is strange indeed, and thus, not surprisingly, Walter compares this moment to a dream, saying he experienced at the time "a sensation oddly akin to the helpless discomfort familiar to us all in sleep, when we recognize but cannot reconcile the anomalies and contradictions of a dream" (59). Walter's remark about the "anomalies and contradictions of a dream" corresponds to Freud's description of dream-distortion (*Entstellung*) in *The Interpretation of Dreams*, in which he argues that resistance or repression can be overcome only if the unconscious reveals itself to us in "a distorted shape" (175). Similarly, as we have seen, Lacan tells us that discontinuity "is the essential form in which the unconscious first appears to us" (*Concepts*, 25), and whatever else might characterize this particular scene, it is defined largely by the distortion and discontinuity it registers. The focus throughout is less on the viewed object, Marian, than on the viewing subject, Walter, who, in writing about his voyeurism, repeats or recovers the very impulses and desires he is describing. "She [Marian] had not heard my entrance into the room," he writes, "and I allowed myself the luxury of admiring her for a few moments" (58). Structured around the dynamics of seeing and watching, this moment is most profitably understood in terms of the gaze as Lacan has described it, getting beyond the eye or what it is that the subject actually sees. The eye, Lacan suggests, is only a metaphor for what he refers to as the seer's shoot or *pousse*, a total intentionality, the very being from which the gaze is being directed. The gaze, as we saw in Thackeray and Gaskell, gathers its power and indeed its very structure from desire, but the object of desire behind our gaze is not what we are looking at, but something else altogether.

This something else eludes or evades us, however, for the full implications of the gaze are not apprehended by the subject, since he or she is screened by what Lacan refers to as the "lure," which makes both the subject who is consciously looking at something and that which is seen in many important respects illusory. "The subject is presented," Lacan observes, "as other than he is, and what one shows him is not what he wishes to see" (*Concepts*, 104). Most important for our understanding of this scene, however, is Lacan's suggestion that the gaze has its origin in a central lack of human experience that is most often expressed in the phenomenon of the castration anxiety: the gaze, he points out, exists in the "form of a strange contingency, symbolic of what we find on the horizon, as the thrust of our experience, namely, the lack that constitutes castration anxiety" (*Concepts*, 72–73). The gaze arises from an unconscious desire on our part, insofar as desire is the desire for the other, for a fullness or totality whose absence is registered in terms of castration anxiety.

As Miller's remarks about the scene's striptease quality suggest, Walter's gaze is directed here toward the female genitals insofar as they have been displaced upward to Marian's head and face. The head and face are particularly described, masculine with a "moustache" on the upper lip and a "large, firm masculine mouth and jaw" (58). But in terms of the anxiety that Walter registers on seeing the head and face, and his rendering of the "thick, coal-black hair, growing unusually low down on her forehead" (58), they invoke the image of Medusa. As Freud argues in his essay on Medusa, "The horrifying decapitated head of Medusa" invokes "a terror of castration linked to the sight of something" (*SE*, 18:273), or, as one of Iris Murdoch's characters puts it in *A Severed Head*, "Freud on Medusa. The head can represent the female genitals, feared not desired" (44). If Anne Catherick exists in the novel as "a multivalent figure who enables multiple, yet linked, levels of reading" (Heller, 119), this moment in the novel similarly invites multiple yet linked readings. It confronts Walter with that which he at once sees and refuses to see, invested with both the horror and the power associated with Medusa. The castration anxiety, as Lacan and others have pointed out, represents not any threatening reality, but rather the thematization of reality, verifying our sense of wanting or lack, a "chronic state of self-insufficiency," to use Lacan's phrase. As Jean Laplanche observes, there is an element of reassurance implicit in any scenario that structures anxiety, and insofar as this scene does give structure to Walter's anxiety, it is finally, at least to some extent, a reassuring one.[18] But he seeks reassurance in other ways as well.

For this moment is also linked in significant ways with the impulses that are at the heart of Walter's narrative. The particular nature of this linkage can best be seen by returning once again to Freud's case history of Dora. Nancy Armstrong argues that the role of analysis in this particular case is one of "supplying the missing parts," that the subject's speech in Freud's communication model has the form of the female body, "that of a disfigured or 'mutilated' male, essentially regressive but at the same time containing the secrets that authorize male discourse" (230). Therefore, Armstrong suggests, Freud's analytic procedures with regard to Dora presuppose "an absence that needs to be filled" (229). Arguing along somewhat similar lines, Toril Moi suggests that Freud's case history of Dora testifies to his conviction that the "possession of knowledge means the possession of power" (194). Although Freud, she argues, displays a curious pride in his "hermeneutical capacities," he is also beset by castration anxieties, for, as in the case of Oedipus, this drive for knowledge carries with it certain risks: "If Freud cannot solve Dora's riddle," Moi observes, "the unconscious punishment for this failure will be castration." Freud's almost obsessive desire to discover the sources, for example, of Dora's knowledge of sexual matters testifies to this anxiety (195). Moi maintains that Dora's "knowledge cannot be conceptualized as a whole; it is dispersed and has been assembled piecemeal from feminine sources. Dora's epistemological model becomes the female genitals, which in Freud's vision emerge as unfinished, diffuse, and fragmentary; they cannot add up to a complete whole and must therefore be perceived as castrated genitals" (196).

Armstrong's and Moi's remarks about Freud's narrative in the case of Dora are especially germane to the anxieties attached to Walter's narrative. As we have seen, Walter also insists that he is presenting a complete and sufficient narrative, that he is concealing nothing from us. Although his narrative has been destabilized from the very beginning by the threat of androgyny and sexually ambiguous subjectivities, Walter tries to persuade us as well as himself that there are no holes or gaps in it, that it has not been feminized. And yet, as we have seen, Walter's narrative is in fact riddled with holes and unfilled spaces. In this respect, Walter's narrative, like Fredrick Fairlie, is problematically gendered, its shapes and textures slippery, at times almost indeterminate, and, as such, it might be regarded as a narrative in drag, to use D. A. Miller's image—but not because of an attempt on Walter's part to deceive us or to keep us off balance through disguises or ambiguous self-representations. On the contrary, he emphatically insists that his narrative is complete, that it has not been castrated; his insistence, however, is qualified, if not belied, by the sense of wanting that haunts the narrative.

Walter's narrative operates in the screen of the lure, presenting itself as something other than what it is. His various attempts to uncover the origins of certain mysteries—Who is Anne Catherick? Who is Percival Glyde? What is the secret?—testify to this desire on his part for wholeness or completion. As we can see, however, in the effect that the "striptease" scene has on Walter, the displaced feminine genitals testify not only to that lack or incompleteness that the text identifies as "wanting," but also to "the power of the woman's gesture," to use Neil Hertz's phrase ("Medusa's Head," 164), a power that Cixous has located in the figure of the Medusa.[19] It is to this "power of the woman's gesture" that I would now like to turn.

As you say, the mystery turns upon your mother.

SIGMUND FREUD, "Fragment of an Analysis of a Case of Hysteria"[20]

In order to more fully, albeit tentatively, explore the wanting or sense of incompleteness that haunts *The Woman in White*, I would like to return, as do so many of the characters in the novel, to Mrs. Fairlie's gravesite. I say tentatively, for *The Woman in White* is not only plotted like a mystery, but, as text, it finally moves into mystery, the interpretation of which must remain provisional. To draw on one of the central metaphors of Collins's text, there is in every interpretive act a labyrinth from which we cannot escape, in whose creation we actually participate through our interpretive gestures.[21] As we have seen earlier, Lacan argues that death tears a hole in the veil of the symbolic, revealing its inadequacy as nothing else can, even as the only access we have to mourning is through the rituals and ceremonies that the symbolic makes available to us ("Desire," 38–39); and in *The Woman in White*, we are drawn, as are the characters themselves, to the central place of mourning in the novel, namely, to Mrs. Fairlie's gravesite. Freud recounts that when Dora visited the Dresden art gallery, "she remained *two hours* in front of the Sistine Madonna, rapt in silent admiration" (116, emphasis Freud's). "When I asked her what had pleased her so much about the picture," Freud writes, "she could find no clear answer to make. At last she said, 'The Madonna'" (116). Collins's text too is enraptured by the site of the mother, moving around it in patterns that always return to it, and, as in Freud's case history, it is around the mother that the mystery of the narrative of *The Woman in White* revolves. Even more than Anne Catherick, Mrs. Fairlie is *the* woman in white, for it is she who first persuades Anne that young girls of her complexion "looked neater and better in white than in anything else" (84). Heller rightly identifies Mrs. Fairlie's gravesite as "the novel's most central symbolic site" (113), but errs, I think, in regarding it as an image of "woman's lack of identity" (113), for it is not an image of lack, but rather of fullness and completeness.

Returning to Ragland-Sullivan's suggestion that Lacan depicts "the unconscious as that memory space created by human language in compensation for separation from the mother" (57), I am arguing that it is this memory space, symbolically centered in the figure of the mother—or, more accurately, the site of her grave—that is specifically registered in Collins's text as wanting or incompleteness, and that is plotted out through its various patterns of repetition and return. Desire testifies to a fundamental human lack and is, as such, metonymic, for since it is rooted in imaginary or infantile scenarios that have been pushed into our unconscious, it is incapable of being satisfied or even named. As we saw in *Ruth*, this desire for the (m)other does not die, but rather continues to express itself through virtually every aspect of our lives. Mrs. Fairlie's gravesite marks, as it were, the locus of this desire and is, as such, the center or hub of many of the novel's crucial moments—for example, Walter's first sight of Anne near the grave and later his seeing Laura there after her escape from the asylum. Marian's dreams, both surreal and prescient, are also haunted by the site, as she dreams of Walter "kneeling by a tomb of white marble" (296), and later sees "the white tomb again, and the veiled woman rising out it by Hartright's side" (310). The veiled woman is a figure of mystery, hiding that which lies on the other side of the symbolic. The phallus in Lacan's terms is the primary signifier of completion or totality, the grounding of language itself, but it can function as such, Lacan points out, only when veiled.[22] In this respect, then, the "veiled woman" of Marian's dreams, rising out of the white tomb by Walter's side, might be seen as the veiled phallus, the primary signifier of completion or fullness that must work unseen or hidden.

But what Collins's text seems to point to is not the veiled phallus, but rather what Kristeva describes as "maternal quietude," which, "more stubborn than even philosophical doubt, with its fundamental incredulity, eats away at the omnipotence of the symbolic" (*Stabat Mater*, 602). Kristeva too invokes the image of the veil, but links it with the maternal, when she asks whether "modern art [is] not a realization of maternal love—a veil over death assuming death's own place and knowing that it does? A sublimated celebration of incest?" (595). In this respect, the figure of the mother in Collins's novel, as in Dickens's and Gaskell's, is associated with death, with the desire, albeit veiled or unconscious, to return to a site beyond language and separation, to a point at which beginning and end, Alpha and Omega, mysteriously merge into each other. "Oh, if I could die, and be hidden and at rest with you," says Anne Catherick, as she "murmured the words close on the gravestone, murmured them in tones of passionate endearment, to the dead remains beneath" (127). Like Anne Catherick, Collins's text is haunted by the grave, moving around it in gestures of "passionate endearment," but finally the figure of Mrs. Fairlie remains a veiled mystery, seen only dimly by us, standing beyond ideologies. And as Collins's characters return, as they do so often, to the site of her grave, they express through their various actions and gestures an unconscious desire that finds articulation only through symptomatic acts and gestures.

Mrs. Fairlie's gravesite possesses its own narrative, "The Narrative of the Tombstone"; situated, as it is, in the midst of the other narratives, its text

tells of the beginning and end of human existence and is thus linked with
other genealogical texts, such as Laura's death certificate and Percival's
church registry. Toward the end of the novel, we are returned to this site,
where we witness a ceremonial act of reinscription in which false narratives
are erased (after they are first traced and thus once again recorded) and true
ones restored by Walter, who gathers together the community to witness
this act of authority and authorship—"I invited all the persons present," he
tells us, "(after thanking them in Laura's name and mine) to follow me to
the churchyard, and see the false inscription struck off the tombstone with
their own eyes" (639). Although Mrs. Fairlie has no narrative of her own
(except for the one Marian constructs when she reads aloud from some of
her letters), she is deeply inscribed in the other narratives. One of the earliest images we have is of Mrs. Fairlie walking between the two young girls,
Laura and Anne, holding each of them by the hand; and throughout the
novel, she remains a figure whose presence (and, although dead, she is very
much present throughout the novel) mediates between completeness and
incompleteness, silence and language, emptiness and fullness, female and
male, life and death. Collins's figures are thrust into a world of division and
lack, and language as trace reminds them of what has been lost, of a secret
that cannot be uncovered. Exploring in necessarily tentative ways the
nature of wanting, as well as the images of fullness or presence that perhaps
make us only more acutely aware of loss, Collins suggests that this presence
is embodied not in images of male power or dominance, but, on the contrary, in the maternal or feminine as an image of (m)other, that from which
we are separated by paternal interdiction and thus by language itself.[23] In this
sense, then, *The Woman in White* moves tentatively beyond either matriar-
chal or patriarchal ideologies in that it attempts to explore the real as a realm
of experience beyond the symbolic, the ground of all ideologies. The book
must, of course, ultimately fail, since, given the absence of any metalanguage, it must draw on language in its attempt to probe beyond language,
but it nevertheless points in the direction of a mystery hauntingly suggested
by the silent and powerful presence of Mrs. Fairlie, a mystery beyond language itself and that world of wanting that haunts this narrative.

5

Yearning and Melancholia

Obscure Objects of Desire in Jude the Obscure

"I want to go back," Daniel says, quietly, with effort.
"Where?" I ask, unsure.
There's a long pause that kind of freaks me out and Daniel finishes his drink and fingers the sunglasses he's still wearing and says, "I don't know. Just back."

BRET EASTON ELLIS, *Less Than Zero*

Not long after Little Father Time comes to live with Sue and Jude, he asks Sue if he might call her "mother," and almost immediately, Hardy writes, "a yearning came over the child and he began to cry" (345). Jude watches this scene with particular interest and later reminds Sue that the boy "called you mother two or three times before he dropped off," adding that he, Jude, thought it "odd that he should have wanted to" (346). Sue, however, does not regard the boy's gestures as "odd," but rather sees them as "significant," and Little Father Time's yearning is indeed significant, not just for this scene, but for the novel as a whole, for Sue and Jude are drawn toward objects of desire that remain obscure, hidden, incapable of being apprehended directly. Marjorie Garson has observed that "Jude Fawley wants" (152), but Sue Bridehead also wants, and in both cases "want" signifies both desire and lack. Desire in *Jude the Obscure* is to be understood as that which remains hidden, distinct from need, and, as such, the novel is driven by a repressed history of desire that is traced through various recurrent signifiers, such as Jude's dreams of Christminster and Sue's desire for unencumbered instinctual freedom. Invoking the ancient voices of Sophocles and Aristophanes in order to develop his own voice more fully, Hardy explores in *Jude* the shapes and sounds of desire, registered in the novel as a sense of loss or want, what the novel refers to as "yearning."

Charles-Pierre Baudelaire's poetry, Walter Benjamin notes, "is devoted to something irretrievably lost" (181), and *Jude*, I argue, is similarly devoted to that which has been "irretrievably lost." And just as Benjamin begins his inquiry into Baudelaire's poetry by examining "the correlation between memory (in the sense of *mémoire involontaire*) and consciousness" in Freud's *Beyond the Pleasure Principle* (160), I will draw on this late Freudian text, for, like Freud and Baudelaire, Hardy examines this correlation and its relationship to modernity itself. I am, however, not interested in the question of influence or indirect borrowings. Freud and Hardy read many of the same writers—Sophocles, Aristophanes, Goethe, Nietzsche, Proust, Schopenhauer, and John Stuart Mill, to name just a few—but it is unlikely that Hardy was familiar with Freud's writings, and there is no evidence that Freud, who seems to have read just about everything, knew Hardy's work.[1] Rather, I am interested in the convergence of certain central questions and images, in particular correspondences of mood and atmosphere, for although they are divided by a quarter of a century, *Jude the Obscure* and *Beyond the Pleasure Principle* both articulate the moods and anxieties that haunt the fin de siècle and the early decades of the twentieth century.

Both texts are argumentative, almost combative, in tone, unwilling to compromise or lighten their dark visions for a potentially hostile audience.[2] Each comes late in the writer's career: Freud wrote *Beyond the Pleasure Principle* when he was sixty-four years old, and although Hardy was to live and write for more than thirty years after *Jude*, he would write no more novels. It is perhaps for this reason that both texts examine the end, seem in fact obsessed by the question of closure. Each text is fascinated by certain patterns in human life and with the connection between these patterns and the tendency of organic life to move toward death or, as Freud puts it, "towards the restoration of an earlier state of things" (*Beyond the Pleasure Principle*, 31–32).

> Do not ghosts prove—even rumours, whispers, stories of ghosts— that the past clings, that we are always going back?

GRAHAM SWIFT, *Waterland*

The text of *Jude* functions as a crypt, as Derrida describes it—that which is meant "to disguise and hide: something, always a body in some way. But also to disguise the act of hiding and to hide the disguise" (*The Wolfman's Magic Word*, xiv). What is hidden (and disclosed) in *Jude* is *somebody* whose death is being mourned. Hardy informs us in the 1895 preface to *Jude* that the novel "was suggested by the death of a woman" in 1886. His comments about this death betray an emotional ambivalence similar to that Freud speaks of in *Totem and Taboo* when he points out that while, on one hand, mourners tend to be "preoccupied with the dead man, to dwell upon his memory and preserve it as long as possible," they also "perform a great number of ceremonies to keep him at a distance or drive him off" (*SE*, 13:57).

Hardy's preface preserves the memory of the dead woman, telling of her presence in the "history of this novel": "The scheme was jotted down in 1890, from notes made in 1887 and onwards, some of the circumstances being suggested by the death of a woman in the former year. The scenes were revisited in October 1892; the narrative written in outline in 1892 and the spring of 1893, and at full length, as it now appears, from August 1893 onwards into the next year" (39). But at the same time, the preface withholds her name, telling us nothing about her relationship with Hardy or how her death figures into the "circumstances" of the novel. Extremely reticent about his private life, Hardy does all he can to avoid mentioning her name, apparently afraid, like Freud's mourners, that such a mention might risk

invoking her presence. And yet, in spite of a testimony that stands both as epi-
taph and incantation to keep the spirits of the dead at a distance, Tryphena
Sparks—let us not withhold her name any longer—makes her presence felt.
For Tryphena (1851–90), Hardy's cousin who lived at Puddletown, near
Hardy's boyhood home, not only shows up in the preface but also is written
into the characters of Sue Bridehead and Arabella Donn, perhaps most
strikingly so in an episode I will have occasion to return to later.[3] In it, Jude,
himself unseen, watches Arabella tending bar and flirting with the customers
and is struck by what seems to him to be the abandoned and sensuous nature
of her behavior and gestures. Jude will later observe that Arabella's behavior
and gestures suggest that her "manners were still more vivacious than before—
more abandoned, more excited, more sensuous" (240). In "My Cicely," a
poem in which Hardy also draws on his relationship with Tryphena, the
speaker watches the woman he loves tending bar:

> I'd looked on, unknowing, and witnessed
> Her jests with the tapsters,
> Her liquor-fired face, her thick accents,
> In naming her fee.
>
>   (*Poetical Works*, 1:70)[4]

Hardy's poetry often reveals more nakedly than his fiction the twisted and
circuitous paths of desire, and in a passage suggesting the aggression and
violence often inherent in idealized projections, the speaker imagines his
Cicely dead, as he fantasizes that "Death stole intact her young dearness /
And innocence," confessing that it is far better to dream of such a death
than "to own the debasement of sweet Cicely" (70). Arabella, of course,
does not succumb to anyone's fantasies, except perhaps her own, and she is
very much alive at the end of the novel.

But there are other ghosts in *Jude* as well. An often ancient past is
woven throughout Hardy's fiction, but its place in *Jude* is unique in that its
site is registered both as absence and as presence.[5] In earlier Hardy novels,
such as *The Return of the Native* and *Tess of the d'Urbervilles*, the past
makes itself known through ancient voices, rituals, and ceremonies, such as
the May Day dance early in *Tess*, for example, or the Druidic rites that
begin *The Return of the Native*, with a bonfire ceremony that makes it seem

"as if these men and boys had suddenly dived into past ages, and fetched there from an hour and deed which had before been familiar with this spot" (12). In *Jude*, however, this ancient past has been erased or obliterated. Jude peers down a well "as ancient as the village itself" (49), but knows nothing of the tales and legends connected with the well's history. Troutham's farm, with its "meanly utilitarian air" (53), has been stripped of "all history beyond that of the few recent months" (53), even though its land once resounded with ancient and multitudinous sounds of human life: "Every clod and stone there really attached associations enough and to spare—echoes of songs from ancient harvest-days, of spoken words, and of sturdy deeds. Every inch of ground had been the site, first or last, of energy, gaiety, horseplay, bickerings, weariness" (53). These echoes, however, have long since died into silence, and just as the rooks regard Troutham's field as nothing more than "a granary good to feed in," Jude finds in it little more than "the quality of a work-ground" (53). Hardy, Gillian Beer remarks, is "a writer who was willing to encounter the activity of forgetting, to let go of origins, and to encompass oblivion—with pain certainly, but without panic. He records that some times are 'silent beyond the possibility of echo'" ("Origins," 81), and in *Jude*, this echo seems unreachable, its silence almost deafening.

But if ancient rituals and ceremonies can no longer be discovered in *Jude*, the past nevertheless makes its presence felt. Kevin Moore observes of *Jude* that "the dead past informs the living present, killing its ability to be fully present or fully alive" (*The Descent of the Imagination*, 32), but the past in *Jude* is not dead, but rather very much alive, inscribed in what Michael Millgate has identified as "old paths inadvertently re-entered" (*Career*, 333), or in what the narrator refers to at one point as Jude's acts of "automatic repetition" (78). Lacan notes of Poe's "The Purloined Letter" that Poe's characters do not possess the letter so much as the unconscious possesses them: "One can say," he writes, "that when the characters get a hold of this letter, something gets a hold of them and carries them along" (*Seminar II*, 196). This same "something" seems to have "a hold" of the figures in *Jude*, carrying them along with it, so that they often seem to be acting in response to some set of invisible psychic coordinates, moving in accord with unconsciously choreographed patterns or designs.

Such patterns, which Freud refers to as the "perpetual recurrence of the same thing" (*Pleasure Principle*, 16), are most evident in Jude's and Sue's behavior—Jude's continuous circling back to Christminster and Arabella, for example, and Sue's repetitive relationships with the undergraduate, Jude, and Phillotson. Both regard themselves as somehow fated or cursed, haunted by stories of their family history and its various scenarios of violence and death. But such patterns are not limited to Sue and Jude. Phillotson and Sue remarry in a ceremony characterized as "a re-enactment by the ghosts of their former selves of the similar scene which had taken place at Melchester years before" (446). Their spectral ceremony invokes in turn familiar reactions to it, as Arabella, somewhat like the fifth little piggy of nursery rhyme fame, "made dimples most successfully all the way home," and a less buoyant Jude in "his misery and depression walked to well-nigh every spot in the city that he had visited with Sue" (451). Immediately after this scene, Arabella once again plies Jude with liquor, softening him up for their second marriage, and her gestures and tactics, even employing once again the help of her father, lead the narrator to observe that "the circumstances were not altogether unlike those of their entry into the cottage at Cresscombe, such a long time before" (454).

Doesn't every narrative lead back to Oedipus?

ROLAND BARTHES, *The Pleasure of the Text*

Such patterns give *Jude* the appearance of a haunted or demonized arena in which unconscious dramas are being played out, and, like Dickens, Hardy suggests that such dramas are reenactments of still earlier dramas, some of ancient origin. In this respect, the House of Atreus is significantly present in *Jude*. And while it is possible that Roland Barthes in the above epigraph overstates the case, there is little doubt that *Jude* leads in the direction of Oedipus.[6] Even the most casual reading of *Jude* discloses the strong smell of incest surrounding Sue and Jude's relationship, creating what Penny Boumelha identifies as "an incestuous *frisson* to their sense of impending and hereditary doom" (141). Jude contemplates the "reasons why [he] must not attempt intimate acquaintances with Sue Bridehead now that his interest in her had shown itself to be unmistakably of a sexual kind" (145), and thus tries to think of her "in the family way, since there were crushing reasons why he should not and could not think of her in any other" (137), including the fact that "marriage with a blood-relation . . . might be intensified to a tragic horror" (137). When Sue tells Jude of hearing from her father of how marriages always ended badly for the Fawleys, the mood is equally foreboding, as she and Jude "stood possessed by the same thought, ugly enough, even as an assumption; that a union between them, had such been possible, would have meant a terrible intensification—two bitters in one dish" (224).[7]

The question, then, is not whether Hardy draws on Sophocles, but rather why. The huge graveyard set aside for failed literary texts is filled with imitations of Greek tragedy, and Hardy, certainly no fool, must have known the risks he was taking. But he takes them nevertheless, and it could be that he does so, as Millgate suggests—in citing Edmund Gosse's famous critique of the novel—in order to leave us "stunned with a sense of the hollowness of existence" (*Career*, 325). There may be other reasons for Hardy's decision to imitate Greek tragedy as well. At one point, Sue refers to Jude as "a dreamer of dreams" (265), and some remarks by Freud, another "dreamer of dreams," may help us identify some of Hardy's reasons. Freud argues that *Oedipus Rex* has its origin in "primeval dream material" and that its power derives from its ability to touch or awaken similar dreams in its audience. *Jude*'s power seems to derive, in part at least, from similar sources, and critical commentary about the novel often suggests as much. Millgate argues, for example, that "Jude's obsession with Christminster should be seen in terms of its relationship to deeper, obscurer needs" (*Career*, 329–30). Similarly, Marjorie Garson refers to Jude's desire as "overdetermined" (168), noting that "the deep concerns [of *Jude*] which are disguised by the moral shape of the main plot will return—obliquely, and as it were under pressure—in figurative ways" (179).

In order to understand the presence of the Oedipus myth in *Jude*, we need to move away from the explicit presence of forbidden desires, whatever *frissons* or shudders they might cause, and look instead at the "deeper, obscurer needs" that are screened by them, at what else the text may be getting at through them. As Ellie Ragland-Sullivan reminds us, Lacan "never tires of repeating that *Totem and Taboo* is wrong and that the Oedipus complex is Freud's own neurosis" (267), that "the Oedipal crisis does not occur because a child wants to possess its mother sexually, but when the child comprehends its society's sexual rules, the crisis is resolved when the rules are acceded to and accepted" (268). Because it intervenes in the mother-child dyad, the Oedipus stands at the juncture of nature and culture, requiring the inscription of the human subject in the symbolic order and its laws and kinship structures. While denying any historical basis for Freud's notion of the primal horde, Claude Lévi-Strauss also sees Freud's theory as occupying that nodal point at which nature and culture clash, and, as such, he argues that the Oedipus embodies the stuff of "an ancient and lasting dream": "The magic of this dream, its power to mould men's thought unbeknown to them, arises precisely from the fact that the acts it evokes have never been committed, because culture has opposed them at all times and in all places" (*Kinship*, 491).

Jude the Obscure explores above all else precisely this conflict between culture and nature, itself, as we saw in *Martin Chuzzlewit*, a problematic cultural construction of the age. In fact, it is this question, rather than those concerning marriage or education, that is truly at the center of the novel, and thus the lingering presence of the Oedipus story as a kind of floating signifier should not surprise us, for it marks the sites where, as Hardy puts it, instinct and nature on one hand and civilization on the other come into conflict with one another. Such a site is seen in *Jude* when Farmer Troutham, after he discovers Jude allowing the rooks to feed on the corn, reminds the young boy that nature and civilization are indeed in conflict—that "what was good for God's birds was bad for God's gardener" (55): "All at once [Jude] became conscious of a smart blow upon his buttock, followed by a loud clack, which announced to his surprised senses that the clacker had been the instrument of offense used. The birds and Jude started up simultaneously, and the dazed eyes of the latter beheld the farmer in person, the great Troutham himself, his red face glaring down upon Jude's cowering frame, the clacker swinging in his hand" (54). "Whilst saluting Jude's ears with his impassioned rhetoric," Hardy continues, "Troutham had seized his left hand with his own left, and swinging his slim frame round him at arms-length, again struck Jude on the hind parts with the flat side of Jude's own rattle, till the field echoed with the blows" (54).

Depicted as phantasmagoric, larger than life, "the great Troutham himself, his red face glaring down upon Jude's cowering frame," is a phal-

lic figure of authority and law, his "clacker swinging in his hand," saluting
Jude with "his impassioned rhetoric."[8] It is not just a matter of either using
your clacker or losing it, as Jude learns, but of having it taken away and
turned against your backside. Although cast in a mock-heroic light, this
moment is also frightening and disturbing, as comedy often is, constituting
a symbolic castration that drives home to Jude a newly registered sense of
lack or loss; he knows that the "magic thread" that once connected his life
with nature's has been cut or severed. Jude, we hear, "walked along the
trackway weeping," burdened by a "shadow on his mind" (55).[9]

But if the relationship between nature and culture seems fairly straightforward in this particular scene, it is nevertheless problematic in *Jude*. After
the death of the children, Sue reminds Jude of an earlier dream that they
had shared: "We said—do you remember?—that we would make a virtue
of joy. I said it was Nature's intention, Nature's law and *raison d'être* that we
should be joyful in what instincts she afforded us—instincts which civilization had taken upon itself to thwart" (413). Sue seems to have in mind here
a prior condition of natural wholeness and joy that has been stripped away
or thwarted by "civilization." But Sue's "Nature," very much like that prefestival world that Rousseau describes, does not exist in *Jude*, or, for that matter, anywhere else.[10] "The very structure at the basis of desire always lends a
note of impossibility to the object of human needs," suggests Lacan ("Desire,"
36), and in Sue's paean to a lost instinctual joy, we hear the articulation of
such an impossibility. What hurts Jude and Sue is not the ache born of a
forbidden or transgressive sexual desire—the text's compulsive patterns
continue after Jude and Sue have become sexually intimate and have had
several children—but rather what the text identifies as a "yearning" for
what necessarily remains a dream, an obscure object of desire.[11]

At one point, Freud writes that Rome, the city of his dreams, had
become "in my dream a cloak and symbol for a number of passionate
wishes," and the city of Jude's dreams, Christminster, is a cloak and symbol
for his own passionate wishes.[12] At one point, Jude notes of Christminster
that Robert Burton, "the great Dissector of Melancholy used to walk here"
(473), and melancholia haunts the pages of *Jude* as well. The 1895 preface
to *Jude* suggests that it might be read as an act of mourning insofar as it
seems to have begun with the death of "a woman"; but because that which
has been lost in *Jude* remains obscure or hidden, it is a novel less about

mourning than about melancholia. Melancholia, as Freud tells us in "Mourning and Melancholia," can be regarded as insufficient or incomplete mourning, when the subject has not accepted what the mourner finally comes to accept through "reality-testing" (*SE*, 14:244), namely the fact of loss itself, that that which is being mourned is dead or gone and will not return. When this fact is accepted, "when the work of mourning is completed," as Freud describes it, "the ego becomes free and uninhibited again" (245). The melancholic's ego does not become "free and uninhibited," for she incorporates the object of loss into herself through a process of identification, and the ambivalence characteristic of mourning itself—namely, feelings of both love and hate or remorse and anger toward the dead person or object—is turned not outward against the deceased, but inward against herself. Thus the melancholic is a person torn, as it were, in two on an unconscious level, the consequence of what Freud characterizes as "a cleavage between the critical activity of the ego and the ego as altered by identification" (249). Evidence of this cleavage is seen in the behavior of the melancholic—namely, a "lowering of the self-regarding feelings to a degree that finds utterance in self-reproaches and self-revilings" (244), but also a sense that he has "been slighted and . . . treated with great injustice" (248). The melancholic "abases himself before everyone," regarding himself as "worthless, incapable of any achievement and morally despicable; he reproaches himself, vilifies himself, and expects to be cast out and punished" (246). Unlike the mourner, who tends to be withdrawn and quiet, melancholics "are not ashamed and do not hide themselves" (248), but, on the contrary, evince "an almost opposite trait of insistent communicativeness which finds satisfaction in self-exposure" (247). And while it is perhaps not surprising that Jude, a man of "tempestuous, self-harrowing moods" (*Jude the Obscure*, 396), should resemble Freud's melancholic, the strength of the resemblance is nevertheless striking. Shortly after receiving the letter of rejection from the Master of Biblioll College, Jude sits in the tavern surrounded by self-reproach and self-revilings, "more or less all the day long, convinced that he was at bottom a vicious character, of whom it was hopeless to expect anything" (170), only to begin, after drinking some more, feeling himself to have "been slighted and . . . treated with great injustice": "I don't care a damn . . . for any Provost, Warden, Principal, Fellow, or cursed Master of Arts in the University! What I know is that I'd lick 'em on their own ground if they'd give me a chance, and show 'em a few things they are not up to yet!" (171). During his final return to Christminster, Jude, we hear, "was not inclined to shrink from open declaration of what he had no great reason to be ashamed of" (398); and he soon speaks in a loud voice to the assembled throng, describing himself to them as "a paltry victim to the spirit of mental and social restlessness, that makes so many unhappy in these days!" (399).

Less vocal and less given to public exposure than Jude, Sue neverthe-less resembles Freud's melancholic. After the death of the children, she tells Jude that she would "like to prick myself all over with pins and bleed out the badness that's in me" (420), wishing, as she puts it, that "something would take the evil right out of me, and all my monstrous errors, and all my sinful ways!" (420). Jude tries to reason with her, telling her that it is "mon-strous and unnatural for you to be so remorseful when you have done no wrong" (425–26), but, as Freud might have told Jude, it is fruitless to argue with such self-reproaches, for the melancholic "must surely be right in some way and be describing something that is as it seems to him" (SE, 14:246). On the other hand, Arabella has mastered the art of "reality-testing" in resilient and imaginative ways, and thus successfully resolves her mourn-ing as she enthusiastically sheds her widow's weeds. She also identifies both the symptoms and etiology of Sue's illness when she observes that "she's took in a queer religious way, just as I was in my affliction at losing Cartlett, only hers is of a more 'sterical sort than mine" (432–33). Jude's affliction is "'sterical" as well, insofar as it is the symptom of unconscious desires, and, in order to understand it, we need to return to Christminster, the city of his dreams.

The epigraph to *Jude* tells us that "the letter killeth," and Christminster is above all else the primary site of the letter and the word.[13] Jude is led to Christminster and Sue by his aunt's "nervously anxious letter," and while working there as a stone mason, repairing old letters or inscriptions and inscribing new ones, he meets Sue Bridehead, who is, like her father before her, "an ecclesiastical worker in metal" (135). It is a demonized necropolis, an "infernal cursed place" (401), as Jude will describe it, inhabited by the ghosts of producers and readers of letters—theologians, playwrights, poets, scientists, and philosophers. "The phantoms [are] all about here," Jude tells Arabella, "in the college archways, and windows" (473). "When I am dead," he tells her, "you'll see my spirit flitting up and down here among these" (474). Sue, haunted by her own demons and thus uneasy in the presence of others, sees Christminster as "a place full of fetishists and ghost-seers" (205), a remark that elicits a confession from Jude: "That's just what I am, too. . . . I am fearful of life, spectre-seeing always" (205). The fetish, a substitute for that which has been lost, is a precise and rich image in this context. For Freud, the fetish registers lack or want, insofar as it is a substitute for the missing penis, but Lacan deepens Freud's definition. Lacan argues that desire itself is fetishistic in that the fetish is a substitute for what Lacan identifies as the phallus—absolutely distinct from the male generative organ, or penis—the primary signifier of completion or wholeness and thus that which all human subjects, female and male alike, lack.[14]

Jude and Sue, two of the age's true melancholics, unconsciously mourn this loss throughout the novel. They both know that a loss has occurred (its presence as absence haunts virtually all of their conversations and actions), but neither knows what has been lost. What has died is what the human subject must necessarily lose, Augustine's completeness closed in on itself, but neither Jude nor Sue can mourn adequately its loss, and are thus destined to reenact it through their wanderings. In this respect, it is only fitting that Christminster is the primary site of the letter or word, for our birth into language constitutes the eternalization of our desire, our movement from the thing itself to the symbol of the thing. Lacan reads Freud's account of the child's "fort-da" game in *Beyond the Pleasure Principle* as parable or fable, indicative of death insofar as it signifies a break in the child's bond with the mother, what John P. Muller characterizes as "the loss incurred in separation from the immediacy of maternal symbiosis" ("Language, Psychosis, and the Subject in Lacan," 31). Not surprisingly, yearning in *Jude* is often associated with the maternal.[15] As we have seen, it is right after Little Father Time asks Sue if he might call her "mother" that a "yearning" comes over him; the older Jude's yearning is also directed toward the maternal, as when, for example, he stumbles drunkenly toward Sue's apartment, not only possessed by "an unreasoning desire," but also "under the influence of a childlike *yearning* for the one being in the world to whom it seemed possible to fly" (173, emphasis mine).

One of the most peculiar manifestations of this yearning, however, takes place during a scene alluded to earlier, in which Jude walks into an inn he has frequented before, only to discover that Arabella has returned from Australia and is now tending bar in its tavern. From where he sits, he is able to watch Arabella without being seen by her, and the whole scene, in fact, has the appearance of a voyeuristic fantasy, as Jude observes a sexually charged exchange between Arabella and an undergraduate student, "a handsome, dissipated young fellow," who has just told her a suggestive story: "'O, Mr. Cockman, now! How can you tell such a tale to me in my innocence!' she cried gaily. 'Mr. Cockman, what do you use to make your moustache curl so beautiful?' As the young man was clean shaven the retort provoked a laugh at his expense" (237). Jude's voyeurism here seems to be fairly uncomplicated, as he listens to and watches the exchange between Arabella and Mr. Cockman (a signifier that rather blatantly suggests the particular focus of their exchange), observing the participants' gestures, faces, and figures in a large mirror that hangs behind the bar. As he does so, he is struck not only by the archness of Arabella's gestures, but also by the fullness of her breasts, noting that "her figure, more developed than formerly, was accentuated by a bunch of daffodils that she wore on her left bosom" (237). The undergraduate student soon leaves, asking for his change in a scene similarly agitated by playful erotic gestures: "She handed the change over the counter, in taking which he caught her fingers and held them. There was a slight struggle and titter, and he bade her goodbye and left" (237).

At this point, however, the scene takes an unusual turn. After watching with what is described as "the eye of a dazed philosopher," Jude moves into the area of the tavern where Arabella is working, and they exchange a few pleasantries, as she "idly" (and suggestively) allows "her fingers to rest on the pull of the beer-engine as she inspected him critically" (238). She then offers him a drink, only to have him decline her offer: "'Thanks, Arabella,' said Jude without a smile. 'But I don't want anything more than I've had.' The fact was that her unexpected presence there had destroyed at a stroke his momentary taste for strong liquor as completely as if it had whisked him back to his milk-fed infancy" (238). This scene begins with an erotic, or even masturbatory, fantasy on Jude's part, in which he inhabits the site of the voyeur, but the grounds of that fantasy shift quickly when another breast makes its presence felt.[16] In one of the most bizarre shifts in Victorian fiction, we move from Jude's rapt attentiveness to Arabella's breasts to a sudden loss of taste for strong liquor on his part, comparable, we are told, to the absence of that taste he would have experienced had he been transported, or "whisked," back in time to a state of "milk-fed infancy." And, as in some of the other scenes we have examined, we get the sense here of a drama occurring at levels not necessarily available to either the central figure or the narrative voice, but nevertheless making itself felt through a language that registers the pressure of occulted signifiers.[17]

How does this reference to "milk-fed infancy," with all of the rich and complex associations of the maternal breast invoked by that phrase, find its way into a scene involving otherwise rather grown-up activities? Both the image and its origin remain problematic, for while Jude's loss of taste for liquor is characterized as a "fact," it is a fact grounded in some rather slippery figural language. Are we to see the image as originating with the narrator or with Jude, or does it perhaps exist in some third ground, between these other two sites? It might also be thought of as a shifting kaleidoscopic combination of all of these, an indeterminate moment that eludes any attempt on our part to fix it in one position. Given the nature of this scene and the fantasy structures embodied by it, such a shifting subjectivity is appropriate, for as Laplanche and Pontalis point out in their essay "Fantasy and the Origins of Sexuality," while reveries and daydreams disclose a subject stabilized and "weighted by the ego" (13), fantasy is characterized by an absence of subjectivization. And thus in a fantasy such as Freud's "the father seduces the daughter," for example, we find "a scenario with multiple entries, in which nothing shows whether the subject will be immediately located as *daughter*; it can as well be fixed as *father*, or even in the term *seduces*" (13–14, Laplanche and Pontalis's emphasis).

But however difficult or impossible it might be to fix with certainty the site of consciousness behind this scene, it is nevertheless clear that the scene discloses Jude's position toward his own unconscious desires. It should not surprise us that Jude's gaze is situated in a field of fantasy, for the sexual relationship from the male perspective is in fact grounded in fantasy, or, as Lacan puts it, what man "relates to is the *objet a* and . . . the whole of his realisation in the sexual relation comes down to fantasy" (Mitchell and Rose, 157). The *objet a*, Lacan writes, "serves as a symbol of the lack . . . of the phallus, not as such, but in so far as it is lacking" (*Concepts*, 103), and therefore, a man makes love not so much with a woman as with an object of his fantasy in an attempt to fill the place of lack. Not surprisingly, Lacan characterizes man's role in the sexual relation as masturbatory, "the *jouissance* of the idiot" (Mitchell and Rose, 152).

In this respect, Marjorie Garson is only partially correct when she observes of Jude that "Hardy's protagonist is always denied access to a female body which would make him whole, and it is always the fault of a woman" (170), for while Jude may indeed seek wholeness through the female body and might even blame the woman for not making it possible, the fact that he looks for wholeness and does not find it is not his fault. We should not look, Hardy tells us, to blame either the man or the woman for this failure. It is simply the way things are, a condition of human subjectivity itself. Arguing along similar lines, Rosemarie Morgan speaks of Jude's ineffectuality as far as his sexual relationship with Arabella is concerned, suggesting that "all this phallic posturing notwithstanding," he appears at times as "an utterly puerile young man," occupying an "infantile" role in their relationship (*Women and Sexuality in the Novels of Thomas Hardy*, 139). And although the novel itself contests Morgan's reading, the scene in the tavern nevertheless seems to explore some of the ambiguous dynamics identified by Morgan.[18] For even as Jude is fascinated, maybe even excited, by the scene, he is also shown to be watching it through "the eye of a dazed philosopher," as if he is thrown off balance by what he sees—not up, as it were, to the blatant sexuality manifested by it. But other things are going on as well. In speaking of what Freud refers to as *Urphantasien*, primal or original fantasies, Laplanche and Pontalis note that such fantasies exist outside of any clearly grounded subjectivity, "beyond the history of the subject but nevertheless in history, a kind of language and symbolic sequence, but loaded with elements of the imagination, a structure, but activated by contingent elements" (*Fantasy*, 10). Primal or original fantasies also postulate retroactivity insofar as they "relate to the origins. Like myth they claim to provide a representation of, and a solution to, the major enigmas which confront the child. Whatever appears to the subject as something needing an explanation or theory, is dramatized as a moment of emergence, the beginning of a history" (11).

Such moments, Laplanche and Pontalis note, are necessarily located "beyond the history of the subject but nevertheless in history, a kind of language and symbolic sequence, but loaded with elements of the imagination" (*Fantasy*, 10). Filled with various and conflicting hungers, this scene in *Jude* registers a desire, primary and originary in nature, that can be articulated only symptomatically through its dimension of loss, as it depicts yet another example of yearning, captured in the psychoanalytically precise and richly layered image of "a milk-fed infancy."[19] Fantasy, Laplanche and Pontalis argue, "tries to cover the moment of *separation* between *before* and *after*, whilst still containing both: a mythical moment of disjunction between the pacification of need (*Befriedung*) and the fulfillment of desire (*Wunscherfüllung*)" (15). This scene in *Jude* moves toward the delineation of such a "mythical moment," as the scene shifts from Arabella's breasts to an inarticulated and much more original "primal hallucination" involving the maternal breast, a shift that would seem to take place in sites explicitly inaccessible both to Jude and to the narrative voice, but nevertheless registered through occulted signifiers that make their presence felt. As such, the scene would seem to testify to a fleeting recognition, lost as soon as it is gained, on Jude's part regarding the nature of his earlier masturbatory fantasies, as he understands that he cannot find either in Arabella or in any sexual relation what it is that he seeks.[20]

In his essay "On the Universal Tendency to Debasement in the Sphere of Love," Freud touches on this question when he speaks of "the possibility that something in the nature of the sexual instinct itself is unfavorable to the realization of complete satisfaction" (*SE*, 11:188–89). Lewis Carroll, in his own fashion, also acknowledges such frustrations in a wonderful scene in *Through the Looking Glass*. In it, the White Queen offers Alice a position as her "lady's-maid," promising her "two pence a week and jam every other day" (247). When Alice declines the offer, letting the queen know that she does not want any jam *today*, the queen tells Alice, "You couldn't have it if you *did* want it. The rule is, jam to-morrow and jam yesterday, but never jam *to-day*" (247). "It *must*," Alice objects, "come sometimes to 'jam today,'" but the queen assures her, "No, it can't. It's jam every *other* day: today isn't any *other* day, you know" (247). Completeness, like the White Queen's jam, can be had only tomorrow, never today, and tomorrow is always beyond the reach of a wounded and fragmented human subjectivity. Shortly after the moment in *Jude* in which Jude loses his taste for liquor, the text returns us to a more stable male gaze, as Jude notices the sexually charged atmosphere of the tavern, observing that "the faces of the barmaidens had risen in colour, each having a pink flush on her cheek; their manners were still more vivacious than before — more abandoned, more excited, more sensuous, and they expressed their sentiments and desires less euphemistically, laughing in a lackadaisical tone, without reserve" (240). However, there is still no jam, only an admittedly fascinating grape jelly.

The baby new to earth and sky,
What time his tender palm is prest
Against the circle of the breast,
Has never thought that "this is I";
But as he grows he gathers much,
And learns the use of "I" and "me,"
And finds "I am not what I see,
And other than the things I touch."
So rounds he to a separate mind
From whence clear memory may begin,
As thro' the frame that binds him in
His isolation grows defined.

ALFRED, LORD TENNYSON, *In Memoriam*

A passage in *Jude* that also shows up in Hardy's *Life* especially captures the nature of the traumatic wound of separation, while exploring its origins and effects.[21] In this scene, we find the young Jude lying on his back "on a heap of litter near a pig-sty," reflecting on the prospect of growing up: "As you got older, and felt yourself to be at the centre of your time, and not at a point in its circumference, as you had felt when you were little, you were seized with a sort of shuddering, he perceived. All around you there seemed to be something glaring, garish, rattling, and the noises and glares hit upon the little cell called your life, and shook it, and warped it. If he could only prevent himself growing up! He did not want to be a man" (57). I come at this scene somewhat indirectly, first turning my attention briefly to Tennyson's *In Memoriam* and Benjamin's remarks about Baudelaire. Written almost half a century later, this scene in Hardy revisits some of the same questions explored by Tennyson. In the lyric that serves as the epigraph for this section,

Tennyson looks at the wound or trauma of separation, focusing on the formation of human subjectivity, as he considers the ways in which we become aware of ourselves as something other than the other, or other than the mother, as the first quatrain makes clear. Tennyson's poem investigates such a moment of emergence or origin, what Laplanche and Pontalis describe as "the beginning of a history" ("Fantasy," 11). At the mother's breast—and here, as in Hardy, the breast is a metonymic signifier identifying a moment, whether real or imaginary does not matter, prior to individualization and subjectivity—the newborn baby "has never thought that 'this is I.'" Anticipating in striking ways the later inquiries by Freud and Lacan, Tennyson suggests that the process of individualization assumes the form of language, making itself felt as we come to know ourselves through the "use of 'I' and 'me.'" Our movement into human subjectivity, he argues, involves both loss and gain, for although we gain a sense of our uniqueness or individuality, we also learn that we are destined to exist apart as separate beings, forever divided from that which is not ourselves—or, as Tennyson puts it, each of us must learn that "I am not what I see / And other than the things I touch." To use Tennyson's language, this emergence of self-consciousness "binds" us in our new identity, dividing us from the world that we previously experienced as an extension of ourselves. Our "isolation grows defined" and is destined, Tennyson implies, to become even more defined, more binding, through nothing other than experience itself.

Even though Tennyson's language registers his ambivalence about this experience, he does not seem to consider it especially destructive or traumatic, in large part because he argues for the ongoing existence of this forged identity or self even beyond death. For although he argues that the human subject is formed or framed at particular moments in our early history, such as weaning from the maternal breast and the acquisition of language, Tennyson must believe (even though, as T. S. Eliot suggested some time ago, his doubt is finally stronger than his belief) that this subjectivity does not dissolve or reform at the moment of death.[22] If this were not the case—and Tennyson is clearly haunted by the possibility that it is not—then life itself, he feels, would be absurd, meaningless. For Hardy, on the other hand, the wound of separation is shattering and traumatic. Unlike Tennyson, he is not concerned with questions of eschatology, and the violence of the language he uses to describe this moment is striking and cryptic: What is the nature of the "sort of shuddering," for example, with which

Jude is "seized," and what is the origin of the "noises and glares" that bombard him? What does Hardy have in mind when he speaks of "the little cell called your life," and in what ways is this cell shook and warped? Similarly, what is the "something" that does all this damage? Although *Jude* itself gives us few answers to these questions, Freud's *Beyond the Pleasure Principle* does, for it too depicts a living cell bombarded, shook, and warped by things that are similarly glaring, garish, rattling.

Exploring further his thesis that "becoming conscious and leaving behind a memory-trace are processes incompatible with each other" (*Pleasure Principle*, 19), Freud imagines "a little fragment of living substance . . . suspended in the middle of an external world charged with the most powerful energies" (21). Pointing out that the "little fragment" would be killed if it did not defend itself against these energies by means of an outside shield or cortex, Freud stresses that the more intense the shocks of these stimuli are, the more alert consciousness has to be in order to protect the organism. However, such experiences, regardless of their intensity, do not have the capacity to linger or to become a part of our memory-traces. In fact, if an organism were able to remember all of the shocks that it received from the outside world, its system would soon become overloaded, and thus incapable of any longer protecting itself (19), dying "of a rose in aromatic pain," as Alexander Pope suggests, "tremblingly alive all o'er, / To smart and agonize at ev'ry pore" (*Essay on Man*, Epistle 1, ll. 197, 200).

In the midst of this violent and painful external reality, Freud argues, the "little fragment" desires to return to a time prior to life itself, to move toward a cessation of such experiences.[23] Lacan reads the death Freud speaks of as metaphorical rather than literal, as testifying to the fragmented or wounded nature of human subjectivity. The scene in *Jude* in which Jude reflects on the prospect of growing up registers the moment in which this wound takes place, but, like the earlier fantasy we looked at involving Arabella's breasts, it exists in a time both inside and outside of human subjectivity, for it is a mythical moment of emergence or origin, albeit one characterized, as the violence of Hardy's language indicates, by pain and trauma. And although Jude imagines a possible way out of all of this—"If he could only prevent himself growing up! He did not want to be a man (57)"—he is not yet ready to flee from that which he is. If I might turn to Lewis Carroll's *Through the Looking Glass* once again, we find in it a rather extended conversation about birthdays and growing older between Alice and Humpty Dumpty, and at one point, Alice observes that "one ca'n't help growing older" (162). Humpty Dumpty, however, tells her that while "one ca'n't perhaps . . . but two can. With proper assistance you might have left off at seven" (162). Alice, a most precocious little girl, understands only too well the drift of Humpty Dumpty's remarks, and immediately changes the subject: "What a beautiful belt you've got on, Alice suddenly remarked" (163). This death joke, so wonderfully embedded in Carroll's text, speaks to Alice about how life can be ended, but not until the end of *Jude* does the end of life come for its main character. Until then he must continue to grow older, repeating in various scenarios the trauma and pain of the originary moment of separation and loss. Jude's movement from circumference to center registers the creation of a wound or lack so profound that he seeks throughout his short life to fill in its emptiness with invariably inadequate substitutes.

Christminster, Jude suggests, "is the center of my universe to me, because of my early dream: and nothing can alter it" (391), but his "early dream" of the city bathed in light and splendor is itself but the image of yet an earlier dream in which beginning and end would merge into each other. "All instincts tend towards the restoration of an earlier state of things," writes Freud (*Pleasure Principle*, 32), in explaining that the repetition compulsion is a manifestation of the death instinct, and Jude confesses, "I should like to go back there [to Christminster] to live, perhaps to die there" (391). Marjorie Garson speaks of Sue as being a rival to Christminster (167), but Jude and Sue both have their own dreams, locating them in different metonymic signifiers— Jude in Christminster, as we have seen, and Sue, as we will see, in capturing once again or reexperiencing what she refers to as "the life of my infancy and its freedom" (191). In this respect, Sue is no more of a rival to Jude's dreams than he is a rival to hers. Sue too desires to be restored to "an earlier state of things," telling Jude at one point, "I like reading and all that, but I crave to get back to the life of my infancy and its freedom" (191). Sue's language here is precise: what she experiences is a craving or hunger, a desire that by its very nature cannot be satisfied. "The memory of that first state of Freedom and paradisaic Unconsciousness has faded away into an ideal poetic dream. We stand here conscious of too many things," wrote Thomas Carlyle in 1831 ("Characteristics," 44), and Sue is indeed conscious of too many things.

In her case, however, one might argue that the worst gift Sue can get is the one she most wants. Earlier in the novel Phillotson tells Gillingham, "I wouldn't be cruel to her [Sue] in the name of the law" (298), but time, his own sufferings, and the lingering echoes of Arabella's agenda-driven advice—"there's nothing like bondage and a stone-deaf taskmaster for taming us women. Besides you've got the laws on your side" (389)—weaken his resolve and he becomes increasingly aligned with the law. And although he does not literally follow Gillingham's advice—"I think she ought to be smacked and brought to her senses" (296)—he does finally attempt to satisfy her desire for penance and punishment. Sue approaches Phillotson's bed as errant daughter/wife, seeking to receive from him, in his capacity as father, lawgiver, and punishing lover, the pain and humiliation she must endure if she is to achieve that impossible redemption she seeks. "I shall try," she promises, "to learn to love him by obeying him" (437). In one ceremonial exchange suffused with ritualistic overtones, Phillotson gives Sue three chances to change her mind about coming into his bed. Especially telling is the exchange that takes place after his second warning:

> "So think again."
> "I have thought—I wish this!"
> "That's a complaisant spirit—and perhaps you are right. With a lover hanging about, a half-marriage should be completed. But I repeat my reminder this third and last time."
> "It is my wish! . . . O God!"
> "What did you say O God for?"
> "I don't know!" (478)

Phillotson is taken aback by God's sudden intrusion into this exchange, and Sue's response—"I don't know"—to his question "What did you say O God for?" is a telling one. In this scene, the identities of God and Phillotson begin to merge, becoming almost indistinguishable, and thus when Sue climbs into Phillotson's bed, hoping to do penance for unnamed sins by opening her heart to God and her legs to Phillotson, she has already acknowledged the ambiguous identity of her bed partners. Most of Hardy's marriages are rather miserable, but there is perhaps a certain perverse fitness or Sadean symmetry about Sue and Phillotson's second marriage, involving, as it does, a coming together of one who wants to be punished with one who wants to punish, a scenario of potentially unspeakable delights.[24]

Plots carry their own logic. There is a tendency of plots to move towards death.

DON DeLILLO, *Libra*

Our cultural neurosis, Freud suggests, is, like sublimation and repression, the price we pay for being human, and thus it is not an illness that can be cured. And yet Jude and Sue seem especially vulnerable, more scarred than most by this experience, and we have to wonder why. The particular violence and self-destructive tendencies associated with their history seem inextricably connected with their susceptibility to what Hardy variously refers to as "the ache of modernism" (*Tess*, 129) and "the modern vice of unrest" (*Jude*, 131).[25] One of the characteristics of modernity is the possession of a historical and philosophical perspective toward one's place in history, what Jürgen Habermas describes in *The Philosophical Discourse of Modernism* as "the reflective treatment of traditions that have lost their quasinatural status" (2), and Jude and Sue are acutely conscious of their place in a particularly defined historical moment. Jude, for example, describes himself as grappling with the questions "which thousands are weighing at the present moment in this uprising time" (398), "a paltry victim," as he puts it, "to the spirit of mental and social restlessness, that makes so many unhappy in these days!" (399).

When Jude refers to Sue as "a product of civilization" (191), she insists, "I am not modern. . . . I am more ancient than medievalism, if you only knew" (187). But Sue, in spite of her protestations, is neither ancient nor medieval, but very much modern. In fact the historical distinctions of ancient, medieval, and modern that she draws on in denying Jude's characterization of her are themselves categories of modern thought, and she, no less than Jude, is defined by and ravaged by "the ache of modernism." By the end of the novel, Jude has found a way of breaking the ice that would not succumb to his earlier imprecations (115), as he visits Sue and insures his own death at the same time. He travels through a landscape of death, the inside turned outward, that mirrors his death-haunted desire, "a dreary, strange, flat scene, where boughs dripped, and coughs and consumption lurked, and where he had never been before" (439). Sue's narrative has been prolonged, but her movement toward the end has also been accelerated, Mrs. Edlin pointing out, for example, that the second marriage between Sue and Phillotson resembles a funeral more than a wedding. Sue, Mrs. Edlin tells Arabella, is tired and miserable, "years and years older than when you saw her last. Quite a staid, worn woman now" (490).

Again, Benjamin's remarks about Baudelaire and the relationship between modernity and the unconscious can help shed light on Hardy's novel, and specifically on Sue and Jude's particular vulnerability to the shocks and warps of the modern world.[26] Benjamin argues that both Proust's *mémoire involontaire* and Baudelaire's *correspondances* refer to a notion of time and memory that can be best understood in the context of Freud's suggestion that "becoming conscious and leaving behind a memory trace are processes incompatible with each other" (*Pleasure Principle*, 19). Noting that only Freud's unconscious, that which has not happened to the subject as an experience (*Erfahrung*), can be a component of the *mémoire involontaire* (160), Benjamin observes that such memories are transindividual insofar as they allow the individual to connect with the past and its rituals and ceremonies. "Put in Proustian terms," Benjamin writes, "this means that only what has not been experienced explicitly and consciously, what has not happened to the subject as an experience, can become a component of the *mémoire involontaire*" (160–61). Such experiences are "the data of remembrance [as opposed to memory]—not historical data, but the data of prehistory. What makes festive days great and significant is the encounter with an earlier life" (182). As Benjamin notes, Baudelaire might have understood the price that the modern age exacts of its citizens, but he could not himself avoid paying it: "He indicated the price for which the sensation of the modern age may be had: the disintegration of the aura in the experience of the shock. He paid dearly for consenting to this disintegration" (190).

In *Jude*, the aura has disintegrated as well, for Hardy's text suggests that what Jude and Sue share in common is precisely this absence of any transindividual memory. The primary festivals in *Jude*—those of fertility and fecundity (the Agricultural Fair) and of memory (Remembrance Day)—stand in sharp contrast to Jude's and Sue's histories. What Baudelaire and Proust both imagine, Benjamin suggests, is an isolation that is unique to modernity, a condition of being severed from "the realm of ritual" (181), the festive days and data of prehistory. Benjamin's remarks bear directly on Hardy's last novel, for what has not been observed emphatically enough, I think, is the profoundly sustained isolation that surrounds both Sue and Jude. Hardy late in his life claimed, "the best way to find a starting point for a piece of writing was to go to some work by a major writer—Carlyle, for instance—and read at random until one came across an image or idea that stimulated one's own inventiveness" (*Biography*, 88); and although it is impossible to find any one "starting point" for *Jude*, Hardy's novel calls to mind Carlyle's earlier description of an isolation and exile from which there is no escape: "The Thinker," writes Carlyle, "must in all senses wander homeless, too often aimless, looking up to a Heaven which is dead for him, round to an Earth which is deaf" (56). Except for their companionship, volatile as it is, Jude and Sue are homeless wanderers, severed from any cultural unit or group (such as trade union, church, neighborhood, extended family) that might create a sense of community or home. This condition, or certainly its severity, is unique to *Jude*; in none of Hardy's other novels, including *The Return of the Native* and *Tess of the d'Urbervilles*, is it so pronounced.

However, this isolation has other implications for *Jude* as well. Mourning, as we have seen earlier, is how we cope with the hole that death creates in the real, the way in which, as Lacan argues, the symbolic order enables us to acknowledge this gap and respond to it, albeit in necessarily inadequate ways. And yet while this whole "system of signifiers" ("Desire," 38), namely the symbolic order itself, is impeached by death, found guilty of being inadequate to the task, mourning is nevertheless all that we have available to us. And, as Lacan points out, the work of mourning is supported—in fact, actualized—by group and community, the "mainstays" of which he, elsewhere in the same essay, refers to as "ritual values," characterized by him as "essential factors in human economy" (38, 40). Proper or sufficient mourning, he suggests, is made possible by the "ritual values" found in "group and community," in that they enable us to deal with the hole in the real and to move finally beyond it. If such values are made inaccessible, then the gap or hole remains open in destructive or damaging ways.

Jude and Sue have been severed from such values, and thus their melancholia—mourning experienced on an unconscious level—remains open-ended, and they are incapable of resolving or completing it. Their isolation from a transindividual past renders them particularly vulnerable to that cultural and spiritual malaise Hardy identifies as "modernism," characterized by the inability to connect with the unconscious powers that Freud would associate with the erotic. Thus it is not surprising that the landscape of *Jude* resembles that of a necropolis, and that, at the end, not only are the children dead, but Jude too is dead, and Sue is essentially dead. The pig's genitals (variously repressed in different editions of *Jude*, but nonetheless returning and making themselves felt) that slap Jude along the side of the face, so rudely awakening him from his daydreams of culture and advancement, are slung not only by Arabella, but by Hardy as well.[27]

It is a crude gesture, perhaps, but an effective one. What is most disturbing about *Jude* is not its criticism of antiquated marriage laws or class-structured university policies—such topics, after all, tend to yellow rather quickly with age—but rather its relentless indictment of Western humanism and its ameliorative beliefs.[28] Arabella not only stands in the way of Jude's youthful aspirations toward refinement and learning, but also exists as a reminder of the text's unsettling critique of Western civilization and its humanistic impulses.[29] But she is more than this. After Jude's death, a scene, as Millgate characterizes it, of "despair, bitterness, and death" (*Career*, 335), what is left and where do we turn—or, more importantly, where does the text turn? Although *Jude* is perhaps more focused on questions of closure than any other nineteenth-century novel, its ending still remains open by virtue of other voices that are heard after Jude has died and Sue has descended into silence, both destined to become narrativized by others. Mrs. Edlin, "the infallible mouth-piece of a wisdom much greater than her own, but which she has confirmed from her own experience," as C. H. Sisson describes her in his introduction to *Jude* (22), is still around, and we hear a good deal of her voice toward the end of the novel.[30]

The final voice we hear is not Mrs. Edlin's, but Arabella's. Sisson calls Arabella "a stupid woman" (24), but her comments are often anything but stupid, and she is, in fact, an astute reader of Sue and Jude. If the text initially attempts to repress Arabella, marginalizing her presence by introducing her as "a complete and substantial female animal, no more, no less" (81), so too have some readers found in her something slightly embarrassing, a kind of textual bad smell that triggers their own censoring tendencies.[31] Perry Meisel suggests that "perhaps Arabella is right when she speaks the last words of the novel" (*Thomas Hardy*, 156). In fact, she speaks not only the last words of the novel, but the final words of the last novel Hardy would write, and there is little doubt that she is indeed right when she says of Sue, "She's never found peace since she left his arms, and never will again till she's as he is now!" (491).[32] Nor can we ignore Vilbert, whose arm steals around her waist at the end of the novel, for if the ancient sounds of ritual and ceremony that once resonated through Farmer Troutham's field are no longer heard by Jude or Sue, they have not disappeared completely. Vilbert tells Arabella, for example, that he created a "love-philtre" from the hearts of doves that he captured by placing rock salt in his dovecote and that he discovered the recipe for this aphrodisiac in the folklore of the ancients through the "study of their writings" (364). Jude learns early on that Vilbert's stories are less than reliable, but even his fictions and tall tales attest to his kinship with the fairy tale and its figures. He is a horny Wordsworthian leech gatherer, a Cumberland beggar gone to seed, and both the speed of his walk and the lust in his heart make him seem an ageless anomaly in a world in which children are born ancient and die young. In a world haunted by death, he seems deathless, protected by the quack medicine he peddles and by the gods of the scam and the road that he worships.

Arabella is a truly chthonic figure, not only making use of Vilbert's aphrodisiac, but also bringing nature into complicity with her cunning and high spirits, both in the production of her dimples and her seduction of various men. She is also one of literature's great genital characters, catching Jude's attention as well as ours in her own unique fashion, and soon afterward telling her girlfriends, "I shall go mad if I can't give myself to him altogether" (93). Later on, as she once again schemes to get Jude to the marriage chapel and into bed, she complains, "Tis hard for a woman to keep virtuous with so many young men" (448). "How hard the sex cops have to work, always having to start over, to block women's threatening return" (69) suggests Hélène Cixous, and Arabella's presence keeps them busy. By repeatedly calling our attention to a picture of Samson and Delilah during moments of conflict between Jude and Arabella (89, 117, 457), an uneasy and repressive narrative voice casts Arabella in the role of a castrating Delilah to Jude's Samson. Garson regards Arabella as a "scapegoat" (160), but also suggests that it is "all too obvious" that "Arabella is a castrating woman" (159). It may be obvious, but not necessarily true. By casting Arabella as a destructive Delilah and Jude as her Samson-like victim, Hardy seems to take part in the fin-de-siècle misogyny that Carolyn J. Dean speaks of: "The misogyny of much fin-de-siècle art and literature—the portrayal of women as monsters, vampires, or abominable criminals and men as their victims—was in many ways a male fantasy of female potency [and male impotence] which linked cultural dissolution and decay to female power" (*The Self and Its Pleasures*, 59).[33] But the text seems to know better, and this analogy is unpersuasive. If Mrs. Gamp informs the world, "Gamp is my name, and Gamp my nater" (367), Arabella, feeling stifled in her widow's weeds, similarly tells her friend Abby, "I must be as I was born!" (387). "Feelings are feelings! I won't be a creeping hypocrite any longer" (386), she confesses. And just as Sairey Gamp's presence is preceded by a wine-scented hiccup borne on the winds, so too is Arabella's attempt to give voice to the cliché-ridden language of orthodoxy subverted by gastrointestinal bubblings that refuse to remain repressed: "'Hang her [Sue]!—I mean, I think she was right,' hiccuped Arabella. 'I've my feelings too, like her; and I feel I belong to you in Heaven's eye, and to nobody else, till death us do part! It is—hic—never too late—hic—to mend!'" (454).

Arabella persists, always landing on her feet and affirming through her gestures and words an allegiance to life rather than death, expression rather than repression. As Arabella leaves Jude's dead body alone in the room and migrates toward the festival and Vilbert, we get the sense that she will survive, enclosed by her own unerring body as well as by the arms of various men.[34] Arabella wrestles finally a begrudging admiration out of a text that half-heartedly tries to resist her charms, for, like that band of itinerants who protest Phillotson's firing by wreaking havoc both on the school and on the stuffed shirts in it, she embodies a folk spirit that only briefly raises its subversive head.

The novel, Bakhtin suggests, struggles against a conventionality, often feudal in structure, in which "all ideological forms, that is, institutions, become hypocritical and false, while real life, denied any ideological directives, becomes crude and bestial" (*The Dialogic Imagination,* 162). If Arabella is "crude and bestial," she is also "real life," the embodiment of a life force that the text locates in the presence of a folk tradition that is so deep and real that Hardy can give no name to it. This folk tradition persists in *Jude,* unwashed and unpolished, but also unvanquished. But if Arabella's attempt to speak the language of orthodoxy is disrupted by symptomatic hiccups that will not remain repressed, the folk language of the carnivalesque, aligned in Hardy and Dickens (as in Freud) with the unconscious, remains for the most part muted in *Jude.* Arabella utters the final words in the last novel Hardy would write, but by the time she does, there are few people around left to hear them.

Notes

Introduction

1. "Desire" is a problematic and ambiguous term that has been used, and arguably even overused, by students of the nineteenth-century novel. Nancy Morrow's *Dreadful Games: The Play of Desire in the Nineteenth-Century Novel* devotes a portion of one chapter to *Jude the Obscure*. Morrow does not acknowledge Freud's and Lacan's theoretical work on desire, but is instead interested in the play of fate and in how the novel's legal structures are able to "crush the spirit of play inherent in Jude's dreams and aspirations" (106). Priscilla L. Walton's *Patriarchal Desire and Victorian Discourse: A Lacanian Reading of Anthony Trollope's Palliser Novels* draws, as do I, on Lacanian theory, but she regards desire as an instrument of patriarchy, identifying it with the wish to be the source of control and meaning. Lacanian desire, I argue, has its origin in an unconscious sense of lack or loss that is at the heart of human subjectivity, and not in the willed attempt to be in control. Except for its chapter on *Wuthering Heights*, Eugene Goodheart's *Desire and Its Discontents* is concerned with modernist writers such as Joseph Conrad, D. H. Lawrence, and Thomas Mann. In a section entitled "The Freudian Narrative and the Case of Jacques Lacan," however, Goodheart finds Lacan guilty of favoring desire, arguing that "like the utopians of desire, though for different reasons, Lacan resolves the conflict in favor of desire" (152). Goodheart characterizes his study calling into question a discourse that regards desire as synonymous with freedom and liberation (3), and groups Lacan with writers such as Norman O. Brown, Herbert Marcuse, and R. D. Laing, whom he sees as making such a connection. The latter three writers can be linked only in the most general of ways, and Lacan definitely does not belong here; he does not regard desire as a movement toward freedom and liberation but rather connects it with the tragic and wounded condition of the human subject.

2. Lacan has in mind here Freud's comment in *The Interpretation of Dreams*: "We have treated as Holy Writ what other writers have regarded as an arbitrary improvisation" (552).

3. Robert Schweik, "The Influence of Religion, Science, and Philosophy on Hardy's Writings," 60.

4. For example, see Kincaid's *Child-Loving: The Erotic Child and Victorian Culture*.

5. Michel Foucault makes much the same point: "If interpretation can never be completed, this is quite simply because there is nothing to interpret. There is nothing absolutely primary to interpret, for after all everything is already interpretation, each

sign is in itself not the thing that offers itself to interpretation but an interpretation of other signs" ("Nietzsche, Freud, Marx," 3).

6. Referring to "the essence of the Freudian discovery, the decentering of the subject in relation to the ego," Lacan writes, "If what I say is false, it becomes extremely difficult to read the slightest of Freud's texts and understand anything about it" (*Seminar II*, 148).

7. Gayatri Spivak, for example, observes that Freud advises us to focus our attention particularly on the spots in a text, spoken or written, where it seems uneven or broken: "Where the subject is not in control of the text, where the text looks supersmooth or superclumsy, is where the reader should fix his gaze, so that he does not merely read but deciphers the text, and sees its play within the open textuality of thought, language, and so forth within which it has only a provisionally closed outline" (translator's preface to Derrrida's *Of Grammatology*, xlvi).

8. "Discontinuity," Lacan writes, "is the essential form in which the unconscious first appears, for in a spoken or written sentence something stumbles." He notes that "Freud is attracted by these phenomena, and it is there that he seeks the unconscious" (*Concepts*, 25).

9. Ian Watt's 1957 *The Rise of the Novel* contains, of course, the classic examination of the mimetic structure of Defoe's *Robinson Crusoe* in light of the capitalistic project of his age. Also see Peter Hulme's more recent *Colonial Encounters: Europe and the Native Caribbean, 1492–1797.*

10. In "The Counterworld of Victorian Fiction and *The Woman in White*," U. C. Knoepflmacher regards this particular aspect of the ending of the novel as "at best pathetic" (5), but Stewart speaks of it as a powerful but also risky artistic choice on Eliot's part (118). Maggie, Stewart suggests, "has worked back to her very first memory, canceling all that has intervened, remaking the birth of consciousness into a single blissful swoon to death" (117), and for her brother, Tom, drowning "takes place in the depths of his long stagnant nature" (119), and he is shattered into life just before the end.

11. Jean Laplanche and J. B. Pontalis provide a nice gloss for this passage. In speaking of Lacanian desire, they point out that while "need is directed towards a specific object and satisfied by it" and demand "is essentially a demand for love," desire itself "appears in the rift which separates need and demand; it cannot be reduced to need since, by definition, it is not a relation to a real object independent of the subject but a relation to phantasy; nor can it be reduced to demand, in that it seeks to impose itself without taking the language or the unconscious of the other into account, and insists upon absolute recognition from him" (*The Language of Psycho-analyis*, 483).

12. Contrasting Luce Irigaray's sense of desire with Lacan's, Kathryn Bond Stockton notes that while "Lacan's tragic sense is now familiar" (*God between Their Lips*, 41), Irigaray breaks with Lacan and "steal[s] Lacan's (theory of) desire: she shaves it (and, thus, puts a new face on it) and claims it as 'woman's own.' The new face she puts on desire is pleasure" (49). Irigaray, Stockton suggests, finds in the "mirrored images of the genital lips" an "identification that enjoys its own splitting" (49).

13. Lacan writes, for example, that desire "is also what is evoked by any demand beyond the need that is articulated in it, and it is certainly that of which the subject

remains all the more deprived to the extent that the need articulated in the demand is satisfied" (*Ecrits*, 263).

14. Freud's account of this game and its implications appears in *Beyond the Pleasure Principle*, 8–9.

15. Jonathan Scott Lee, *Jacques Lacan*, 11.

16. Lacan writes, "I compare it [Freud's discovery of the unconscious] with the approach of a Newton, an Einstein, a Planck, an a-cosmological approach in the sense that all these fields are characterized by tracing in the real a new furrow in relation to the knowledge that might from all of eternity be attributed to God" (*Concepts*, 127).

17. See, for example, Copjec's discussion of Foucault's remarks concerning the "pleb" and "plebness" (6–7).

18. In her chapter entitled "The Education of Desire and the Repressive Hypothesis," Stoler examines "the tangled coexistence of Freud and Foucault . . . in analyses of race relations" (169), noting that "saying 'yes' to Foucault has not always meant saying 'no' to Freud, not even for Foucault himself" (168). She adds that "the differences are striking but so are some of the points on which they are complementary, if not the same" (169).

19. Foucault argues that because psychoanalysis moves in the same direction as the other sciences, but with "its gaze turned the other way," it can move "toward the moment—*by definition inaccessible to any theoretical knowledge of man*, to any continuous apprehension in terms of signification, conflict, or function—at which the contents of consciousness articulate themselves, or rather stand gaping, upon man's finitude" (*Order*, 374, emphasis mine).

20. Cf. Joan Copjec on this point: "Language's opacity is taken as the very *cause* of the subject's being, that is desire, or want-to-be. The fact that it is materially impossible to say the whole truth—that truth always backs away from language, that words always fall short of their goal—*founds* the subject" (35, emphasis Copjec's).

21. Ronald R. Thomas, for example, suggests not only that psychoanalysis is "a particularly insistent and demanding intertext for literary analysis," but also that "the nineteenth century novel was the fiction that allowed psychoanalysis to be thought" (*Dreams of Authority*, 9, 14). For James Mellard, "It is Lacan's imperative to study language that makes Lacanian theory so amenable to the reading of works of literature, especially in the analysis of the subject and of human subjectivity in fiction" (*Using Lacan, Reading Fiction*, 4); and Juliet McCannell even more emphatically maintains that "it is literature and not language or linguistics that is the proper model for figuring Lacan" (*Figuring Lacan*, 14). Eugene Goodheart makes a point similar to McCannell's, but sees literariness as a limitation of Lacanian theory, when he suggests, "It should hardly surprise the reader of Lacan to discover that his main audience is a literary one, for the Lacanian subject—or more accurately Lacanian desire—is ultimately the matter of literature" (148). Actually, Lacan's original audience, namely, those who attended his lectures and seminars, was made up of a diverse group of individuals—writers, students, lawyers, doctors, anthropologists, philosophers, artists, and many others—and while his audience today includes students of literature, it is by no means limited to them. Lacanian desire has a great deal to do with language and thus indirectly with literature, but it is hardly just "the matter of literature." In any case, as Lacan points out, Freud some

time ago recognized this connection (admittedly a problematic one) between literature and psychoanalysis; he suggests (in his "In the Question of Lay Analysis") that the disciplines that would make up his ideal faculty of psychoanalysis include "the history of civilization, mythology, the psychology of religions, literary history, and literary criticism" (*Ecrits*, 76). For more on the relationship between literature and psychoanalysis, see Shoshana Felman's introduction to *Literature and Psychoanalysis*.

22. For example, see Steven Weinberg's *The First Three Minutes: A Modern View of the Origin of the Universe*.

23. Florence Emily Hardy, *The Later Years of Thomas Hardy*, 117.

24. Ibid., 42.

Chapter 1

1. "Fragment of an Analysis of a Case of Hysteria" (1905), better known as the case history of Dora. In *The Standard Edition of the Complete Psychological Works of Sigmund Freud*, 7:77–78. Unless otherwise noted, all future references to Freud's writings are to this edition, hereafter cited as *SE*. Both volume and page number will be cited.

2. Bakhtin observes that the "most important of all human features for the grotesque is the mouth. It dominates all else. The grotesque face is actually reduced to the gaping mouth" (*Rabelais and His World*, 317).

3. Lacan will later make much the same point, albeit somewhat less graphically: "The unconscious is that chapter of my history that is marked by a blank or occupied by a falsehood: it is the censored chapter. But the truth can be rediscovered; usually it has already been written down elsewhere. Namely: in monuments: this is my body" (*Ecrits*, 50).

4. Freud makes no distinction between daydreams and fantasies, actually suggesting that "the best-known productions of phantasy are the so-called 'day-dreams,'" for, as he puts it, "imagined satisfactions of ambitious, megalomanic, erotic wishes . . . flourish all the more exuberantly the more reality counsels modesty and restraint" (*SE*, 16:372).

5. In speaking of Dickens's veiled references to masturbation in *Oliver Twist* and *Great Expectations*, William Cohen has observed of the Victorian novel that it "encrypts sexuality not in its plot or its announced intentions, but in its margins, at the seemingly incidental moments of its figurative language, where, paradoxically, it is so starkly obvious as to be invisible" (*Sex Scandal*, 32).

6. The rather cumbrous original title of *Martin Chuzzlewit*, used only during its serial publication, explicitly identified the concern of the novel with questions of kinship structures, filiation, and inheritance: "The Life and Adventures / of Martin Chuzzlewit / His Relatives, Friends, and Enemies / Concerning / All His Wills and Ways; / With a Historical Record of What He Did, / And What He Didn't: / Showing, Moreover, / Who Inherited the Family Plate, Who Came in for the Silver Spoons, / And Who for the Wooden Ladles. / The Whole Forming a Complete Key to the House of Chuzzlewit." Dickens never did use his motto, dropping it on the advice of John Forster, who feared that it might offend Dickens's readers.

7. Steig regards the Pinch-Pecksniff story line as a "detailed parody of the oedipal conflict" ("Pinch and Pecksniff," 184), suggesting that in Tom Pinch we find evidence of how one can "successfully resolve his Oedipus complex" (185). Dickens's novel seems to know better than this.

8. Copjec argues here, as elsewhere in her book, for "metalanguage's impossibility" and thus for the fact that society cannot be revealed or disclosed in an analytic moment, since its being, or generative principle (the "real," in Lacanian terms) necessarily escapes or transcends the relations and facts constituted by society.

9. Estella is, of course, younger than Charity when she secretly watches the fight between Pip and Herbert, but the scene nevertheless suggests that she is excited by what she sees. Several critics have spoken of this scene as disclosing a precocious sexuality fueled by violence on Estella's part, thus perhaps helping account for her later marriage to Bentley Drummle. (See Darby, "Listening to Estella," 218, and Garnett, "The Good and the Unruly in *Great Expectations*—and Estella," 37–38.)

10. David-Ménard notes that the question of "how a thought can be diverted into bodily innervation [e.g., in cases of hysteria] while at the same time it remains a thought" constitutes one of the central problems of psychoanalysis from Freud to Lacan. See *Hysteria*, 13. In his case history of Dora, Freud observes, "We must recall the question that has so often been raised, whether the symptoms of hysteria are of psychical or somatic origin, or whether, if the former is granted, they are necessarily all of them psychically determined" (*SE*, 7:40). Ned Lukacher suggests that David-Ménard, in trying to find a way out of this epistemological paradox, locates the "body of jouissance" neither in the psychical or physiological, but rather in "the realm of signifying discourse" (*Hysteria*, x). She writes, for example, "Reality exists for us only inasmuch as language structures our desire, inasmuch as grammar contributes its resources to the construction of that desire. If this is true of our relation to objects of the world, it is hard to see how our relation to our own bodies could be any different" (66). Or, as she puts it, "Our bodies exist for us inasmuch as we symbolize them" (66).

11. Steig suggests that "the point is clearly that 'no harm' means no danger of sexual feelings" ("Pinch and Pecksniff," 182).

12. In comparing Dickens to Charlotte Brontë and George Eliot, John Kucich notes in *Repression in Victorian Fiction* that Dickens often "seems closest to making the explicit connection between self-negating libido and death that is formulated in the later Freud, in Bataille, and elsewhere" (204). Kucich also suggests that I, along with Garrett Stewart and several others, "continue to see death as a purely negative, empty moment," one that "Dickens and his characters strive to overcome" (205n12). However, drawing on Heidegger's concept of death as that which gives authenticity to our lives, my essay on *David Copperfield* ("Remembrances of Death Past and Future") argues that although David's narrative may attempt to erect a wall of words between himself and death, the power and haunting beauty of the novel derives in large part from his inability to do so. Death in Dickens is never empty or "negative," but rather that which causes us to experience human anguish in front of ourselves.

13. See chapter 5, "Paradise Lost," of Alexander Welsh's *From Copyright to Copperfield* for further discussion of the significance of Milton's text in Dickens's novel.

14. George Ford argues that the first chapter of *Martin Chuzzlewit* alienated Dickens's readers by turning its satirical impulses in the same direction as the discarded epigraph—namely, on the Victorian family itself (*Dickens and His Readers*, 43–54). See Bowen, Wales, Sadoff, and Ser for further discussion of the opening chapter of *Martin Chuzzlewit*.

15. Although John Bowen regards "the nature of inheritance and family obligation" to be "of only marginal concern to the book that follows" (*Other Dickens*, 181), he nevertheless notes that the first chapter of *Martin Chuzzlewit* "is one of the most remarkable of any novel" and that it has been treated with "contempt" by most critics of the novel (185). Like Bowen, I am convinced that we need to take this wonderful first chapter seriously, but I am also persuaded that questions of inheritance and family obligation are more than marginal concerns in this novel.

16. If Dickens came across the idea of acquired characteristics indirectly through the writings of Erasmus Darwin or Jean Baptiste Lamarck, the questions of genealogy and origin remain problematic, for notions of genealogy, as Loren Eiseley suggests in *Darwin's Century*, seem to have had their origin in ancient hypotheses and folk beliefs. "What Erasmus Darwin and Lamarck both did," writes Eiseley, "was to apply a very ancient hypothesis, one might almost say a folk-belief, to the explanation of continuing organic change and modification" (50). Dickens's ideas may have had other sources as well. As Fred Kaplan notes, Dickens's friendship with the mesmerist John Elliotson began sometime in 1838, and Elliotson's influential *Human Physiology* (1835–40) had started as a translation of *Institutiones Physiologicae*, by the German physician J. F. Blumenbach (*Dickens and Mesmerism*, 21). Blumenbach is reduced to a series of footnotes in the later editions of Elliotson's work, but Dickens nevertheless refers to him in the opening chapter of *Martin Chuzzlewit* when he speaks of his theory about the swinish qualities of "the descendants of Adam'" (21). In addition to Myron Magnet's study "*Martin Chuzzlewit* in Context," Jerome Meckier's *Innocent Abroad: Charles Dickens's American Engagements* considers these questions. See Meckier's chapter entitled "Dickens Discovers Dickens."

17. See Jacques Derrida's "That 'Simple Movement of the Finger,' Writing and the Prohibition of Incest," in *Of Grammatology*, 255–68. Paul De Man argues, however, in *Blindness and Insight*, that Derrida carries out deconstructive activities on a text by Rousseau that already deconstructs itself (102–41).

18. Marx writes, for example, that "this communism, as fully developed naturalism, equals humanism, and as fully developed humanism, equals naturalism" ("Economic and Philosophic Manuscripts of 1844," 84).

19. Magnet points out, for example, that *Martin Chuzzlewit* focuses "on how radically far from being a pure production of nature the truly human being is" (321).

20. See R. S. Pengelly's 1921 "*Martin Chuzzlewit*: Elijah Pogram," 389.

21. This excrementality is evident in the names that Dickens gives to the American newspapers being hawked. While some of the papers, the *Keyhole Reporter*, the *Family Spy*, the *Private Listener*, the *New York Peeper*, and so on, suggest the voyeuristic and salacious nature of the American press, it is the *New York Sewer* that comes in for his special attention. "Here's the Sewer, Here's the Sewer! Here's the wide-awake Sewer; always on the look-out; the leading Journal of the United States, now in its twelfth thousand, and still a printing off: Here's the New York Sewer" (220).

22. For a more extensive examination of abjection and how it is inscribed in the site of the feminine, albeit in another novel by Dickens, see my essay, "Filth, Liminality, and Abjection in Charles Dickens's *Bleak House.*"

23. In speaking of *Great Expectations,* Robert M. Polhemus points out that "sexuality in the novel lurks at the edge of consciousness and in the murk of nature, symbolized by low forms of life or rotten matter." However, Polhemus does not identify this "murk of nature" as feminine, but associates it with Bentley Drummle and Orlick, arguing that the meaning of such images is that "women and their bodies are menaced and exploited by the force of the sex drive" (*Erotic Faith,* 153). Rodney S. Edgecombe, on the other hand, speaks of the malaise or "topographic disaffection" that we find in *American Notes* and traces its origins to Dickens's repugnance at the practice of slavery he found during his American visit ("Topographic Disaffection in Dickens's *American Notes* and *Martin Chuzzlewit*).

24. This dream is centrally important because it was on the basis of it, or rather his interpretation of it, that Freud came to the conclusion that dreams are in fact "the fulfillment of a wish." As he tells us, it was through this particular dream that "the Secret of Dreams" was revealed to him (*Interpretation,* 153).

25. Freud writes, "During the summer of 1895 I had been giving psycho-analytic treatment to a young lady who was on very friendly terms with me and my family" (*SE,* 6:106).

26. Although Freud indicates that disgust usually has "not one but . . . several causes," he also stresses the fact that its etiology is invariably sexual. See, for example, his case history of Dora ("Fragment," *SE,* 7:31).

27. The male-dominated world of Elijah Pograms, Scadders, Hannibal Chollops, and Major Pawkins anticipates the homoerotic bonds that Leslie Fiedler and others have located in nineteenth-century American fiction. Equally striking, however, is the virtual absence in the American sections of women as either subjects or the objects of erotic desire. Women are either parodically and asexually represented, like the famous literary ladies, or barely represented at all. When found, women in the American sections exist outside of the ambivalent paths of desire seen in the Pecksniff and Chuzzlewit clans. The only woman who plays a fairly important role in the American episodes is an Englishwoman whose family Mark Tapley befriends on the ship bound for America and whom he runs into again in Eden. Although she and her family are also suffering from the disease-ridden atmosphere of Eden (see chapter 33 of *Martin Chuzzlewit*), they help nurse Martin and then Mark back to health. Like Martin and Mark, they return to England.

28. In the introduction to her edition of *American Notes,* Patricia Ingham notes that it, like other forms of travel writing, "carried much ideological baggage," observing, for example, that "whereas the Orient stood to the West as female to male, the significance of this rebellious offspring of the 'mother country' was a source of confusion and even fear" (xiii). America as a site of confusion and fear—and desire—continues to haunt Dickens's writing in the pages of *Martin Chuzzlewit.* But in the novel, I would argue, we find America's anger and aggression being directed along Oedipal lines toward England as the site of paternal authority and prestige, while the female is situated not in the Orient, but in the topography of America itself.

29. Aggressivity, Lacan argues, is inherent to our condition, given the fact that our ego or *moi* is structured on imaginary objects that we fear or suspect possess a wholeness or stability that we lack. See "Aggressivity in Psychoanalysis," in *Ecrits*, 8–29.

30. Barbara Hardy suggests in "Change of Heart" that although young Martin's transformation is slow and complex, Dickens's rendering of it makes it seem like "a single leap of vision," while Stuart Curran focuses on the Adamic overtones of the Eden episodes, arguing that what we find in the case of young Martin is nothing less than a quest for his own soul ("The Lost Paradises of *Martin Chuzzlewit*").

31. Meckier suggests of this dialogue that "Dickens struggled . . . to reconcile his allegiance to the revolutionary theories of Rousseau with a growing awareness of himself as a middle-class Englishman" (10). He also writes, "Disappointments in America separated him [Dickens] permanently not just from thinkers like Rousseau but from Marx, Engels, and other indiscriminate admirers of the proletariat" (18). As I argued earlier, I do not believe that Dickens does in fact separate himself from the arguments of Rousseau and Marx, and I would not characterize Marx as an indiscriminate admirer of the proletariat.

32. See Jacques Lacan, "Desire and the Interpretation of Desire in *Hamlet*," 15. Lacan argues that the phallus is the primary signifier, not only anchoring language itself, but also serving as the major metaphor for a loss or lack that all, men and women alike, experience by virtue of being human. Also see Lacan's "The Signification of the Phallus," in *Ecrits*, 281–91.

Chapter 2

1. In *The Works of William Makepeace Thackeray* 14:350. Unless otherwise noted, all future references to *Notes of a Journey from Cornhill to Grand Cairo*, cited by page number, will be from this particular volume and edition.

2. A disclaimer here is in order. Although I am concerned with certain psychological dynamics found in Thackeray's essay, I am also aware of Emile Durkheim's 1901 suggestion that "whenever a social phenomenon is directly explained by a psychological phenomenon, we may be sure that the explanation is false" (quoted in Fredric Jameson, "Imagery and Symbolic in Lacan," 339). As Jameson reminds us, "We will do well to keep Durkheim's stern warning constantly before us as a standard against which to assess the various models psychoanalytic criticism has provided" (339). Questions involving the nature, characteristics, and implications of the presence of imperialism in nineteenth-century British literature do not lend themselves to easy causalities, unambiguous generalizations, or single voices, and I am not arguing that the imperialistic urges or dynamics in Thackeray's essay can be "directly explained by a psychological phenomenon" (Durkheim, in Jameson, 339), or by any other single phenomenon, for that matter. Rather I am concerned with the ambiguous and complex impulses and desires behind the narrative of his text and with how their presence creates tensions and unresolved conflicts, while giving his essay a disturbing power (and sadness) that neither Thackeray nor Ray acknowledges.

3. See, for example, Patrick Brantlinger and Deborah Thomas.

4. The full title of Kinglake's book is *Eothen; or, Traces of Travel, Brought Home from the East* (New York: Wiley and Putnam, 1845).

5. Edward Said notes that the "memory of the modern Orient disputes imagination, sends one back to the imagination as a place preferable, for the European sensibility, to the real Orient" (*Orientalism*, 100–1).

6. Cf. Freud, who observes in his "General Theory of Neuroses" that "the true artist . . . makes it possible for other people once more to derive consolation and alleviation from their own sources of pleasure in their unconscious which have become inaccessible to them" (*SE*, 16:376).

7. As Laplanche and Pontalis write, Freud "had pointed out from the beginning that the subject revises past events at a later date ('nachtraglich'), and that it is this revision which invests them with significance and even with efficacity or pathogenic force" (*Language*, 112).

8. Lukacher does not, in his words, "restrict 'primal scene' to the conventional psychoanalytic understanding of the term: the child's witnessing of a sexual act that subsequently plays a traumatic role in his or her psychosexual life" (24).

9. Lacan considers Sartre's discussion of the gaze to be "one of the most brilliant passages in *Being and Nothingness*" (*Concepts*, 84), but he nevertheless takes exception to Sartre's representation of the gaze as a "seen gaze," arguing instead that "it is not the annihilating subject, correlative of the world of objectivity, who feels himself surprised, but the subject sustaining himself in a function of desire" (84–85; also see 89, 102).

10. Said, for example, notes that for the Western traveler the Orient seemed to contain "sexual promise (and threat), untiring sensuality, unlimited desire, deep generative energies . . . eliciting complex responses, sometimes even a frightening self-discovery" (*Orientalism*, 188). Deborah Thomas similarly argues that "Thackeray's imagination was undoubtedly stimulated by the secrecy and eroticism associated with the proximity of harems and the sight of veiled women in the streets" (45).

11. Such a fantasy exists in history and yet also outside history, or, as Laplanche and Pontalis put it, "it lies beyond the history of the subject but nevertheless in history; a kind of language and symbolic sequence, but loaded with elements of the imagination; a structure, but activated by contingent elements" ("Fantasy," 10).

12. In writing of the transformations of puberty, Freud notes that "psycho-analytic investigation shows . . . how intensely the individual struggles with the temptation to incest during his period of growth and how frequently the barrier is transgressed in phantasies and even in reality" (*SE*, 7:225n3).

13. The foregoing of subjectivity is impossible, that is, unless we are talking of psychosis, the failure of the subject to move into and assume language.

Chapter 3

1. Bonaparte observes, for example, that we often find in Gaskell's fiction evidence of her "turning her own life into a matter of her art" (11). In *Bearing the Word*, Margaret

Homans finds in Gaskell a writer in conflict with the male voices of Romantic poetry. See, for example, her reading (33–39ff.) of Gaskell's 1836 letter written from Sandelbridge (*Letters*, 5–8).

2. "What is important in the work," Pierre Macherey observes, "is what it does not say. What the work *cannot say* is important, because there the elaboration of the utterance is acted out, in a sort of journey to silence" (*A Theory of Literary Production*, 87).

3. *Ruth* has its origin, at least in part, in Gaskell's concern with prostitution—going back at least as far as 1849 or 1850, when she wrote to Dickens about Angela Burdett-Coutts's emigration plan for prostitutes and, more specifically, her concerns about the plight of a Miss Pasley, a sixteen-year-old prostitute who had been seduced by a physician, fallen into the hands of a female procurer, and turned to prostitution to support herself. Gaskell befriended her in 1849, after Pasley was incarcerated in the Manchester jail for theft, only to discover, to her horror, that the prison doctor was the same man who had seduced her. Gaskell's letter to Dickens about Pasley's history and situation appears in her *Letters*, 98–100. For an account of the relationship between Gaskell and Pasley, see Winifred Gérin's *Elizabeth Gaskell*, 127–29. Gérin argues that Gaskell wrote *Ruth* because "the total injustice of such a situation shocked her inexpressibly, and moved her to write the book which was to be a plea for a different and workably Christian morality" (128). It is almost certain that Gaskell was also familiar with W. R. Greg's influential 1850 essay, "Prostitution," because of its references to *Mary Barton*; for an examination of the possible influence of this essay on Gaskell, see Sally Mitchell's *The Fallen Angel: Chastity, Class, and Women's Reading, 1835–1880*.

4. Jenny Uglow observes, for example, that "the atmosphere of the final volume of *Ruth* has a peculiar disconcerting intensity. Ruth's guilt and self-torment appear ludicrously out of proportion to her offence" (336). Rosemarie Bodenheimer too points out the contradictions that have been noted in the novel, even though she argues that the novel itself rebukes these contradictions (153).

5. George Eliot suggests that *Ruth* "will not be an enduring or classical fiction. . . . Mrs. Gaskell seems to me to be constantly misled by a love of sharp contrasts" (*Letters*, 86).

6. Sigmund Freud, "Mourning and Melancholia," in *SE*, 14:246.

7. In comparing George Eliot and Gaskell, Jenny Uglow observes that "in the fiction of both writers the maternal positive has a dark, sexual negative. If women can be creators, they can also be destroyers—or, more often, the destroyed" (467).

8. Homans argues, for example, that Gaskell and Woolf can show such language and only by depicting it as "dependent on interruption and silencing" (21).

9. Bodenheimer notes that Gaskell regarded the history of Pasley, the young prostitute she befriended, as "a story of parental abandonment" (152), and that "with its elements rearranged and romanticized, this story, and its emotional focus, formed the basis for *Ruth*" (152). Also see Schor, "Plot," 32–37, for a discussion of the importance of the mother, and especially the dead mother, in Gaskell.

10. "Feminism," writes Jacobus, "has tried to supply this lack by making the mother the unremembered heroine of the psychoanalytic text—she who would make it whole if we could only tell the entire unexpurgated story" (16). But, as Jacobus notes, "there was never a prior time, or an unmediated relation for the subject (whether masculine

or feminine), except as the oedipal defined it retroactively. The mother is already structured as division by the oedipal" (18).

11. Benjamin makes this remark in his essay "Some Motifs in Baudelaire," in which he also cites Proust's remark about Baudelaire: "There is no one else who pursues the interconnected *correspondances* with such leisurely care, fastidiously and yet nonchalantly—in a woman's smell, for instance, in the fragrance of her hair or her breasts" (*Illuminations*, 183).

12. For Proust, Benjamin reminds us, "only what has not been experienced explicitly and consciously, what has not happened to the subject as an experience, can become a component of the *mémoire involontaire*" (160–61).

13. For example, Bodenheimer argues that "Ruth haunting the Welsh landscapes is, if anything, even more a solitary child of nature than she was before the seduction" (157).

14. Schor remarks, for example, that "Ruth's innocence, when it fits so absolutely with natural right and natural beauty, *is* perfect" (65, emphasis Schor's), that "Ruth's 'loving heart' makes her innocent as well as a victim" (66). Jill Matus similarly suggests that "Gaskell must present Ruth as innocent and unknowing" (*Unstable Bodies*, 119), and Amanda Anderson speaks of Ruth as "so innocent that only some time after the seduction does she become aware of her morally and socially compromised position" (*Tainted Souls and Painted Faces*, 127).

15. Uglow refers to Ruth's "hidden sexuality" (328). I am arguing, of course, that little is hidden in this scene.

16. Copjec echoes Ruth's remarks here in her discussion that Lacan's idea of love is that of "giving what you do not have." As she notes, "We accept someone's gifts and ministrations because we love him; we do not love him because he gives us gifts" (143).

17. R. W. B. Lewis includes the "Fragment of Beatrice Palmato" as an appendix to his *Edith Wharton: A Biography* (548). Carol de Chellis Hill makes imaginative use of this fragment in her novel *Henry James's Midnight Song*. In his "Flowers of Manhood: Race, Sex, and Floriculture from Thomas Wentworth Higginson to Robert Mapplethorpe," Christopher Looby argues that flowers are often associated with male genitalia as well.

18. Although she is speaking specifically of the blush in Gaskell's *North and South*, Mary Ann O'Farrell's comment in *Telling Complexions* is also applicable to Ruth's flushed skin: "As an interpretation of capillary action, the blush is an attribution of desire to the body, a fantasy of the body that conceives of the body as writing its desire on itself, as if—blushing—the body is asking to be read" (81).

19. Amanda Anderson writes of the "apparent noneffect on Ruth of her entry into sexuality," arguing along with Rosemarie Bodenheimer that such omissions "signal Gaskell's insistence on fallenness as a social construction" (133). Anderson is primarily interested in how "the novel stresses Ruth's unconsciousness and then reroutes her redemptive entry into judgement through maternity" (129), but her Ruth, unlike Gaskell's, is a strikingly incorporeal figure.

20. Although she errs, I think, in dividing *Ruth* into narratives of liberation and repentance, Jeanette Shumaker does note that "Ruth is vibrantly sexual during the liberationist narrative" ("Gaskell's *Ruth* and Hardy's *Tess* as Novels of Free Union," 158), but without suggesting how and where we see this vibrant sexuality.

21. Jenny Uglow also notes that Ruth's hair suggests "restless energy, unfocused yearning, and sensuality" (328). In the one scene, however, that especially lingers over Ruth's languorous wildness and the sensuality of her hair, the male gaze is absent. As Sally approaches Ruth to crop her hair, she "walked up to the beautiful, astonished Ruth, where she stood in her long, soft, white dressing gown, with all her luxuriant brown hair hanging dishevelled down her figure" (144).

22. If Schor speaks of Ruth's "aesthetic prostitution," Lansbury argues that if Ruth had been sharper, she might have turned her good looks to financial advantage: "Had she been quick-witted she would have made her appearance her fortune, but her beauty and stupidity, coupled with extreme poverty, made her a predestined victim" (26). In any case, Gaskell must have known when she put the orphaned Ruth in a dressmaker's establishment that such places and the girls who worked in them were frequently associated by the nineteenth-century public with prostitution. In many respects, in fact, the circumstances of Gaskell's Ruth correspond rather closely to the profile of the nineteenth-century prostitute. Judith Walkowitz, for example, points out that prostitutes often began quite young (around sixteen years old), often because of seduction, although not necessarily by upper-class men; that they were frequently orphans; and that often a woman turned to prostitution as "a part time or seasonal activity to supplement her meager salary, as shopgirl, needlewoman, or domestic servant" (*Prostitution and Victorian Society*, 16–18, 46).

23. In speaking of his wife, he tells Jemima, "I have trained her to habits of accuracy very unusual in a woman" (222).

24. Coral Lansbury, for example, observes that "the sexual implications of the scene are made explicit when, after cropping Ruth's hair as short as a boy's, Sally cannot bear to part with her trophy" (26).

25. Jill Matus regards Jemima as a young woman whose knowledge of Ruth's past serves as a "powerful catalyst for examining her own ardent and passionate nature" (127), but nevertheless speaks of Ruth herself as falling from "pure unknowingness" and thus as passionless (126).

26. Critics as well find evidence of this transformation. Shumaker, for example, writes, "Through being a competent and kindly nurse, Ruth regains much of the status she had lost through scandal" (162).

27. Cf. Corbin, 212, Goodwin, 158. In *David Copperfield*, a novel almost contemporary with Gaskell's, Dickens gives us a vivid description of the filth and decay of London: a river site "looked as if it had gradually decomposed into that nightmare condition, out of the overflowings of the polluted stream." Dickens writes that a prostitute, Martha, seems "a part of the refuse it had cast out, and left to corruption and decay" (626).

28. Hilary Schor comments about this passage, "While the novel . . . at moments seems to yearn for such stability—both of self and perception—it is finally committed to a world of shifting, active, changeful response" (74).

29. This section of the novel creates difficulties for Anderson's argument that Ruth moves toward redemption through maternity—"which, for Gaskell, constitutes a form of heightened consciousness sympathetic at its origin, non-instrumental because self-negating" (129)—for, by the end of the novel, Leonard is no longer even in the picture, having been negated, as far as his mother is concerned. Patsy Stoneman finds in *Ruth*

"significant failures of ideological coherence" (*Elizabeth Gaskell*, 100), noting that "of all the critics who have written of Ruth's 'unnecessary' death, not one has noticed that she dies insane. Yet her madness signals the failure of the novel's conscious ideological project" (116). But Shumaker similarly notes that "Ruth's insanity conflicts with the notion that her death reinforces the penitential narrative" (164), finding the ending of the novel to be "even more torn than is the rest of the novel" (165).

Chapter 4

1. He says of this week, "The history of the interval which I pass thus over must remain unrecorded" (433). In *Dead Secrets*, Tamar Heller notes that "as editor-in-chief of the novel's many narratives, Hartright has the power to solicit writing from other characters, to arrange the order of the narrative, and even to delete what seems extraneous" (115).

2. Jenny Bourne Taylor writes that Walter Hartright undergoes a "process of reperception and detection" and that this "forms a more tangled web" in the text (*Secret Theatre*, 110–11). She also suggests that Walter must suppress parts of his narrative in order to appear as a "resolution agent" (127). Similarly, Gloria Jean Masciarotte argues that the three voices in the novel undercut one another, thus undermining not only the reader's capacity to judge what is actually happening, but the very notion of self or subjectivity itself.

3. Given the numerous ways in which *The Woman in White* calls attention to its own gaps, fissures, and rough edges, it is worth noting that Collins himself speaks of the "smoothness" of his text—of the "hundreds of little 'connecting links'" in his narrative as helping maintain "the smoothness, the reality, and the probability of the entire narrative." Cited by Philip O'Neill, *Wilkie Collins*, 98.

4. "Fragment of an Analysis of a Case of Hysteria," in *SE*, vol. 7. All future references to this case history, hereafter cited by page number, will be to this edition and volume.

5. The death of the father, Freud points out, does not remove his power, but rather increases it, since his paternal interdictions become internalized, translated into acts of deferred obedience: "The dead father became stronger than the living one had been—for events took the course we so often see them follow in human affairs to this day. What had up to then been prevented by his actual existence was thenceforward prohibited by the sons themselves, with the psychological procedure . . . of 'deferred obedience.'" (*SE*, 13:143).

6. Albert D. Hutter suggests, for example, that "what is stolen from Rachel is both the actual gem and her symbolic virginity" ("Dreams, Transformations, and Literature," 242).

7. In his case history of the Wolf Man, as he explores the unconscious connections made by the Wolf-Man between the castration complex and faeces, Freud notes that "'faeces,' 'baby,' and 'penis' thus form a unity, an unconscious concept (*sit venia verbo*)—the concept, namely, of 'a little one' that can be separated from one's body" (*SE*, 17:84). Freud uses the German word *Kleinen*, variously translated into English as "little one" or "little thing": "Der Kot, das Kind, der Penis ergeben also eine Einheit,

einen unbewußten Begriff—sit venia verbo—den des vom Körper abtrennbaren Kleinen" (*Gesammelte Schriften von Sigmund Freud*, vol. 8 [Leipzig: Internationaler Psychoanalytischer Verlag, 1924], 526).

8. In the same passage in *Totem and Taboo*, Freud develops this ambivalence more fully: "In their unconscious there is nothing they would like to do more than violate [taboos], but they are afraid to do so; they are afraid precisely because they would like to, and the fear is stronger than the desire" (31). Desire, in this case, as Freud points out, is also unconscious.

9. D. A. Miller regards this scene as "the novel's 'primal scene,'" which "it obsessively repeats and remembers . . . as though this were the trauma it needed to work through" (190). Also see G. Pederson-Krag's "Detective Stories and the Primal Scene." Although *The Woman in White* is not a detective novel in the same sense, for example, as is *The Moonstone*, Geoffrey Hartman's comparison of the scene of suffering or pathos in detective fiction to Freud's primal scene is still pertinent. He suggests that both resemble "a highly condensed, supersemantic event like riddle, oracle, or mime," what he identifies as "a spectacle we can't interpret or a dumbshow difficult to word" ("Literature High and Low," 207).

10. While recently teaching *The Woman in White* to a small group of undergraduate honors students, I had an opportunity to test Lacan's definition of metaphor. I asked the students, about fourteen in all, to describe Laura's first entrance into the novel, relying solely on their memory of the scene. After some slipping and sliding—"She was in the room with Marian," "Walter sees her in another room"—the students were drawn into commentary by my refusal to help them out. One student suggested, somewhat uneasily, that she thought it had something to do with "female problems." After a few seconds of embarrassed silence, another student spoke up, recalling that, yes, the scene does mention female troubles, or "something like that," and that she had been puzzled by the strange language of the scene. At this point, a number of the other students chimed in, their own recollections, bewilderment, and curiosity engaged, and the group soon retrieved the occulted term, moving toward the conclusion that the passage could be referring to menstruation.

11. The authors of *Corrupt Relations* note, for example, that "as a daughter" Laura "is the victim of a father empowered by a patriarchal authority that defines women as appendages" (115).

12. Tamar Heller suggests that Walter's "assertion of his 'manliness' in establishing a pseudofamily (for all it looks like a Romantic *ménage à trois*) reverses the situation at the beginning of the novel, when he was forced to share the genteel poverty of his mother and sister" (137).

13. Heller describes it as "an extraordinarily feminist . . . work" (112), and Maurice Richardson, in his introduction to the Dutton edition of *The Woman in White* (New York: Dutton, 1972), characterizes Collins as a "radical feminist" (vii).

14. Anne Cvetkovich sees this "something wanting" as "not a thing but a relation" between Anne and Laura, the appearance of Laura significant only because of its relationship—what Cvetkovich identifies as a "deferred action," Freud's *Nachträglichkeit*—to the earlier appearance of Anne Catherick. Cvetkovich too finds something uncanny about this aspect of the novel (84–86).

15. Cvetkovich notes, for example, that in *The Woman in White* the female body "powerfully sensationalizes or embodies other meanings" (93). She also observes that "the crime of the father [Mr. Fairlie] gets written on the bodies of the two women, which bear the traces of his secret in an immediately visible form" (90), arguing that the mystery created by the female body in this text "can be connected to Marx's description of commodity fetishism as the production of a secret" (91).

16. D. A. Miller, in arguing for the presence of "male homosexual desire" in *The Woman in White*, perhaps reinforces the phallic presence of Fosco in remarking on the relative size of Fosco's and Walter's swords (188). Heller finds in Fosco's relationship with Percival a betrayal of his revolutionary origins and of feminism, as well as an embodiment of homoerotic desire (130–31).

17. Nuel Pharr Davis's *The Life of Wilkie Collins* describes the nature of Collins's own physical deformities (52–54).

18. See Neil Hertz's "Medusa's Head: Male Hysteria under Political Pressure," 166.

19. In "Dora's Secrets, Freud's Techniques," Neil Hertz suggests that the problematics of this case history extend beyond the questions of transference and countertransference. "Suppose," he asks, "what Freud missed, or did not wish to see, was not that he was drawn to (or repelled by) Dora, but that he 'was' Dora, or rather that the question of who was who was more radically confusing than even nuanced accounts of unacknowledged transferences and countertransferences suggest?" (126).

20. SE, 7:69–70. The place of the mother in Collins's text suggests some other interesting correspondences between *The Woman in White* and Freud's case history of Dora. In Collins's novel, the mother is neither heard directly nor seen, but her presence is nevertheless crucial. Similarly, as one critic has observed, mothers in Freud's case histories (including that of Dora) are often problematically missing: "It is as if Freud could not bring himself to look closely at the mother, the figure his theory proclaims to be so central. . . . They all appear as silhouettes against the rich background of other relationships; other entanglements" (Iza Erlich, "What Happened to Jocasta," *Bulletin of the Menninger Clinic* 41 [1977]: 284. Quoted in Madelon Sprengnether, "Enforcing Oedipus," 54n).

21. J. Hillis Miller examines the implications of this particular metaphor in his "Ariadne's Broken Thread: Repetition and the Narrative Line." Also see his "Arachne's Broken Woof." Nancy K. Miller's "Arachnologies: The Woman, the Text, the Critic" examines some of the same issues from a feminist perspective.

22. Cf. Lacan: "It [the phallus] can play its role only when veiled, that is to say, as itself a sign of the latency with which any signifiable is struck, when it is raised (*aufgehoben*) to the function of signifier. The phallus is the signifier of this *Aufhebung* itself, which it inaugurates (initiates) by its disappearance" ("The Signification of the Phallus," *Ecrits*, 288). Jonathan Scott Lee's remarks are helpful in glossing Lacan's comments: "The phallus," Lee points out, "is the ultimate *point de capiton*, the signifier that fixes the meaning of the signifying chains of every subject's discourse, by virtue of its being 'veiled' or repressed. The phallus is present beneath every signifier as the signifier that has been repressed, and as such every signifier in effect is a metaphor substituting for the phallus" (*Jacques Lacan*, 66–67).

23. Ellie Ragland-Sullivan makes this point rather nicely: "Desire cannot be chased

beyond the navel of the dream into the Real nor beyond the primordial signifying chain of repressed representations. Certain things can never be known" (117).

Chapter 5

1. Although Hardy was not familiar with Freud's work on the unconscious, in the late 1890s he was reading the writings of Arthur Schopenhauer and Eduard von Hartmann, and was familiar with von Hartmann's work on the will as unconscious. But, as Schweik notes in addressing the question of the influence of Schopenhauer and von Hartmann on Hardy's thought, "What can be said with greatest certainty is that Hardy's readings of and about Schopenhauer and von Hartmann confirmed some ideas he had arrived at independently or that he might earlier have derived from Mill, Spencer, Huxley, and others" ("Influence," 70). Freud too was familiar with Schopenhauer's work. In speaking of the unconscious, Peter Gay notes that Freud "could discover very similar formulations in the memorable epigrams of Schopenhauer and Nietzsche" (*Freud*, 128), and that Freud actually points out in the preface to the fourth edition of the *Three Essays on Sexuality* (1920) that "it is some time since Arthur Schopenhauer, the philosopher, showed mankind the extent to which their activities are determined by sexual impulses— in the ordinary sense of the word" (*SE*, 7:134).

2. In his introduction to *Beyond the Pleasure Principle*, Gregory Zilboorg notes that "the tone of the book, the mannerisms of its style are vigorous, poignant, almost controversial; Freud it seems was still combatting his opponents rather than trying to instruct his proponents" (viii).

3. In *Thomas Hardy: A Biography*, Michael Millgate describes Tryphena as "pretty, lively, and intelligent," noting that "the absence of her name from the pages of *Early Life* has in recent years been highlighted (rather than made good) by suggestions that she had a passionate love affair with Hardy during the summer of 1867 and bore him an illegitimate son in 1868, but did not marry him because they were in fact not cousins but uncle and niece" (105). Millgate also adds, however, that there is no "evidence capable of withstanding scholarly or even common-sensical scrutiny" (105) for any of these speculations.

4. For compelling evidence that this poem refers to Tryphena Sparks, see Samuel Hynes's explanatory notes in his edition of *The Complete Poetical Works of Thomas Hardy*, 1:364–65.

5. J. Hillis Miller, *Thomas Hardy: Distance and Desire*, passim. Miller's study examines the ways in which we find inscribed in Hardy's writings a desire for that which is in the distance, that is to say, removed from the desiring subject. However, it does not look specifically at *Jude*.

6. Sophoclean echoes are heard throughout *Jude*, from the image of the family curse and Sue's references to the House of Atreus, to Arabella's statement at the end of the novel that Sue has "never found peace since she left his arms, and never will till she's as he is now" (491)—an observation that, as Millgate points out (*Career*, 324), echoes the closing lines of *Oedipus Rex*. Jude's characterization of himself as "neither a dweller among men nor ghosts" similarly invokes Antigone's description of herself as "alive to

the place of corpses, an alien still, / never at home with the living nor with the dead" (188).

7. As if all of this were not enough, Hardy also invokes (295) Bernardin de Saint-Pierre's *Paul and Virginie* (1821), an immensely popular story of two young people who are raised together as children of nature, calling each other brother and sister and finally becoming lovers.

8. For an interesting reading of this particular scene in *Jude*, see James Kincaid's "Girl-Watching, Child-Beating and Other Exercises in *Jude the Obscure*." Kincaid reads this scene as a variation of the classic pornographic scene of the child being beaten, arguing in fact that "all of Jude's punishments . . . amount to direct or displaced versions of the spanking of children, highly erotic and infinitely repeatable" (141).

9. "The order of the law," Lacan notes, "can only be conceived on the basis of something more primordial, a crime" ("Desire," 42), and, he adds, each of us must repeat this crime in our own lives, reenacting it and thus suffering, through the law, the punishment of symbolic castration: "Oedipus and each one of us potentially at some point of our being, when we repeat the Oedipal drama—renews the law on the level of tragedy, and, in a sort of baptism, guarantees its rebirth" (42).

10. Ramón Saldívar argues, for example, that "natural law" in *Jude* is an illusory construction ("*Jude the Obscure* and the Spirit of the Law").

11. Hardy maintained that he was not permitted to "dwell upon" the fact that "though she has children, [Sue's] intimacies with Jude have never been more than occasional" (Florence Emily Hardy, *Later Years*, 42). But he is stressing here the point that Sue dreads marriage because of the irrevocable sexual commitment that it would seem to involve. In "Compromised Romanticism in *Jude the Obscure*," Michael E. Hassett sees Jude and Sue as Romantics whose vision of life is unattainable, and Marjorie Garson similarly speaks of Jude's desire as "being intrinsically unrealizable" (*Hardy's Fables*, 157), but connects it to Hardy's feelings about the body.

12. Freud makes this remark in his *The Interpretation of Dreams* (SE, 4:197). Earlier, he had written to Wilhelm Fliess (3 December 1897): "My longing for Rome is, by the way, deeply neurotic. It is connected with my high school hero worship of the Semitic Hannibal, and this year I did not reach Rome any more than he did from Lake Trasimeno." See *The Complete Letters of Sigmund Freud and Wilhelm Fliess, 1887–1904*, 285. For an examination of Rome as the city of Freud's dreams, see Carl Schorske's *Fin-de-Siècle Vienna: Politics and Culture*, 190.

13. Maria Dibattista observes of *Jude the Obscure* that "the murderous force of the literal everywhere prevails in this novel intellectually fascinated and morally bound by the laws governing the origin, development, and obsolescence of letters" ("Eroteleptic Narrative," 93).

14. Jonathan Lee points out that for Lacan the phallus as signifier "is not anything that any man or woman could possibly 'have,'" and thus, "precisely because no one can *have* the phallus, it becomes that which all want to *be*" (*Lacan*, 67). This particular aspect of Lacan's theory has generated a great deal of discussion, especially among feminist theorists. See, for example, Richard Feldstein and Judith Roof's *Feminism and Psychoanalysis*. In their respective introductions to *Feminine Sexuality* (1–26, 27–57), Juliet Mitchell and Jacqueline Rose provide a judicious review of this controversy. Also see

Ragland-Sullivan's "Beyond the Phallus," in *Jacques Lacan and the Philosophy of Psychoanalysis*, 267–308.

15. As Ragland-Sullivan notes, "The tragedy of the human condition is implicit in Lacan's theory that both the object and goal of the drive towards constancy converge in the Desire to be desired; in other words, to be recognized by the mother so that the infant feels one with her" (73).

16. Rosemarie Morgan argues that Hardy introduces masturbatory fantasies into the novel much earlier, when Jude is sexually aroused as he dwells on his first encounter with Arabella. In speaking of the passage in which Hardy writes—suggestively, she argues—that "a compelling arm of extraordinary muscular power seized hold" of Jude and pulled him away from his study of the New Testament, she notes that in Jude's case, "no amount of urging hand and mind to the Testament will harden the spirit against roused flesh" (139).

17. "The creative spark of the metaphor," Lacan writes, "flashes between two signifiers, one of which has taken the place of the other in the signifying chain, the occulted signifier remaining present through its (metonymic) connexion with the rest of the chain" (*Ecrits*, 157).

18. When Arabella sees Jude looking "alive and lusty" (363) at the Agricultural Fair, she immediately asks Vilbert for a potion of his love philter, eager to get Jude back into bed.

19. Laplanche and Pontalis provide a footnote that nicely glosses this particular scene from *Jude*: "The Freudian model [of fantasy] is incomprehensible unless one understand that it is not the real object, but the lost object; not the milk, but the breast as signifier which is the object of primal hallucination" ("Fantasy," 15n36).

20. Christopher Lane similarly notes that "Hardy's psychological wisdom stems from his suspicion, to quote Lacan, that 'there is no sexual relation' without the fantasy of complementarity, and that the sexes fundamentally are riven by asymmetry" (*The Burdens of Intimacy*, 274n34).

21. See Ian Gregor's reading of this passage, identified by him as something of an anthology piece, and what he sees as "the shifting relationship of the narrator to his protagonist" (*The Great Web*, 28–29). Perry Meisel too alludes to this passage, noting that "the cell of the young Jude's consciousness . . . is shaken by the calls of both the spirit and the flesh" (*Thomas Hardy*, 141).

22. I have in mind T. S. Eliot's remark that *In Memoriam* "is religious not because of the quality of its faith, but because of the quality of its doubt. Its faith is a poor thing, but its doubt is a very intense experience" ("In Memoriam," 200–201).

23. Arguing that "all instincts tend towards the restoration of an earlier state of things" (32), namely, a time prior to consciousness itself, Freud suggests that the repetition compulsion is a manifestation of the death instinct: "We shall be compelled to say," writes Freud, "that the aim of all life is death" (32).

24. Kincaid writes that "for Sue, there are no grandly expiring days or nights, just a humiliating surrender to Phillotson's punishments, which she, like the child of the comic strips . . . believes are deserved" ("Girl-Watching," 146). When Phillotson discovers Sue hiding in the closet in order to avoid his sexual advances, she attributes her behavior to what she identifies as "the universe, I suppose. Things in general, because

they are horrid and cruel" (282). Kincaid seems to regard Sue Bridehead as a victim—if not of the universe or things in general, then of the reader, Jude, men in general.

25. See David DeLaura's article "'The Ache of Modernism' in Hardy's Later Novels" for a further examination of what he identifies as the "contemporary matrix" of Hardy's modernism, especially as it is found in such figures as Clymn Yeobright of *The Return of the Native* and Angel Clare of *Tess of the d'Urbervilles*.

26. For a fuller examination of Charles-Pierre Baudelaire and Walter Benjamin and their particular place in regard to the question of modernity, see Habermas, 8–16 passim.

27. Comparing the 1895 first English edition of *Jude the Obscure* (Osgood and McIlvaine) with the 1903 "new edition" brought out by Hardy's new English publishers, Macmillan and Company, Robert C. Slack points out that the most striking textual revisions were those Hardy made to the scene in which Arabella throws the pizzle of a pig at Jude ("The Text of Hardy's *Jude the Obscure*"). Another nineteenth-century novelist, Mrs. Oliphant, said of this scene that it was "more brutal in depravity than anything which the darkest slums could bring forth" (331), and Slack suggests that Hardy, "no doubt sensitive to the many outcries like Mrs. Oliphant's, deliberately emasculated the passage in his revision" (331). "In his revision," writes Slack, Hardy "consistently shied away from 'that piece o' the pig,' and the scene is of course weakened" (335). As Slack also points out, however, Hardy had had to make concessions for serial publication before, and "by comparison this was a minor yielding" (335). Although Hardy's textual revisions made this first exchange between Arabella and Jude, as well as the description of the piece of the pig that initiated it, considerably less graphic than in the original edition, there can be little doubt in the attentive reader's mind about what is going on in this scene.

28. In this respect, as well, Hardy and Freud have something in common. Toward the end of *Beyond the Pleasure Principle*, Freud dismisses the notion of "an instinct toward perfection at work in human beings" (36). "I have no faith," he writes, "in the existence of any such internal instinct and I cannot see how this benevolent illusion is to be preserved" (36).

29. Peter A. Dale regards Hardy's work as "a definite rejection" of both evolutionary meliorism and scientific humanism, insisting on Hardy's pessimism against modern attempts to read him as a meliorist ("Thomas Hardy and the Best Consummation Possible," 202, 208).

30. Mrs. Edlin's presence—as well as that of Jude's aunt—would seem to weaken Garson's suggestion that "the female voice is a sinister presence in the novel" (163), unless Garson intends to suggest that only young female voices are sinister.

31. T. R. Wright, for example, speaks of Arabella "and the degrading sexuality for which she stands" (*Hardy and the Erotic*, 122). Millgate observes that "Arabella herself, with her sexuality, her vulgarity, her instinct for survival, is richly imagined and created" (*Career*, 323–24).

32. Garson notes that "Arabella indeed has the final word," and addresses the reasons why this is so (178).

33. For further discussion of male anxiety and the subsequent demonization of the female, see Elaine Showalter's *Sexual Anarchy: Gender and Culture at the Fin de Siècle*

and Nina Auerbach's *Woman and the Demon: The Life of a Victorian Myth* (Cambridge, Mass.: Harvard University Press, 1982).

34. Compare Penny Boumelha's comment: "While Sue's sexuality all but destroys her, Arabella's is the very guarantee of her survival. She, neither enigma nor conundrum, is clear-sighted about her means of economic survival, and barters her sexuality accordingly" (*Thomas Hardy and Women*, 151).

Works Cited

Adorno, Theodor W. "On Proust." In *Notes to Literature*, vol. 2, translated by Shierry Weber Nicholsen, edited by Rolf Tiedemann. New York: Columbia University Press, 1992.

Anderson, Amanda. *Tainted Souls and Painted Faces: The Rhetoric of Fallenness in Victorian Culture*. Ithaca, N.Y.: Cornell University Press, 1993.

Armstrong, Nancy. *Desire and Domestic Fiction: A Political History of the Novel*. New York: Oxford University Press, 1987.

Arnold, Matthew. *The Portable Matthew Arnold*. Edited by Lionel Trilling. New York: Penguin, 1980.

Atwood, Margaret. *The Handmaid's Tale*. New York: Ballantine Books, 1985.

Auerbach, Nina. "The Power of Hunger: Demonism and Maggie Tulliver." *Nineteenth-Century Fiction* 30 (1975): 150–71.

Baker, William. "Afterword: Diversity in Victorian Studies and the Opportunities of Theory." In *Victorian Identities: Social and Cultural Formations in Nineteenth-Century Literature*, edited by Ruth Robbins and Julian Wolfreys, 230–32. London: Macmillan, 1996.

Bakhtin, Mikhail. *The Dialogic Imagination*. Edited by Michael Holquist. Translated by Caryl Emerson and Michael Holquist. Austin: University of Texas Press, 1981.

———. *Rabelais and His World*. Translated by Hélène Iswolsky. Bloomington: Indiana University Press, 1984.

Barickman, Richard, Susan MacDonald, and Myra Stark. *Corrupt Relations: Dickens, Thackeray, Trollope, Collins, and the Victorian Sexual System*. New York: Columbia University Press, 1982.

Barthes, Roland. *The Pleasure of the Text*. Translated by Richard Miller. New York: Hill and Wang, 1975.

Bataille, Georges. *Erotism: Death and Sensuality*. Translated by Mary Dalwood. San Francisco: City Lights Books, 1986.

Beer, Gillian. *Darwin's Plots: Evolutionary Narrative in Darwin, George Eliot, and Nineteenth-Century Fiction*. London: Routledge and Kegan Paul, 1983.

———. "Origins and Oblivion in Victorian Narrative." In *Sex, Politics, and Science in the Nineteenth-Century Novel*. Edited by Ruth Bernard Yeazell, 63–87. Baltimore: Johns Hopkins University Press, 1986.

Benjamin, Walter. *Illuminations*. Edited by Hannah Arendt. Translated by Harry Zohn. New York: Schocken Books, 1968.

Bernheimer, Charles, and Claire Kahane, eds. *In Dora's Case: Freud—Hysteria—Feminism.* New York: Columbia University Press, 1985.

Bernstein, Stephen. "Reading Blackwater Park: Gothicism, Narrative, and Ideology in *The Woman in White.*" *Studies in the Novel* 25 (1993): 291–305.

Bersani, Leo. *Baudelaire and Freud.* Berkeley and Los Angeles: University of California Press, 1977.

Blake, William. *The Poetry and Prose of William Blake.* Edited by David V. Erdman. Commentary by Harold Bloom. New York: Doubleday and Co., 1970.

Bodenheimer, Rosemarie. *The Politics of Story in Victorian Social Fiction.* Ithaca, N.Y.: Cornell University Press, 1988.

Boheemen, Christine van. "*Bleak House* and the Victorian Family Romance." In *The Novel as Family Romance: Language, Gender, and Authority from Fielding to Joyce,* 101–31. Ithaca, N.Y.: Cornell University Press, 1987.

Bonaparte, Felicia. *The Gypsy-Bachelor of Manchester: The Life of Mrs. Gaskell's Demon.* Charlottesville: University Press of Virginia, 1992.

Boose, Lynda E. "The Father's House and the Daughter in It." In *Daughters and Fathers,* edited by Lynda E. Boose and Betty S. Flowers, 19–74. Baltimore: Johns Hopkins University Press, 1988.

Boumelha, Penny. *Thomas Hardy and Women: Sexual Ideology and Narrative Form.* Brighton, UK: Harvester Press, 1982.

Bowen, John. *Other Dickens: Pickwick to Chuzzlewit.* Oxford: Oxford University Press, 2000.

Brantlinger, Patrick. *Rules of Darkness: British Literature and Imperialism, 1830–1914.* Ithaca, N.Y.: Cornell University Press, 1988.

Bronfen, Elisabeth. *Over Her Dead Body: Death, Femininity, and the Aesthetic.* New York: Routledge, 1992.

Brontë, Charlotte. "Preface to the 1850 Edition." In *Wuthering Heights,* by Emily Brontë, edited by Pauline Nestor. New York: Penguin, 1995.

Brooks, Peter. *Reading for the Plot: Design and Intention in Narrative.* New York: Vintage, 1985.

Brown, Norman O. *Life against Death: The Psychoanalytic Meaning of History.* Middletown, Conn.: Wesleyan University Press, 1959.

Browning, Robert. *The Poetical Works of Robert Browning.* London: Oxford University Press, 1962.

Bunyan, John. *The Pilgrim's Progress.* Edited by Roger Sharrock. New York: Penguin, 1965.

Burke, Edmund. *A Philosophical Enquiry into the Origin of Our Ideas of the Sublime and Beautiful.* Edited by James T. Boulton. Notre Dame, Ind.: University of Notre Dame Press, 1968.

Byatt, A. S. *Possession.* New York: Vintage, 1990.

———. *Still Life.* New York: Collier, 1985.

Carlyle, Thomas. "Characteristics." In *Victorian Literature: Prose,* edited by G. B. Tennyson and Donald J. Gray, 43–62. New York: Macmillan, 1976.

Carroll, Lewis. *Alice in Wonderland: Authoritative Texts of Alice's Adventures in Wonderland, Through the Looking-Glass,* and *The Hunting of the Snark with Back-*

grounds and Essays in Criticism. Edited by Donald J. Gray. 2nd ed. New York: Norton, 1992.

Cixous, Hélène. "Sorties: Out and Out: Attacks/Ways Out/Forays." In *The Newly Born Woman,* translated by Betsy Wing, 63–132. Minneapolis: University of Minnesota Press, 1986.

Clément, Catherine. *The Lives and Legends of Jacques Lacan.* Translated by Arthur Goldhammer. New York: Columbia University Press, 1983.

Coetzee, J. M. *Foe.* New York: Viking, 1986.

——. *Waiting for the Barbarians.* New York: Penguin, 1982.

Cohen, William. *Sex Scandal: The Private Parts of Victorian Fiction.* Durham, N.C.: Duke University Press, 1996.

Collins, Wilkie. *The Woman in White.* Edited by Julian Symons. New York: Penguin, 1986.

Copjec, Joan. *Read My Desire: Lacan against the Historicists.* Cambridge, Mass.: MIT Press, 1994.

Corbin, Alain. "Commercial Sexuality in Nineteenth-Century France: A System of Images and Regulations." Translated by Katherine Streip. In *The Making of the Modern Body: Sexuality and Society in the Nineteenth Century,* edited by Catherine Gallagher and Thomas Laquer, 209–19. Berkeley and Los Angeles: University of California Press, 1987.

Curran, Stuart. "The Lost Paradises of *Martin Chuzzlewit.*" *Nineteenth-Century Fiction* 25 (1970): 51–67.

Cvetkovich, Anne. *Mixed Feelings: Feminism, Mass Culture, and Victorian Sensationalism.* New Brunswick, N.J.: Rutgers University Press, 1992.

Dale, Peter A. "Thomas Hardy and the Best Consummation Possible." In *Nature Transfigured: Science and Literature, 1700–1900,* edited by John Christie and Sally Shuttleworth, 201–21. Manchester, UK: Manchester University Press, 1989.

Darby, Margaret Flanders. "Listening to Estella." *Dickens Quarterly* 16, no. 4 (December 1999): 215–29.

David-Ménard, Monique. *Hysteria from Freud to Lacan: Body and Language in Psychoanalysis.* Translated by Catherine Porter. Foreword by Ned Lukacher. Ithaca, N.Y.: Cornell University Press, 1989.

Davis, Nuel Pharr. *The Life of Wilkie Collins.* Introduction by Gordon N. Ray. Urbana: University of Illinois Press, 1956.

Davis, Robert Con. *The Fictional Father: Lacanian Readings of the Text.* Amherst: University of Massachusetts Press, 1981.

Dean, Carolyn J. *The Self and Its Pleasures: Bataille, Lacan, and the History of the Decentered Subject.* Ithaca, N.Y.: Cornell University Press, 1992.

Defoe, Daniel. *Robinson Crusoe.* Edited by Angus Ross. New York: Penguin, 1985.

DeLaura, David J. "'The Ache of Modernism' in Hardy's Later Novels." *Journal of English Literary History* 34 (1967): 380–99.

DeLillo, Don. *Libra.* New York: NAL / Dutton, 1987.

——. *Underworld.* New York: Scribners, 1997.

——. *White Noise.* New York: Penguin, 1985.

Deleuze, Gilles. *Masochism: An Interpretation of Coldness and Cruelty.* Translated by Jean McNeil. New York: George Braziller, 1971.

De Man, Paul. *Allegories of Reading: Figural Language in Rousseau, Nietzsche, Rilke, and Proust.* New Haven: Yale University Press, 1979.

——. *Blindness and Insight.* New York: Oxford University Press, 1971.

——. *Resistance to Theory.* Minneapolis: University of Minnesota Press, 1986.

Derrida, Jacques. Foreword to *The Wolfman's Magic Word,* by Nicholas Abraham and Maria Torok, translated by Nicholas Rand. Minneapolis: University of Minnesota Press, 1986. xi–xlviii.

——. *Of Grammatology.* Translated by Gayatri Chakravorty Spivak. Baltimore: Johns Hopkins University Press, 1974.

——. *The Post Card: From Socrates to Freud and Beyond.* Translated by Alan Bass. Chicago: University of Chicago Press, 1987.

——. "The Principle of Reason: The University in the Eyes of its Pupils." *Diacritics* 13 (Fall 1983): 3–20.

Deutsch, Felix. "A Footnote to Freud's 'Fragment of an Analysis of a Case of Hysteria.'" *Psychoanalytic Quarterly* 26 (1957): 159–67. Reprinted in Bernheimer and Kahane, eds., *In Dora's Case,* 33–43.

Dibattista, Maria. "Eroteleptic Narrative: Hardy's *Jude the Obscure.*" In *First Love: The Affections of Modern Fiction,* 93–111. Chicago: University of Chicago Press, 1991.

Dickens, Charles. *American Notes.* New York: Penguin, 2000.

——. *Bleak House.* Edited by Norman Page. New York: Penguin, 1985.

——. *David Copperfield.* Edited by Jeremy Trambling. New York: Penguin, 1996.

——. *Great Expectations.* Edited by Angus Calder. New York: Penguin, 1965.

——. *The Letters of Charles Dickens,* vol. 3. Edited by Madeline House, Graham Storey, and Kathleen Tillotson. Oxford: Clarendon Press, 1974.

——. *Martin Chuzzlewit.* Edited by Margaret Cardwell. New York: Oxford University Press, 1982.

——. *Our Mutual Friend.* New York: New American Library, 1964.

Dickinson, Emily. *The Complete Poems of Emily Dickinson.* Edited by Thomas H. Johnson. Boston: Little, Brown, and Co., 1960.

Didion, Joan. *The White Album.* New York: Simon and Schuster, 1979.

Donaghy, Mary, and Pamela Perkins. "A Man's Resolution: Narrative Strategies in Wilkie Collins's *The Woman in White. Studies in the Novel* 22, no. 4 (1990): 392–402.

Easson, Angus. *Elizabeth Gaskell.* London: Routledge and Kegan Paul, 1979.

Eckstein, Barbara J. *The Language of Fiction in a World of Pain: Reading Politics as Paradox.* Philadelphia: University of Pennsylvania Press, 1990.

Edgecombe, Rodney S. "Topographic Disaffection in Dickens's *American Notes* and *Martin Chuzzlewit.*" *JEGP* 93 (1994): 35–54.

Eiseley, Loren. *Darwin's Century: Evolution and the Men Who Discovered It.* New York: Doubleday, 1958.

Eliot, George. *Adam Bede.* Edited by Stephen Gill. New York: Penguin, 1980.

——. *The George Eliot Letters,* vol. 2 (1852–1858). Edited by Gordon Haight. New Haven: Yale University Press, 1954.

——. *Middlemarch*. Edited by Rossemary Ashton. New York: Penguin, 1994.

——. *The Mill on the Floss*. Edited by A. S. Byatt. New York: Penguin, 1981.

Eliot, T. S. "In Memoriam." In *Essays Ancient and Modern*, 186–203. New York: Harcourt, Brace and Company, 1936.

Ellis, Bret Easton. *Less Than Zero*. New York: Penguin, 1986.

Faulkner, William. *Lion in the Garden: Interviews with William Faulkner, 1926–1962*. Edited by James Meriwether and Michael Millgate. New York: Random House, 1968.

Feldstein, Richard, and Judith Roof, eds. *Feminism and Psychoanalysis*. Ithaca, N.Y.: Cornell University Press, 1989.

Felman, Shoshana, ed. *Literature and Psychoanalysis: The Question of Reading, Otherwise*. Baltimore: Johns Hopkins University Press, 1982.

Fink, Bruce. "The Subject and the Other's Desire." In *Reading Seminars I and II: Lacan's Return to Freud*, edited by Richard Feldstein, Bruce Fink, and Maire Jaanus, 76–97. Albany: State University Press of New York, 1996.

Flaubert, Gustave. *Madame Bovary*. Translated by Eleanor Marx Aveling. New York: Dover, 1996.

Ford, George. *Dickens and His Readers: Aspects of Novel-Criticism since 1836*. Princeton, N.J.: Princeton University Press, 1955.

Foucault, Michel. *Discipline and Punish: The Birth of the Prison*. Translated by Alan Sheridan. New York: Vintage, 1979.

——. *The History of Sexuality*, vol. 1. Translated by Robert Hurley. New York: Vintage, 1990.

——. *Madness and Civilization: A History of Insanity in the Age of Reason*. Translated by Richard Howard. New York: Pantheon Books, 1965.

——. "Nietzsche, Freud, Marx." In *Critical Texts* 3, no. 2 (1986): 1–6.

——. *The Order of Things: An Archeology of the Human Sciences*. Translated by A. M. Sheridan Smith. New York: Vintage, 1973.

Freud, Sigmund. *Beyond the Pleasure Principle*. Edited by James Strachey. Introduction by Gregory Zilboorg. New York: Norton, 1961.

——. *Civilization and Its Discontents*. Edited by James Strachey. New York: Norton, 1961.

——. *The Complete Letters of Sigmund Freud and Wilhelm Fliess, 1887–1904*. Translated and edited by Jeffrey Moussaieff Masson. Cambridge, Mass.: Harvard University Press, 1985.

——. *The Interpretation of Dreams*. Translated by James Strachey. New York: Avon Books, 1965.

——. *Jokes and Their Relation to the Unconscious*. Translated and edited by James Strachey. Introduction by Peter Gay. New York: Norton, 1989.

——. *The Standard Edition of the Complete Psychological Works of Sigmund Freud*. James Strachey, general editor. 24 vols. London: Hogarth Press, 1955–74.

Gallagher, Catherine. "George Eliot and *Daniel Deronda:* The Prostitute and the Jewish Question." In *Sex, Politics, and Science in the Nineteenth-Century Novel*, edited by Ruth Bernard Yeazell, 39–62. Baltimore: Johns Hopkins University Press, 1986.

——. *The Industrial Reformation of English Fiction: Social Discourse and Narrative Form, 1832–1867.* Chicago: University of Chicago Press, 1985.

Gallop, Jane. *Reading Lacan.* Ithaca, N.Y.: Cornell University Press, 1985.

Garnett, Robert R. "The Good and the Unruly in *Great Expectations*—and Estella." *Dickens Quarterly* 16, no. 1 (March 1999): 24–41.

Garson, Marjorie. *Hardy's Fables of Integrity: Woman, Body, Text.* Oxford: Clarendon Press, 1991.

Gaskell, Elizabeth. *The Letters of Mrs. Gaskell.* Edited by J. A. V. Chapple and Arthur Pollard. Cambridge, Mass.: Harvard University Press, 1967.

——. *The Life of Charlotte Brontë.* Edited by Alan Shelston. New York: Penguin, 1985.

——. *North and South.* Edited by Patricia Ingham. New York: Penguin, 1995.

——. *Ruth.* Edited by Alan Shelston. Oxford: Oxford University Press, 1981.

Gay, Peter. *Freud: A Life for Our Time.* New York: Doubleday, 1988.

Gérin, Winifred. *Elizabeth Gaskell: A Biography.* Oxford: Clarendon Press, 1976.

Ghosh, Amitav. *The Shadow Lines.* Delhi: Ravi Dayal, 1988.

Goodheart, Eugene. *Desire and Its Discontents.* New York: Columbia University Press, 1991.

Goodwin, Sarah Webster. "Romanticism and the Ghost of Prostitution: Freud, *Maria*, and 'Alice Fell.'" In *Death and Representation*, edited by Sarah Webster Goodwin and Elisabeth Bronfen, 152–73. Baltimore: Johns Hopkins University Press, 1993.

Greg, W. R. "Prostitution." *Westminster Review* 53 (1850): 448–506.

Gregor, Ian. *The Great Web: The Forms of Hardy's Major Fiction.* London: Faber and Faber, 1974.

Habermas, Jürgen. *The Philosophical Discourse of Modernism.* Translated by Frederick G. Lawrence. Cambridge, Mass.: MIT Press, 1987.

Hanzo, Thomas. "Paternity and the Subject in *Bleak House*." In *The Fictional Father: Lacanian Readings of the Text*, edited by Robert Con Davis, 27–47. Amherst: University of Massachusetts Press, 1981.

Hardy, Barbara. "The Change of Heart in Dickens's Novels." *Victorian Studies* 5 (1961): 49–67.

Hardy, Florence Emily. *The Early Life of Thomas Hardy, 1840–1891.* New York: Macmillan, 1928.

——. *The Later Years of Thomas Hardy, 1892–1928.* New York: Macmillan, 1930.

Hardy, Thomas. *The Complete Poetical Works of Thomas Hardy*, vol. 1. Edited by Samuel Hynes. Oxford: Clarendon Press, 1982.

——. *Jude the Obscure.* Edited by C. H. Sisson. New York: Penguin, 1985.

——. *The Return of the Native.* Edited by James Gindin. New York: Norton, 1969.

——. *Tess of the d'Urbervilles.* Edited by Juliet Grindle and Simon Catrell. New York: Oxford University Press, 1988.

Hartman, Geoffrey. "Literature High and Low: The Case of the Mystery Story." In *The Fate of Reading and Other Essays*, 203–22. Chicago: University of Chicago Press, 1975.

Hassett, Michael E. "Compromised Romanticism in *Jude the Obscure*." *Nineteenth-Century Fiction* 25 (1971): 432–43.

Hawking, Stephen W. *A Brief History of Time: From the Big Bang to the Black Hole*. New York: Bantam Books, 1988.

Heller, Tamar. *Dead Secrets: Wilkie Collins and the Female Gothic*. New Haven: Yale University Press, 1992.

Hendershot, Cyndy. "A Sensation Novel's Appropriation of the Terror-Gothic: Wilkie Collins's *The Woman in White*." *Clues: A Journal of Detection* 13, no. 2 (1992): 127–33.

Henkle, Roger B. *Comedy and Culture: England, 1820–1900*. Princeton, N.J.: Princeton University Press, 1980.

Hertz, Neil. "Dora's Secrets, Freud's Techniques." In Hertz, *The End of the Line: Essays on Psychoanalysis and the Sublime*, 122–43. New York: Columbia University Press, 1985.

———. "Medusa's Head: Male Hysteria under Political Pressure." In Hertz, *The End of the Line*, 161–93.

Hill, Carol de Chellis. *Henry James's Midnight Song*. New York: Norton, 1995.

Holbrook, David. *Charles Dickens and the Image of Woman*. New York: New York University Press, 1993.

Homans, Margaret. *Bearing the Word: Language and Female Experience in Nineteenth-Century Women's Writing*. Chicago: University of Chicago Press, 1986.

Hughes, Winifred. *The Maniac in the Cellar: Sensation Novels of the 1860s*. Princeton, N.J.: Princeton University Press, 1980.

Hulme, Peter. *Colonial Encounters: Europe and the Native Caribbean, 1492–1797*. New York: Routledge, 1992.

Hutter, Albert D. "Dreams, Transformations, and Literature: The Implications of Detective Fiction." In *The Poetics of Murder: Detective Fiction and Literary Theory*, edited by Glenn W. Most and William W. Stowe, 230–51. New York: Harcourt, 1983.

Ingham, Patricia. Introduction to *American Notes* by Charles Dickens. New York: Penguin, 2000.

Irwin, John T. *Doubling and Incest/Repetition and Revenge: A Speculative Reading of Faulkner*. Baltimore: Johns Hopkins University Press, 1975.

Jacobus, Mary. "Freud's Mnemonic: Screen Memories and Feminist Nostalgia." In *First Things: The Maternal Imaginary in Literature, Art, Psychoanalysis*, 1–22. New York: Routledge, 1995.

Jameson, Fredric. "Imagery and Symbolic in Lacan: Marxism, Psychoanalytical Criticism, and the Problem of the Subject." In Felman, *Literature and Psychoanalysis*, 338–456.

Johnson, Barbara. "Apostrophe, Animation, and Abortion." *Diacritics* 16 (1986): 29–39.

Kaplan, Fred. *Dickens and Mesmerism: The Hidden Springs of Fiction*. Princeton: Princeton University Press, 1975.

Kincaid, James R. *Child-Loving: The Erotic Child and Victorian Culture*. New York: Routledge, 1992.

———. "Girl-Watching, Child-Beating, and Other Exercises in *Jude the Obscure*." In *The Sense of Sex: Feminist Perspectives on Hardy*, edited by Margaret E. Higonnet, 132–48. Urbana: University of Illinois Press, 1993.

Kinglake, Alexander William. *Eothen; or, Traces of Travel, Brought Home from the East.* London: J. Olliver, 1844.

Knoepflmacher, U. C. "The Counterworld of Victorian Fiction and *The Woman in White.*" In *The Worlds of Victorian Fiction*, edited by Jerome H. Buckley, 351–69. Cambridge, Mass.: Harvard University Press, 1975.

———. *Laughter and Despair.* Berkeley and Los Angeles: University of California Press, 1971.

Knox, Bernard. *The Oldest Dead White European Males and Other Reflections on the Classics.* New York: Norton, 1993.

Kristeva, Julia. *Powers of Horror: An Essay on Abjection.* Translated by Leon S. Roudiez. New York: Columbia University Press, 1982.

———. "Stabat Mater" (1977). In *Contemporary Critical Theory*, edited by Dan Latimer, 579–603. New York: Harcourt Brace Jovanovitch, 1989.

Kucich, John. *Repression in Victorian Fiction: Charlotte Brontë, George Eliot, and Charles Dickens.* Berkeley and Los Angeles: University of California Press, 1987.

Kundera, Milan. *The Book of Laughter and Forgetting.* Translated by Michael Henry Heim. New York: Penguin, 1980.

———. *The Unbearable Lightness of Being.* Translated by Michael Henry Heim. New York: Harper Collins, 1985.

Lacan, Jacques. "Desire and the Interpretation of Desire in *Hamlet.*" In Felman, *Literature and Psychoanalysis*, 11–52.

———. *Ecrits.* Translated by Alan Sheridan. New York: Norton, 1977.

———. *The Four Fundamental Concepts of Psychoanalysis.* Translated by Alan Sheridan. New York: Norton, 1981.

———. "God and the Jouissance of The Woman." Translated by Jacqueline Rose. In *Feminine Sexuality: Jacques Lacan and the Ecole Freudienne*, edited by Juliet Mitchell and Jacqueline Rose, 137–48. New York: Norton, 1985.

———. *The Seminar of Jacques Lacan, Book II: The Ego in Freud's Theory and in the Technique of Psychoanalysis, 1954–1955*, edited by Jacques-Alain Miller, translated by Sylvana Tomaselli, 191–205. New York: Norton, 1988.

Lane, Christopher. *The Burdens of Intimacy: Psychoanalysis and Victorian Masculinity.* Chicago: University Chicago Press, 1999.

Langbauer, Laurie. "Women in White, Men in Feminism." *Yale Journal of Criticism* 2 (1989): 219–43.

Lansbury, Coral. *Elizabeth Gaskell.* Boston: Twayne, 1984.

Laplanche, Jean, and J. B. Pontalis. "Fantasy and the Origins of Sexuality." *International Journal of Psychoanalysis* 49 (1968): 1–17.

———. *The Language of Psycho-analyis.* Translated by Donald Nicholson-Smith. New York: Norton, 1973.

Lee, Jonathan Scott. *Jacques Lacan.* Amherst: University of Massachusetts Press, 1990.

Lemaire, Anika. *Jacques Lacan.* Translated by David Macey. Boston: Routledge and Kegan Paul, 1977.

Lévi-Strauss, Claude. *The Elementary Structures of Kinship.* Translated by James Harle

Bell and John Richard von Sturmer. Boston: Beacon Press, 1969. Originally published in French in 1949.

——. *Tristes Tropiques: An Anthropological Study of Primitive Societies in Brazil.* Translated by John Russell. New York: Atheneum, 1973.

Lewis, R. W. B. *Edith Wharton: A Biography.* New York: Harper, 1975.

Looby, Christopher. "Flowers of Manhood: Race, Sex, and Floriculture from Thomas Wentworth Higginson to Robert Mapplethorpe." *Criticism* 37 (Winter 1995): 109–56.

Lougy, Robert E. "Filth, Liminality, and Abjection in Charles Dickens's *Bleak House.*" *English Literary History* 69 (2002): 473–500.

——. "Remembrances of Death Past and Future: A Reading of *David Copperfield.*" *Dickens Studies Annual* 6, edited by Robert B. Partlow Jr., 72–102. Carbondale: Southern Illinois University Press, 1977.

Lukacher, Ned. *Primal Scenes: Literature, Philosophy, Psychoanalysis.* Ithaca, N.Y.: Cornell University Press, 1986.

Macey, David. *The Lives of Michel Foucault: A Biography.* New York: Pantheon Books, 1993.

Macherey, Pierre. *A Theory of Literary Production.* Translated by Geoffrey Wall. London: Routledge and Kegan Paul, 1978.

Magnet, Myron. "*Martin Chuzzlewit* in Context." In *Dickens and the Social Order,* 203–37. Philadelphia: University of Pennsylvania Press, 1985.

Marcus, Steven. "Freud and Dora: Story, History, Case History." In Bernheimer and Kahane, *In Dora's Case,* 56–91.

Marx, Karl. "Economic and Philosophic Manuscripts of 1844." In *The Marx-Engels Reader,* edited by Robert C. Tucker, 66–125. New York: Norton, 1978.

Masciarotte, Gloria Jean. "The Madonna with Child, and Another Child, and Still Another Child . . . : Sensationalism and the Dysfunction of Emotions." *Discourse* 14, no. 1 (1991–92): 88–125.

Matus, Jill. *Unstable Bodies: Victorian Representations of Sexuality and Maternity.* Manchester, UK: Manchester University Press, 1995.

McCannell, Juliet Flower. *Figuring Lacan: Criticism and the Cultural Unconscious.* London: Croon Helm, 1986.

Meckier, Jerome. *Innocent Abroad: Charles Dickens's American Engagements.* Lexington: University Press of Kentucky, 1990.

Meisel, Perry. *Thomas Hardy: The Return of the Repressed: A Study of the Major Fiction.* New Haven: Yale University Press, 1972.

Mellard, James M. *Using Lacan, Reading Fiction.* Urbana: University of Illinois Press, 1991.

Miller, D. A. "Cage aux Folles: Sensation and Gender in Wilkie Collins's *The Woman in White.*" In *Novel and the Police,* 186–215. Berkeley and Los Angeles: University of California Press, 1988.

Miller, J. Hillis. "Arachne's Broken Woof." *Georgia Review* 31 (Spring 1977): 36–48.

——. "Ariadne's Broken Thread: Repetition and the Narrative Line." In *Interpretation of Narrative*, edited by Mario J. Valdés and Owen J. Miller, 148–66. Toronto: University of Toronto Press, 1979.

——. *Charles Dickens: The World of His Novels*. Cambridge, Mass.: Harvard University Press, 1958.

——. "The Search for Grounds in Literary Studies." In *Rhetoric and Form: Deconstruction at Yale*, edited by Robert Con Davis and Ronald Schleifer, 19–36. Norman: University of Oklahoma Press, 1985.

——. *Thomas Hardy: Distance and Desire*. Cambridge, Mass.: Harvard University Press, 1970.

Miller, Nancy K. "Arachnologies: The Woman, the Text, the Critic." In *The Poetics of Gender*, edited by Nancy K. Miller, 270–95. New York: Columbia University Press, 1986.

Millgate, Michael. *Thomas Hardy: A Biography*. New York: Random House, 1982.

——. *Thomas Hardy: His Career as a Novelist*. New York: Random House, 1971.

Mitchell, Juliet, and Jacqueline Rose, eds. *Feminine Sexuality: Jacques Lacan and the Ecole Freudienne*. New York: Norton, 1985.

Mitchell, Sally. *The Fallen Angel: Chastity, Class, and Women's Reading, 1835–1880*. Bowling Green, Ohio: Bowling Green University Popular Press, 1981.

Moi, Toril. "Representation of Patriarchy: Sexuality and Epistemology in Freud's *Dora*." In Bernheimer and Kahane, *In Dora's Case*, 181–99.

Moore, Kevin. *The Descent of the Imagination: Postromantic Culture in the Later Novels of Thomas Hardy*. New York: New York University Press, 1990.

Morgan, Rosemarie. *Women and Sexuality in the Novels of Thomas Hardy*. London: Routledge, 1988.

Morrow, Nancy. *Dreadful Games: The Play of Desire in the Nineteenth-Century Novel*. Kent, Ohio: Kent State University Press, 1988.

Muller, John P. "Language, Psychosis, and the Subject in Lacan." In *Interpreting Lacan*, edited by Joseph H. Smith and William Kerrigan, 21–32. New Haven: Yale University Press, 1983.

Mulvey, Laura. "Visual Pleasure and Narrative Cinema." *Screen* 16 (1975): 6–18.

Murdoch, Iris. *A Severed Head*. Harmondsworth, UK: Penguin, 1976.

Musselwhite, David E. *Partings Welded Together: Politics and Desire in the Nineteenth-Century English Novel*. New York: Methuen, 1987.

Newman, S. J. *Dickens at Play*. New York: St. Martin's Press, 1981.

Nietzsche, Friedrich. *The Portable Nietzsche*. Translated by Walter Kaufmann. New York: Viking Press, 1968.

O'Farrell, Mary Ann. *Telling Complexions: The Nineteenth-Century English Novel and the Blush*. Durham, N.C.: Duke University Press, 1997.

O'Neill, Philip. *Wilkie Collins: Women, Property, and Propriety*. London: Macmillan, 1988.

Orwell, George. "Charles Dickens." In *The Collected Essays, Journalism, and Letters of George Orwell*, edited by Sonia Orwell and Ian Angus, 1:413–60. New York: Harcourt, Brace, and World, 1968.

Page, Norman. "Art and Aesthetics." In *The Cambridge Companion to Thomas Hardy*, edited by Dale Kramer, 38–53. Cambridge: Cambridge University Press, 1999.

Paglia, Camille. *Sexual Personae: Art and Decadence from Nefertiti to Emily Dickinson.* New York: Vintage, 1991.

Pater, Walter. "The Child in the House." In *English Prose of the Victorian Era,* edited by Charles Frederick Harrold and William D. Templeman, 1469–78. New York: Oxford University Press, 1938.

Pederson-Krag, G. "Detective Stories and the Primal Scene." *Psychoanalytical Quarterly* 18 (1949): 207–14.

Pengelly, R. S. "*Martin Chuzzlewit:* Elijah Pogram." *Notes and Queries* 8 (1921): 389.

Plato. *The Symposium and Other Works.* Translated by Michael Joyce. Introduction by John Warrington. London: Dent, 1964.

Polhemus, Robert M. *Comic Faith: The Great Tradition from Austen to Joyce.* Chicago: University of Chicago Press, 1980.

———. *Erotic Faith: Being in Love from Jane Austen to D. H. Lawrence.* Chicago: University of Chicago Press, 1990.

Poovey, Mary. *Making a Social Body: British Cultural Formation, 1830–1864.* Chicago: University of Chicago Press, 1995.

Pope, Alexander. *The Poems of Alexander Pope.* Edited by John Butt. New Haven: Yale University Press, 1963.

Ragland, Ellie. "Lacan, the Death Drive, and the Dream of the Burning Child." In *Death and Representation,* edited by Sarah Webster Goodwin and Elisabeth Bronfen, 80–102. Baltimore: Johns Hopkins University Press, 1993.

Ragland-Sullivan, Ellie. *Jacques Lacan and the Philosophy of Psychoanalysis.* Urbana: University of Illinois Press, 1987.

Ray, Gordon N. *Thackeray: The Uses of Adversity, 1811–1846.* New York: McGraw-Hill, 1955.

Ritchie, Anne Thackeray. "Mrs. Gaskell." In *Blackstick Papers,* 217–18. London: Smith, Elder, 1908.

Rose, Jacqueline. *States of Fantasy.* Oxford: Clarendon Press, 1996.

Roudinesco, Elisabeth. *Jacques Lacan and Co.: A History of Psychoanalysis in France, 1925–1985.* Translated by Jeffrey Mehlman. Chicago: University of Chicago Press, 1990.

Rousseau, Jean-Jacques. *Confessions.* Translated by J. M. Cohen. New York: Viking Penguin, 1953.

———. *On the Origin of Language: Two Essays by Jean-Jacques Rousseau and Johann Gottfried Herder.* Translated by John H. Moran and Alexander Gode. Chicago: University of Chicago Press, 1966.

Ruskin, John. *The Complete Works of John Ruskin,* vol. 27. Edited by E. T. Cook and Alexander Wedderburn. London: George Allen, 1907.

Sadoff, Diane. *Monsters of Affection: Dickens, Eliot, and Brontë on Fatherhood.* Baltimore: Johns Hopkins University Press, 1982.

Said, Edward W. *Beginnings: Intention and Method.* New York: Columbia University Press, 1985.

———. "The Mind of Winter: Reflections on Life in Exile." *Harpers,* September 1984, 49–55.

———. *Orientalism.* New York: Vintage, 1979.

Saldívar, Ramón. "*Jude the Obscure* and the Spirit of the Law." *English Literary History* 50 (1983): 607–25.

Schor, Hilary M. "The Plot of the Beautiful Ignoramus: *Ruth* and the Tradition of the Fallen Woman." In *Scheherezade in the Marketplace: Elizabeth Gaskell and the Victorian Novel*, 45–79. New York: Oxford University Press, 1992.

Schorske, Carl. *Fin-de-Siècle Vienna: Politics and Culture.* New York: Knopf, 1980.

Schweik, Robert. "The Influence of Religion, Science, and Philosophy on Hardy's Writings." In *The Cambridge Companion to Thomas Hardy*, edited by Dale Kramer, 54–72. Cambridge: Cambridge University Press, 1999.

Ser, Cary D. "The Function of Chapter I of *Martin Chuzzlewit.*" *Dickens Studies Newsletter* 10 (1979): 45–47.

Shklar, Judith N. *The Faces of Injustice.* New Haven: Yale University Press, 1990.

Showalter, Elaine. *Sexual Anarchy: Gender and Culture at the Fin de Siècle.* New York: Viking, 1990.

Shumaker, Jeanette. "Gaskell's *Ruth* and Hardy's *Tess* as Novels of Free Union." In *Dickens Studies Annual* 28, edited by Stanley Friedman, Edward Guiliano, and Michael Timko, 151–72. New York: AMS Press, 1999.

Sisson, C. H. Introduction to *Jude the Obscure* by Thomas Hardy. New York: Penguin, 1985.

Slack, Robert C. "The Text of Hardy's *Jude the Obscure.*" *Nineteenth-Century Fiction* 11 (1957): 261–75. Reprinted in *Jude the Obscure*, edited by Norman Page, Norton Critical Editions, 331–39. New York: Norton, 1978.

Sophocles. *Antigone.* Translated by Elizabeth Wyckoff. In vol. 2 of *The Complete Greek Tragedies*, edited by David Grene and Richard Lattimore, 159–206. Chicago: University of Chicago Press, 1957.

Spivak, Gayatri Chakravorty. Translator's preface to *Of Grammatology* by Jacques Derrida, ix–xc. Baltimore: Johns Hopkins University Press, 1974.

Sprengnether, Madelon. "Enforcing Oedipus: Freud and Dora." In *The (M)other Tongue: Essays in Feminist Psychoanalytic Interpretation*, edited by Shirley Nelson Garner, Claire Kahane, and Madelon Sprengnether, 51–71. Ithaca, N.Y.: Cornell University Press, 1985.

Steig, Michael. "The Intentional Phallus: Determining Verbal Meaning in Literature." *Journal of Aesthetics and Art Criticism* 36 (1977): 51–61.

——. "*Martin Chuzzlewit*: Pinch and Pecksniff." *Studies in the Novel* 1 (1969): 181–88.

Stewart, Garrett. *Death Sentences: Styles of Dying in British Fiction.* Cambridge, Mass.: Harvard University Press, 1984.

Stockton, Kathryn Bond. *God between Their Lips: Desire in Women in Irigaray, Brontë, and Eliot.* Palo Alto, Calif.: Stanford University Press, 1994.

Stoler, Ann Laura. *Race and the Education of Desire: Foucault's History of Sexuality and the Colonial Order of Things.* Durham, N.C.: Duke University Press, 1995.

Stoneman, Patsy. *Elizabeth Gaskell.* Brighton, UK: Harvester Press, 1987.

Swift, Graham. *Waterland.* New York: Vintage, 1992.

Swinburne, Algernon Charles. *The Poems of Algernon Charles Swinburne*, vol. 1. London: Chatto and Windus, 1904.

Taylor, Jenny Bourne. *In the Secret Theatre of Home: Wilkie Collins and the Female Gothic*. New Haven: Yale University Press, 1992.

———. "Representing Illegitimacy in Victorian Culture." In *Victorian Identities: Social and Cultural Formations in Nineteenth-Century Literature*, edited by Ruth Robbins and Julian Wolfreys, 119–42. London: Macmillan, 1996.

Taylor, Jenny Bourne, and Sally Shuttleworth, eds. *Embodied Selves: An Anthology of Psychological Texts, 1830–1890*. Oxford: Clarendon Press, 1998.

Thackeray, William Makepeace. *A Journey from Cornhill to Grand Cairo*. In *The Works of William Makepeace Thackeray*, 14:347–514. London: Smith, Elder, 1869.

———. *Vanity Fair: A Novel without a Hero*. Edited by Geoffrey and Kathleen Tillotson. Boston: Houghton Miflin, 1963.

Thomas, Deborah A. *Thackeray and Slavery*. Athens: Ohio University Press, 1993.

Thomas, Ronald R. *Dreams of Authority: Freud and the Fictions of the Unconscious*. Ithaca, N.Y.: Cornell University Press, 1990.

Uglow, Jenny. *Elizabeth Gaskell: A Habit of Stories*. New York: Farrar, Straus Giroux, 1993.

Wales, Kathleen. "The Claims of Kinship: The Opening Chapter of *Martin Chuzzlewit*." *Dickensian* 83 (1987): 167–79.

Walkowitz, Judith. *Prostitution and Victorian Society: Women, Class, and the State*. Cambridge: Cambridge University Press, 1980.

Walton, Priscilla L. *Patriarchal Desire and Victorian Discourse: A Lacanian Reading of Anthony Trollope's Palliser Novels*. Toronto: University of Toronto Press, 1995.

Watt, Ian. *The Rise of the Novel: Studies in Defoe, Richardson and Fielding*. Berkeley and Los Angeles: University of California Press, 1957.

Webb, Beatrice. *My Apprenticeship*. London: Longmans Green, 1950.

Weinberg, Steven. *The First Three Minutes: A Modern View of the Origin of the Universe*. New York: Basic Books, 1977.

Welsh, Alexander. *From Copyright to Copperfield: The Identity of Dickens*. Cambridge, Mass.: Harvard University Press, 1987.

White, Allon. "Language and Location in *Bleak House*." In *Carnival, Hysteria, and Writing: Collected Essays and Autobiography*, 88–110. Oxford: Clarendon Press, 1993.

Wordsworth, William. *Poetical Works*. Edited by Thomas Hutchinson. New edition, revised by Ernest de Selincourt. London: Oxford University Press, 1966.

Wright, T. R. *Hardy and the Erotic*. London: Macmillan, 1989.

Index

Adorno, Theodor, 64
Anderson, Amanda, 175n14, 175n19, 176n29
Arabian Nights, 61–62
Atwood, Margaret, 120

Baker, William, 3
Bakhtin, Mikhail, 24, 48, 163–64
Bataille, Georges
    animal aspect of woman, 96, 102
    eroticism and continuity, 86, 111
    eroticism and death, 81, 92, 169n12
    eroticism and religious sensibility, 105–6
    eroticism and violence, 31
    nature and human nature, 48
Barthes, Roland, 36, 130, 142
Baudelaire, Charles, 102, 138, 153, 159–60, 175n11
Benjamin, Walter
    on Baudelaire, 89, 138, 153, 159–60, 175n11, 183n26
    on Freud's *Beyond the Pleasure Principle*, 159
    on Proust, 175nn11–12
Beer, Gillian, 4, 84, 141
Bernheimer, Charles, 115
Blake, William, 56, 95
Bodenheimer, Rosemarie, 80, 174n4, 174n9, 175n13, 175n19
Bonaparte, Felicia, 80–81, 91–92
Boose, Lynda, 121, 123
Boumelha, Penny, 142, 184n34
Bowen, John, 17, 41, 170nn14–15
Brantlinger, Patrick, 58, 173n3
Bronfen, Elizabeth, 107
Brontë, Charlotte, 5, 81, 169n12
Brontë, Emily, 10
Brooks, Peter, 7, 27, 38, 59, 71–72
Browne, Hablot K., 33, 39

Burke, Edmund, 91
Byatt, A. S., 91–92

Carlyle, Thomas, 58, 156, 160
Carroll, Lewis, 152, 155–56
Clément, Catherine, 47, 52
Cixous, Hélène, 93, 125, 162
Cohen, William, 168n5
Collins, Wilkie
    The Moonstone, 117, 178n9
    See also The Woman in White
Copjec, Joan, 13
    historicism and psychoanalysis, 15–16
    language and subjectivity, 29–30, 167n17, 167n20, 169n8
    love and giving, 175n16
    primal father, 29–30
Corbin, Alain, 103–4, 108, 110, 176n27
Curran, Stuart, 54, 172n30
Cvetkovich, Anne, 121–22, 124, 178–79nn14–15

Dale, Peter A., 183n29
Darby, Margaret Flanders, 169n9
Darwin, Charles, 3
David-Ménard, Monique, 32, 95, 169n10
Davis, Robert Con, 119
Dean, Carolyn J., 163
Defoe, Daniel: desire in *Robinson Crusoe*, 5–9, 48, 166n9
Deleuze, Gilles, 51
DeLillo, Don
    Underworld, 1–2, 11, 44
    White Noise, 79
    Libra, 158
De Man, Paul, 114, 170n17
Derrida, Jacques, 3–4, 43, 91, 139, 170n17
Dibattista, Marie, 181n13
Dickens, Charles, 19, 23–24

Dickens, Charles (*continued*)
  and America, 41–42
  American Notes, 42, 171n23, 171n28
  Bleak House, 38, 47, 125
  David Copperfield, 3–4, 33, 116
  Great Expectations, 31, 168n5, 169n9,
    171n23
  Letters, 41–42
  See also *Martin Chuzzlewit*
Dickinson, Emily, 95
Didion, Joan, 113
Durkheim, Emile, 172n2

Easson, Angus, 85
Einstein, Albert, 3
Eiseley, Loren, 170n16
Eliot, George
  Adam Bede, 127
  and Elizabeth Gaskell, 174n7
  The Mill on the Floss, 10
  remarks about *Ruth*, 174n5
Eliot, Thomas Stearns, 154, 182n22
Ellis, Bret Easton, 137

Faulkner, William, 19
Fink, Bruce, 72
Flaubert, Gustave, 98
Ford, George, 170n14
Foucault, Michel, 3
  Discipline and Punish, 124
  discourses, 75
  and Freud, 15–17, 167n18
  History of Sexuality, 103–4, 113–14
  on interpretation, 18, 165n5
Freud, Sigmund, 3, 7
  Beyond the Pleasure Principle, 14, 22,
    52–53, 90, 138–39, 141; consciousness
    and memory traces, 155; "fort-da"
    game, 14, 49, 148; repetition and
    death instinct, 53, 90, 156; tone of
    work, 180n2
  child at mother's breast as image of love,
    71
  Civilization and Its Discontents, 29–30
  daydreams and fantasy, 168n4
  death of the father, 29–30, 177n5
  "délirer du toucher," 120
  "Fragment of an Analysis of a Case of
    Hysteria," 23, 25, 115–16, 179nn19–20
  From the History of an Infantile Neurosis,

  67, 177n7; "Nachträglichkeit," or
    deferred action, 67, 173n13; primal
    scene, 67
  The Interpretation of Dreams, 2, 18, 50,
    72; condensation in dreams, 84; dis-
    tortion in dreams, 130; "The Dream
    of Irma's Injection," 50–51, 171n24;
    navel of dream, 72, 179n23; Rome as
    city of Freud's dreams, 145, 181n12
  *Jokes and Their Relation to the
    Unconscious*, 19
  "little thing," 119, 177n7
  Medusa and castration anxiety, 131–32
  "Mourning and Melancholia," 85, 146
  "On the Universal Tendency to
    Debasement in the Sphere of Love,"
    152
  primal fantasies, 71, 150–51
  The Psychopathology of Everyday Life, 33
  Three Essays on Sexuality, 71–72; and
    adolescent fantasies, 72; visual
    impressions and libido, 68
  Totem and Taboo, 29–30, 120–21, 139,
    178n8
  "The Uncanny"; and homesickness,
    51–52; patterns of repetition in, 66
  unconscious as a "new place," 5
  unconscious in language, 7, 79, 115

Gallagher, Catherine, 4, 82–83, 105
Gallop, Jane, 87
Garnett, Robert R., 169n9
Garson, Marjorie, 22, 138, 143, 151, 156, 163,
    181n11, 183n30
Gaskell, Elizabeth
  on Charlotte Brontë's art, 81
  Letters, 82
  Mary Barton, 100
  Miss Pasley, 174n3, 174n8
  on *Ruth*, 80, 82–83
  See also *Ruth*
Gérin, Winifred, 174n3
Ghosh, Amitav: *The Shadow Lines*, 10–11
Goodheart, Eugene, 165n1, 167n21
Goodwin, Sarah Webster, 21, 81–82, 101, 105,
    176n27

Habermas, Jürgen, 158
Hanzo, Thomas, 125

Hardy, Barbara, 32–33, 54, 172n30
Hardy, Thomas
    Biography, 160
    and Einstein's Theory of Relativity, 3
    Later Years, 181n11
    Life, 153
    "My Cicely," 140
    The Return of the Native, 140, 160
    Tess of the d'Urbervilles, 140, 160
    on Turner and Wagner, 21
    See also *Jude the Obscure*
Hartman, Geoffrey, 178n9
Hawking, Stephen, 18
Heller, Tamar, on *The Woman in White*
    Catherick, Anne, 132
    Fairlie, Mrs., gravesite of, 134
    and female and male plots, 129
    as feminist text, 178n13, 179n16
    Walter Hartright, 116, 119; manliness of,
        178n12; narrative of, 177n1
Herrick, Robert, 94
Hertz, Neil, 133, 179nn18–19
Holbrook, David, 38
Homans, Margaret, 87, 173n1, 174n8
Hughes, Winifred, 116
Hutter, Albert D., 177n6

Ingham, Patricia, 171n28
Irwin, John, 14

Jacobus, Mary, 87, 174n10
Jameson, Fredric, 172n2
Johnson, Barbara, 88
Jude the Obscure (Hardy), 4, 10, 21–22, 137–64
    ancient past in, 141
    and *Beyond the Pleasure Principle*
        (Freud), 22, 138–39, 148, 155
    Bridehead, Sue, 137, 141–42; as melan-
        cholic, 147–48
    Christminster, 145, 147–48, 156
    Donn, Arabella, 22, 140–42; as chthonic
        figure, 162–64; as judge of Sue
        Bridehead, 147; and pig's genitals, 161,
        183n27; and undergraduate student,
        148–49
    Edlin, Mrs., 161
    Fawley, Jude: and Arabella's breasts, 10,
        149–50; and masturbatory fantasies,
        182n16; as a melancholic, 145–47; and
        Sue Bridehead, 142–43

Greek tragedy in, 143–44
isolation in, 159–61
Little Father Time, 137
loss in, 148
modernism and, 22, 158, 161, 183n25
nature and culture in, 144–45
preface, 139–40, 145
pig-sty scene, 153–55
Phillotson, 157–58
repetition in, 141–42
Sparks, Tryphena, 139–40, 180n3
Troutham, 144–45
unconscious in, 180n1
Vilbert, 162
yearning in, 137–38, 148–53

Kael, Pauline, 64
Kaplan, Fred, 170n16
Keats, John, 3
Kincaid, James, 3, 165n4, 181n8, 182n24
Kinglake, William, 5, 59–60
Knoepflmacher, U. C., 166n10
Kristeva, Julia, 3, 49, 135
Kucich, John, 169n12
Kundera, Milan
    The Unbearable Lightness of Being, 10
    The Book of Laughter and Forgetting,
        46–47

Lacan, Jacques
    castration anxiety, 131
    corps morcelé, 13, 129
    desire, as distinct from need and
        demand, 12–13, 166n13
    "Desire and the Interpretation of Desire
        in *Hamlet*," 7
    desire as fetishistic, 148
    "The Direction of the Treatment and the
        Principles of Its Power," 12–14
    discontinuity of unconscious, 130, 166n8
    discovery of the unconscious, 8, 167n16
    "Dream of Irma's Injection," 50–51
    *Four Fundamental Concepts of
        Psychoanalysis*, 8–9, 68
    on Freud's "fort-da" game, 148
    on the gaze, 68, 131
    on Jean Paul Sartre and the gaze, 173n9
    jouissance, 72
    "*jouissance* of the idiot," 151
    metaphor, 96, 182n17

Lacan, Jacques (*continued*)
  "The Mirror Stage," 12–13
  "Name of the Father," 29, 54
  objet a, 8, 150
  Oedipal crisis, 143–44
  on *Oedipus at Colonus*, 112
  on the order of the law, 181n9
  and the phallus, 135, 148, 150, 172n32,
    179n22, 181n14
  on Poe's "The Purloined Letter,"141
  the site of the unconscious, 5
  structure of desire, 11–14, 17, 39, 117–18,
    145
  text as Holy Writ, 2, 165n2
  the unconscious as censored chapter,
    168n3
Lane, Christopher
  on Freud and Foucault, 15–17
  on Thomas Hardy, 182n20
Langbauer, Laurie, 115
Lansbury, Coral, 81, 92, 176n22, 176n24
Laplanche, Jean, 70, 132
  deferred memory, 173n7
  Freudian model of fantasy, 182n19
  Lacanian desire, 166n11
  primal fantasies, 150–52, 154
Lee, Peggy, 38
Lévi-Strauss, Claude, 60, 144
Looby, Christopher, 175n17
Lukacher, Ned, 17, 19, 67, 169n10, 173n8

Macherey, Pierre, 18–19
Magnet, Myron, 42, 170n16
Marryat, Frederick, 42
Martin Chuzzlewit (Dickens), 1, 3, 9, 19–20,
    23–56
  America, 19–20, 41–56
  America and England, 45–46
  American legends and traditions, 44–45
  Bevan, Mr., 45–46
  debt in, 54–55
  Eden, 46, 49–53
  English travel writers, 41–42
  fantasy in, 25–26, 53
  female body in, 51–52
  Gamp, Mrs., 19, 22, 25
  Choke, General, 52
  Chollop, Hannibal, 45
  Chuffey and Lewsome, 30
  Chuzzlewit, Anthony, 30, 53

Chuzzlewit, Jonas, 19, 26–31, 35
Chuzzlewit, Martin (junior), 9, 24,
    36–37, 46, 53–55
Chuzzlewit, Martin (senior), 31, 38–39, 55
Graham, Mary, 27
homesickness, 51–52
illustrations, 33–34, 38–40
incest, 36–39, 44
institutions, 53–54
joke, novel as, 19
jouissance, 26, 32, 36
Kedgwick, Captain, 46
myths of origin, 55–56
natural freedom, 44–45
nature in America, 55–56
orgiastic feeding, 47–49
Pawkins, Mrs., 47–49
Pecksniff, 39
Pecksniff, Charity, 19, 26, 28, 31–32, 35
Pinch, Ruth, 36–39
Pinch, Tom, 9, 19, 26–28, 32–39
Pogram, Elijah, 45, 53–54
Tapley, Mark, 46
Tigg, Montague, 28, 30, 53
title and first chapter, 26, 28–29, 41, 168n6
women, their absence in America, 171n27
Martineau, Harriet, 42
Marx, Karl, 43–44
Matus, Jill, 104, 175n14, 176n25
Meckier, Jerome, 24, 42, 170n16, 172n31
Meisel, Perry, 162, 182n21
Mellard, James, 167n21
Miller, D. A., on *The Woman in White*, 65,
    116, 124
  male homoerotic desire, 179n16
  primal scene, 116, 178n9
  Walter and Laura, 124
  Walter and Marian, 130–31, 133
Miller, J. Hillis, 2, 179n21, 180n5
Millgate, Michael, 141, 143, 161, 180n3, 180n6,
    183n31
Mitchell, Juliet, 14
Morgan, Rosemarie, 151, 182n16
Muller, John P., 148
Mulvey, Laura, 100

Nelson, Willie, 88
*Notes of a Journey from Cornhill to Grand
    Cairo* (Thackeray), 5, 9–10, 20, 57–78

Arabian Nights, 61–62
   British ladies in, 74
   Carlyle's remarks about, 58
   and "The Child in the House," 73–74
   cities visited, 60
   Constantinople, 63–64, 76
   English tourist, 76–77
   Eothen, 59–60
   fantasy and daydream, 70–73
   harem, 68–73
   homesickness in, 77–78
   Jews, description of, 74–75
   language of, 58–59, 61–64, 69, 76
   madness, 77
   modern criticism of, 58–59
   Orient and sexuality, 69–70
   origin of trip, 57–58
   pyramids of Egypt, 76–77
   reception of book, 58
   and sensation novelists, 64–65
   sensations of boyhood, 63–68, 72
   Smyrna, 61–62, 76
   Stansfield's panorama, 68
   trapdoor and dancing women, 9–10,
      68–69

O'Farrell, Mary Ann, 175n18
Orwell, George, 36

Paglia, Camille, 51
Paradise Lost, 39
Pater, Walter, "The Child in the House," 10,
   11, 73–74, 78
Polhemus, Robert
   Comic Faith, 2, 19, 49
   Erotic Faith, 171n23
Pontalis, J. B. *See* Laplanche, Jean
Poovey, Mary, 100
prostitute, figure of, 21, 81–82, 101
   woman writer and, 82–83
Proust, Marcel, 159–60, 175nn11–12

Rabelais, François, 24
Ragland, Ellie. *See* Sullivan, Ellie Ragland
Ray, Gordon N., 58
Richardson, Maurice, 178n13
Ritchie, Anne Thackeray, 80
Rose, Jacqueline, 7, 25–26, 39, 45, 181n14
Rossetti, Christina, 63

Rousseau, Jean-Jacques, 4, 42–43
Ruskin, John, 121
Ruth (Gaskell), 4, 20–21, 79–112
   Bellingham, 92–96; as Donne, 97–101
   Benson, Faith, 94
   Benson, Thurstan, 88–90, 109
   Bradshaw, Jemima, 104–7
   Bradshaw, Mr., 102–4
   Bradshaw, Mrs., 102
   cholera epidemic, 110–11
   female sexuality in, 104–5
   gifts and giving in, 94–95
   guilt in, 84–85
   Hilton, Ruth: body of, 95–97; as corpse,
      109–10; desire for death, 109–12;
      dream of, 83–84; erotics of death and
      dying, 109–11; erotic moments,
      92–102; hair of, 92–94, 96–99, 105;
      madness of, 112, 176n29; mother of,
      85, 87–90, 108; as mother, 82, 112; as
      naughty, 82, 103, 110; as prostitute,
      81–83, 85–86, 100–4, 109–11, 176n22;
      sexual desire of, 97–98; sexuality of,
      92–95; and taboo, 86, 109–10
   origin of novel, 174n3
   Romantic project of novel, 81
   Romantic sublime, 91
   Sally, 105, 176n21, 176n24
   scents and memory in, 89–90
   Wales, 92–96
   See also Gaskell, Elizabeth; Schor,
      Hilary; Uglow, Jenny

Said, Edward, 36, 57–60, 69, 75, 77
Saint-Pierre, Bernardin de, *Paul and
   Virginie,* 181n7
Saldívar, Ramón, 181n10
Schor, Hilary, on *Ruth*
   aesthetic prostitution, 92–95
   changefulness in, 176n28
   dead mother, importance of, 174n9
   divided and contradictory work, 80–81
   guilt of Ruth, 84, 176n22
   innocence of Ruth, 175n14
   Ruth and power, 99
Schweik, Richard, 180n1
Shklar, Judith N., 43
Shumaker, Jeanette, 97, 175n21
Sisson, C. H., 161

Slack, Robert C., 183n27
Spivak, Gayatri, 166n7
Sprengnether, Madelon, 179n20
Steig, Michael, 27
Stewart, Garrett, 10, 166n10
Stockton, Kathryn Bond, 166n12
Stoler, Ann Laura, 16, 167n18
Stoneman, Patsy, 176n29
Sullivan, Ellie Ragland, 41
    body and language, 95
    desire, dreams, language, 179n23
    Lacan and the Oedipal crisis, 143–44
    Lacanian death drive, 108–9
    primordial separation drama, 126
    tragedy of human condition, 182n15
    unconscious as memory space, 127, 134
Swift, Graham, 139
Swift, Jonathan, 24

Taylor, Jenny Bourne, 121, 124, 177n2
Tennent, James, 57
Tennyson, Alfred Lord, 153–54
Thackeray, William
    as exile, 77
    James Tennent and Reform Club, 57–58
    as Michael Angelo Titmarsh, 57
    See also Notes of a Journey from Cornhill
        to Grand Cairo
Thomas, Deborah, 58
Thomas, Ronald R., 167n21
Trollope, Frances Milton, 42

Uglow, Jenny, on Ruth
    final volume of novel, 174n4
    George Eliot and Gaskell, 174n7
    motive beneath the writing, 79–80
    private identification in, 105
    repression in, 82

Ruth's hair, 176n21
Ruth's innocence, 175n14
Ruth's sexuality, 175n15
Ruth's wildness, 96
sexualized landscape of, 96

Walkowitz, Judith, 109–10, 176n22
Watt, Ian, 166n10
Welsh, Alexander, 169n13
Wharton, Edith, 95
The Woman in White (Collins), 1, 21, 65,
    113–36
    and Adam Bede, 127–28
    Catherick, Anne: entrance into novel,
        120; and taboo, 120
    Fairlie, Laura, 120–24; and asylum,
        124–25; as child/woman, 124; and
        father, 122–23; menstruation, 122; and
        taboo, 121
    Fairlie, Mrs.: gravesite, 134–36; letters, 126
    Fosco, 128–29; and homoerotic desire,
        179n16; and phallic presence, 128,
        179n16
    Glyde, Percival, 124; and scarred male
        body, 128
    Halcombe, Marian, 113; dreams, 135
    Hartright, Mrs., 118–19
    Hartright, Sarah, 118–19
    Hartright, Walter, 114; and dead father,
        116–20; as errant son, 124–25; and
        male desire, 121–22; and Marian
        Halcombe, 129–32; and narrative, 21,
        115, 132–33; and Theseus, 125–26
    Pesca, 118–19
    wanting in, 126–27
    and Wordsworth, 126–27
    See also Heller, Tamar; Miller, D. A.
Wright, T. R., 183n31